NATIONAL SECURITY

Preparing for the Possibility of a North Korean Collapse

Bruce W. Bennett

Prepared for the Smith Richardson Foundation

The research described in this report was prepared for the Smith Richardson Foundation.

Library of Congress Cataloging-in-Publication Data is available for this publication.

ISBN: 978-0-8330-8172-8

Preface

This report addresses the potential consequences of a North Korean government collapse that could lead to Korean unification. It explains how appropriate preparations now could reduce the negative consequences that could otherwise occur. These preparations need to address North Korean attitudes toward unification, providing humanitarian assistance to North Korea, demobilizing the North Korean military and security services, handling potential Chinese intervention in a collapse, and other key issues.

The Smith Richardson Foundation sponsored this research. This research was conducted within the International Security and Defense Policy Center of the RAND National Security Research Division (NSRD). NSRD conducts research and analysis on defense and national security topics for the U.S. and allied defense, foreign policy, homeland security, and intelligence communities and foundations and other nongovernmental organizations that support defense and national security analysis.

For more information on the International Security and Defense Policy Center, see http://www.rand.org/nsrd/ndri/centers/isdp.html or contact the director (contact information is provided on the web page).

Contents

CHAPTER SEVEN

Challenges of and Responses to Security Services and Human Rights Disasters

Figures

Tables

Summary

North Korea is a failing state. Its government could collapse in the coming months or years, causing an immense humanitarian disaster and potentially other, even more serious consequences. This report assumes that the Republic of Korea (ROK) would decide to intervene in such a crisis with U.S. assistance and seek Korean unification. Neither the ROK nor the United States is adequately prepared for such an intervention. Inadequately prepared, the ROK and the United States could suffer many serious consequences, including a failed or aborted intervention, a destabilization of the region, and possibly broader warfare.

It is therefore incumbent on the ROK and the United States to prepare for a North Korean collapse. To explain the reasons for preparations and the areas needing preparations, this report examines the potential negative consequences of a North Korean collapse and the challenges that cause or contribute to them. It then turns to proposing the actions the ROK and the United States could take to ameliorate the various consequences of a North Korean government collapse and the preparations needed to empower these actions.

Background

There is a reasonable probability that North Korean totalitarianism will end in the foreseeable future, with the very strong likelihood that this end will be accompanied by considerable violence and upheaval.[1] The immediate past U.S. commander in Korea, GEN Walter Sharp, summarized the North Korean situation this way:

> Combined with the country's disastrous centralized economy, dilapidated industrial sector, insufficient agricultural base, malnourished military and populace, and developing nuclear programs, the possibility of a sudden leadership change in the North could be destabilizing and unpredictable.[2]

Such a sudden change could occur if the current North Korean leader, Kim Jong-Un, is assassinated,[3] leaving no clear successor and the potential division of the senior North Korean leadership into factions that would likely wage civil war against each other. Such a government collapse would develop into a humanitarian disaster, one that would likely force ROK, U.S., and Chinese intervention to resolve the resulting threats both within the region and beyond.[4]

Unification as the Objective

The costs of intervening in a North Korean government collapse will be high for the ROK and its partners. If the ROK is to pay such costs, it will likely decide to make Korean unification the ultimate objective of the intervention. The presidents of both the United States and the ROK established peaceful unification as the objective for Korea in

---

[1]   See, for example, Andrew Scobell, "Making Sense of North Korea: Pyongyang and Comparative Communism," *Asian Security,* Vol. 1, No. 3, 2005, pp. 245–266.

[2]   "USFK Commander Warns of Possible N.K. Instability," *Korea Herald,* March 26, 2010.

[3]   He reportedly survived such an assassination attempt in Pyongyang in 2012, "during a power struggle in a military bureau." See Chang Se-jeong and Ser Myo-ja, "Attempt to Kill Jong-un Took Place in 2012: Source," *JoongAng Ilbo,* March 14, 2013.

[4]   For example, North Korean factions could use weapons of mass destruction (WMD) against the ROK, Japan, and China or could proliferate WMD or WMD expertise to third parties (especially terrorist groups) that would be prone to use the weapons against the United States. North Korean possession of WMD could thus force U.S. military intervention in a North Korean government collapse.

their 2009 and 2013 summit meetings.[5] A North Korean collapse may well provide the very best chances for unification. For a ROK and U.S. intervention to succeed in achieving unification, substantial preparations are required beforehand. While unification has been the alliance strategic guidance, the planning and preparation for unification appear to have been inadequate thus far.

The Potential Consequences of Collapse and Subsequent Intervention

The most immediate consequences of a North Korean government collapse will occur in North Korea. The division of the North into factions would likely precipitate civil war, as at least some of the factions will seek primacy and eventual control of all of North Korea, and none of the factions are likely to have the resources, such as food, needed for survival throughout the area that they control.[6] Compared to today, the even more serious lack of food, medicine, and other supplies in North Korea would lead to a humanitarian disaster likely worse than the famine of the mid-1990s in North Korea, when several hundred

---

[5] In 2009, the "Joint Vision" statement from the U.S.-ROK Presidential Summit said, "Through our Alliance we aim to build a better future for all people on the Korean Peninsula, establishing a durable peace on the Peninsula and leading to peaceful reunification on the principles of free democracy and a market economy" ("Joint Vision for the Alliance of the United States of America and the Republic of Korea," Washington, D.C.: The White House, Office of the Press Secretary, June 16, 2009). The 2013 Summit concluded, "We pledge to continue to build a better and more secure future for all Korean people, working on the basis of the Joint Vision to foster enduring peace and stability on the Korean Peninsula and its peaceful reunification based on the principles of denuclearization, democracy and a free market economy" ("Joint Declaration in Commemoration of the 60th Anniversary of the Alliance between the Republic of Korea and the United States of America," Washington, D.C.: The White House, Office of the Press Secretary, May 7, 2013).

[6] North Korea already suffers from starvation in relatively stable circumstances. In the unstable circumstances of a collapse, many will likely hoard food, and much more food than normal will be wasted.

thousand to potentially several million died of starvation.[7] The break-down of central authority would allow the North Korean military and security services to prey on the North Korean civilian population, stealing food and taking away the modest level of individual security that exists today. In turn, potentially millions of North Koreans would become refugees,[8] seeking to cross into China and the ROK in search of food and security. Such huge numbers of refugees would be desta-bilizing in both the ROK and China. China, in particular, has been quite clear that it does not want any such refugee flow. China also does not want U.S. forces operating near its territory.

The horrendous nature of these consequences would likely drive both a ROK-U.S. and a Chinese intervention into North Korea. The large size of the North Korean military would require that both inter-ventions be led by military forces, seeking to reestablish security and provide humanitarian aid that is not immediately stolen from the people. The forces of both sides would have significant incentives to advance rapidly into the North, leading to a risk of accidental combat between them. In the zeal of the moment, the inevitable accidents could escalate into major combat between the ROK and U.S. forces and the Chinese forces, one of the worst possible outcomes. And even

---

[7] According to one report, the North Korean

> government has acknowledged that 220,000 North Koreans died of starvation between 1995 and 1998, the height of the catastrophe. At the other end of the spectrum, Hwang Jong Yup, the highest-ranking defector from North Korea, has stated that North Korean agricultural officials estimated internally to the government itself that 2.5 million people perished between 1995 and 1997, including 500,000 in 1995, one million in 1996, and another one million in 1997. Andrew Natsios's review of several independent studies concludes that there is significant evidence to support Hwang Jong Yup's estimates. There have been plausible, fact-based estimates as high as 3.5 million deaths, although these estimates are regarded with skepticism by several scholars.

Vaclav Havel, Kjell Magne Bondevik, and Elie Wiesel, *Failure to Protect: A Call for the UN Security Council to Act in North Korea*, Washington, D.C.: U.S. Committee for Human Rights in North Korea, October 30, 2006, p. 22. See also Andrew Natsios, "The Politics of Famine in North Korea," special report, Washington, D.C.: U.S. Institute of Peace, August 2, 1999.

[8] Na Jeong-ju, "3 million NK Refugees Expected in Crisis: BOK," *Korea Times*, January 26, 2007. The 3 million is the estimate for refugees trying to cross into the ROK; an even larger number of refugees trying to cross into China can be expected.

if such conflict is avoided, the North Korean military forces would almost certainly oppose both interventions in some combination of regular combat, insurgency, and criminal behavior. This combat could lead to significant damage to the ROK, as North Korean artillery and missiles could be used against the ROK, and North Korean special forces could infiltrate the ROK and seek to wreck havoc. The North Korean military attacks could be made worse by the use of WMD. Even Japan and the United States would not be immune from North Korean attacks, let alone follow-on terrorist attacks.

If the worse consequences develop, the ROK-U.S. intervention in the North could fail. Alternatively, China could take political control of much of the North, likely in cooperation with one or more North Korean factions. A failure to achieve Korean unification in these circumstances could doom Korea to division for at least many more decades.

Preparing North Koreans for Unification

For six decades, North Korea has indoctrinated its people, describing the United States as the enemy of the North Korean people and the source of all the problems in North Korea. The ROK is described both as the lackey of the United States and as a determined enemy of the North Korean people. This North Korean diversionary effort is needed to deflect criticism from the regime for all its failings. If North Koreans sustain these feelings after a North Korean government collapse, it will be extremely difficult to perform the functions needed to achieve unification. Indeed, outright opposition can be expected from many in the North.

A ROK-U.S. information operations campaign is a key starting point for overcoming North Korean hatred and fear of the United States and the ROK across almost all the potential consequences. The ROK and the United States must change how North Koreans think about unification and their individual prospects after unification. Information is already leaking into North Korea that at least challenges North Korean indoctrination claiming that people in the ROK live even worse lives than people in the North. But the North Korean people need to be given hope that the United States and the ROK are not enemies but are rather preparing policies that will make unification advantageous for the North Koreans. And these policies need to be communicated to the North Koreans. This will be particularly important with the North Korean elites who could oppose unification in very serious ways. Policies are needed for such issues as provision of humanitarian aid and jobs, selective amnesty, and property rights. These need to be transmitted to the North Korean people over time to adjust North Korean expectations. The ROK and the United States must be prepared to provide the North Koreans a favorable life after unification;[9] otherwise, many North Koreans will become disaffected and likely rebel against the development of a stable and prosperous unified Korea that treats them poorly.

Responses to Humanitarian Disaster

A first step in improving the lives of North Koreans would be for the ROK and the United States to prepare to deliver humanitarian aid throughout North Korea promptly and in significant quantities. This aid needs to be delivered throughout the country to avert North Koreans from displacing from their homes in search of food and security and thereby posing a more serious humanitarian aid requirement. Prompt delivery of humanitarian aid will require ROK and U.S. military forces to take a major role in aid delivery because of the magnitude of deliveries required and the desire to avoid misappropriation of the aid by the North Korean military, security services, or criminal personnel. Intervening ROK and U.S. forces should "lead with aid" across the demilitarized zone and along the coasts of North Korea. Because about one-half of the North Korean populace lives in the interior of North Korea, rapid action should be taken to neutralize the North Korean

---

[9]   When the East German government collapse developed into a West German–led unification, many of those in East Germany expected that such a unification would be good for them, which is not the case in North Korea.

air defense network so that aircraft can also be used for aid delivery (including encouraging North Korean military personnel to destroy the air defenses).[10]

Responses to Conflict and Military Forces in North Korea

After a North Korean government collapse, all conflict that occurs in North Korea poses risks of spilling over into the ROK and China and worsening the humanitarian disaster in the North. The ROK and U.S. forces should therefore seek prompt ceasefires for these conflicts and to avoid having to fight the North Korean forces.

Today, most of the North Korean military personnel will likely be hostile to unification. In aggregate, they pose far larger and more serious threats to the Korean unification process than was the case in German unification, including North Korean possession and potential use of WMD. Thus, ROK and U.S. forces moving into North Korea to secure the delivery of humanitarian aid will need to begin their work with the local North Korean military commanders, trying to co-opt the commanders and their units. With North Korean commanders facing the pressures of a North Korean collapse, it may be possible to avoid conflict and insurgency in some local areas, especially if more has been done to help the North Koreans perceive that unification offers them a reasonable future. But the ROK and U.S. forces need to prepare to do more, promptly disarming most North Korean forces and sending mobilized North Korean reservists back to their civilian jobs, while keeping some North Korean units lightly armed to assist in the demilitarization, weapon security, and countering insurgent actions. The disarmed former North Korean units should be transferred to public-service efforts to rebuild North Korean infrastructure and other critical capabilities, hopefully providing training for at least some North Koreans in future jobs that will support Korean economic growth and

---

[10] The ROK and/or U.S. presidents may order airborne delivery of humanitarian aid before the military is satisfied with the safety of the environment. Thus, the military needs to make every effort to prepare the environment and to be able to respond to any threats that still develop.

stability. Officially retaining former North Korean military personnel in the combined Korean military for a year or more will allow imposition of military discipline, completion of debriefings, and imposition of biometrics that will both help deter criminal behavior and provide a means of countering that behavior when it develops.[11]

The elimination of North Korean WMD would be another objective for ROK and U.S. forces entering North Korea. The North Korean WMD could cause serious damage in North Korea and beyond and could be proliferated to third parties, including terrorist groups, many of which would delight in attacking the United States. Unfortunately, the North Korean WMD appear to be dispersed among a large number of facilities, at least some of which have not yet been identified or located, making it difficult to quickly eliminate the WMD threat. Because of the severity of the damage WMD could do, ROK and U.S. forces need to be prepared to secure and then eliminate this threat as promptly as possible. This would be a major reason for ROK-U.S. military intervention into a North Korean collapse and also a reason for ROK-U.S. cooperation with China in resolving this threat.

Responses to Security Services and Human Rights Disasters

The North Korean security services will be more difficult to deal with because many of their members will be guilty of criminal activities. In practice, however, the ROK judicial system will lack the capacity for criminal action against most of these personnel, and thus the ROK will need to decide how many criminal cases it can handle and prepare to grant selective amnesty for lesser offenses that the judicial and prison systems are unprepared to handle. Amnesty may be applied to those guilty of accepting bribes and other forms of corruption, giving pre-

---

[11] The imposition of biometrics may not initially be very effective in deterring criminal behavior because few North Koreans will understand the capabilities of biometrics at first. Biometrics will be useful in catching criminals and, over time, will have a deterrent effect as criminals and others learn how other criminals were caught.

cedence to the criminal prosecution of those guilty of serious human rights abuses, such as torture, murder, and serious abuse.

The ROK and U.S. forces must also pay particular attention to the North Korean prisons, especially the political prisons. Potentially hundreds of thousands of North Koreans are incarcerated in these facilities. While some prisoners may be guilty of crimes and justly imprisoned, many are imprisoned because of political offenses. As ROK and U.S. forces advance into North Korea, the prison camp commanders and guards may try to execute many of the prisoners to prevent their eventual testimony against the prison staffs. ROK and U.S. forces will need to reach these prisons quickly to stop such executions and save many lives. At least some of the prisoners may prove useful to postunification governance of the North, having served in the North Korean government but then been imprisoned for "political unreliability."

Responses to Ownership Issues

In North Korea, the state technically owns the vast majority of the property. Once unification occurs, decisions must be made on who should assume property ownership.[12] As in the case of East Germany, there will be conflict between those currently occupying the property and the families that held ownership before the North Korean regime took control.

The combined Korean government needs to establish policies for how property rights will be conferred. In general, the most favorable outcome with personal property (e.g., homes) will be to convey ownership to the current residents, requiring them to remain in place for some number of years to obtain property rights; the ROK government should plan to compensate pre–North Korea landowners. The vesting period will keep many North Koreans in their homes to reduce the potential refugee flows. It will also avoid some of the abuses of people selling their property immediately to achieve a financial windfall

---

[12] Ownership issues arise as a result of ROK efforts to unify the peninsula in the aftermath of a North Korean collapse, not directly from the collapse itself.

but then suffering from the longer-term consequences of not owning property—consequences that would lead to significant dissatisfaction with and blame of the combined Korean government. Similar problems developed in East Germany after German unification.

With regard to North Korean businesses, most are in such serious deterioration that they have little value. The East German government suffered similar problems; it decided to have a national organization take ownership of these firms and to "sell" them to private ownership under specific rules that would promote the needed capital investments. Indeed, in some cases, the East German government had to pay private companies to take ownership of the firms. A similar approach for North Korea seems warranted.

Responses to Chinese Intervention

A North Korean collapse raises Chinese fears of both U.S. intervention into the area directly adjoining China's border and a massive influx of North Korean refugees. China recognizes, for example, that the United States will want to reach the North Korean WMD sites north of Pyongyang promptly to prevent WMD use or proliferation, and this threat will potentially force China to seek to secure these facilities before the United States can reach them. And the best way to reduce an influx of desperate refugees is for China to establish a buffer zone inside North Korea and keep the refugees in camps within the buffer zone. China would also have other reasons for intervening in the North, including Chinese economic interests, such as in North Korean ports on the East Sea (Sea of Japan) and in North Korean mineral wealth.

The view of Chinese intervention changes significantly in future years. The ROK Army is planned to reduce from 22 active duty divisions today to roughly 12 by 2022 due to severe ROK demographic problems. With 12 active duty divisions, the ROK will have insufficient forces, even with significant U.S. participation, to fully handle the various challenges of North Korean collapse. China could help, but the ROK worries that Chinese intervention in the North might not be reversible and that, as a result, unification after a North Korean collapse may only be partial, with China annexing some significant portion of the North.

This future should force the ROK and the United States to work more closely with China in preparing for a North Korean collapse and developing cooperative plans for this effort. This will be a major undertaking, especially since China has sought to avoid preparations for a North Korean collapse, because these would make China appear to be disloyal to its North Korean ally. But China appears to be increasingly ready to address this difficult issue. The ROK and the United States should take every opportunity to share perspectives with China and seek to develop at least common perspectives on how to handle a North Korean collapse.

Addressing the Prerequisites of Collapse Preparation

The ROK, especially, needs to make progress in two critical areas to accomplish the preparations discussed above. The first is convincing the ROK populace that the ROK should prepare for a North Korean collapse and subsequent unification. Many in the ROK oppose such preparation, fearing that it will sour relations with North Korea and increase the likelihood of a collapse, outcomes that they wish to avoid. In practice, however, most preparation for unification would reduce its costs, whether it occurs peacefully or as the result of a North Korean collapse. And with the failing character of North Korea, a North Korean government collapse appears to be more an issue of when it occurs and not whether it occurs. Thus, preparations would most likely accelerate rather than cause a collapse, and by accelerating collapse would hasten the time when the North Korean people would be freed from their abusive government. These trade-offs need to be more actively discussed in the ROK to help encourage the people to support preparation for a collapse.

The other critical issue is preparing the ROK Army to sustain more combat power as its size declines in the coming years. As noted above, the ROK Army is planned to decline from 22 active duty divisions to about 12 over the next ten years. The reduction does not need to be that severe if the current 21-month conscription period is retained, as opposed to reducing the period to 18 months, as ROK President Park Geun-Hye promised in her 2012 election campaign. But critical to sustaining and even enhancing ROK Army capabilities will be better use of the ROK reserves, whose effectiveness is constrained today by the limitation of only three days of training per year for the reservists.[13] Selected reservists could be organized into reserve battalions or regiments serving in active duty divisions or into key specialty forces and could be provided financial incentives for agreeing to enough training time each year to keep the force effective. Some third-country forces could also be brought into plans for unification.

---

[13] All ROK reserve divisions have an active duty cadre, which would be more qualified.

Acknowledgments

The author acknowledges the substantial help provided in performing this research by Dr. Rhee Sang-Woo and LTG(R) Park Yong-Ok. They helped identify consequences of collapse in various areas and options for addressing the consequences. Many other audiences have listened to the ideas presented here and provided valuable suggestions. Dr. Andrew Scobell and COL(R) David Maxwell provided very helpful substantive reviews. The author appreciates the help he has received but accepts responsibility for the content herein.

Abbreviations

ABC	atomic, biological, and chemical
BCT	brigade combat team
CBRN	chemical, biological, radiological, and nuclear
CIA	Central Intelligence Agency
CINCUNC	Commander in Chief, United Nations Command (a historical title no longer used)
DDR	disarmament, demobilization, and reintegration
DIA	Defense Intelligence Agency
DMZ	demilitarized zone
DPRK	Democratic People's Republic of Korea
DRP	Defense Reform Plan
FAO	Food and Agriculture Organization
GDP	gross domestic product
GPS	Global Positioning System
ICBM	intercontinental ballistic missile
IISS	International Institute for Strategic Studies
KEF	Korea Employers Federation

KTX	Korea Train eXpress
MND	Ministry of National Defense
MR	military region
NCO	noncommissioned officer
NK	North Korea
PDC	Pyongyang Defense Command
PLA	People's Liberation Army
PSI	Proliferation Security Initiative
ROK	Republic of Korea
SAM	surface-to-air missile
SLBM	submarine-launched ballistic missile
SOF	special operations forces
UGF	underground facility
UN	United Nations
WMD	weapons of mass destruction
WMD-E	WMD elimination

CHAPTER ONE

Introduction

In the aftermath of the death of North Korean leader Kim Jong-Il in December 2011, there has been increasing discussion of the possibility of a North Korean collapse.[1] Indeed, many argue that it is only a matter of time because North Korea is a failing state.[2] Still, others argue that the North Korean regime has survived very difficult circumstances in the past when many predicted collapse and appears to be stable now.[3] In reality, we do not know how stable the North Korean government is. Moreover, it is extraordinarily difficult to predict a collapse, as many observers came to realize with both the collapse of East Germany and the collapse of the Soviet Union (which also ended Soviet hegemony over Eastern Europe). It is impossible to predict a North Korean government collapse other than to say it could happen, perhaps even in

---

[1] This report focuses on a North Korean government collapse. It is also possible that the North Korean regime could collapse and be replaced with a new North Korean government, likely constituted from the North Korean military. Such a regime collapse is outside of the scope of this effort.

[2] According to one observer, "At some point in the next 12–24 months, the underpinnings of control will come undone, followed by a rapid collapse of North Korea as we know it and movement toward reunification" (Jack Pritchard, "My New Year's Predictions for North Korea," The Peninsula blog, Korea Economic Institute, December 21, 2011). See also "Kim Jong-nam Says N.Korean Regime Won't Last Long," *Chosun Ilbo*, January 17, 2012.

[3] See, for example, "Defense Officials of S. Korea, U.S., Japan Say N. Korea 'Stable,'" *Korea Herald*, January 31, 2012. According to one observer, "[t]he new regime is stable, dynamic, and here to stay. This is also the prevailing view that is shared by South Korea and Japan, as well as by China and Russia. As Russian Foreign Minister Sergei Lavrov noted last week, there are no signs of instability" (Mark P. Barry, "A Window of Opportunity with North Korea," World Policy Blog, January 31, 2012).

the next few years. Nevertheless, as the collapse of the East German and Soviet governments demonstrated, the consequences of a collapse can be substantial even if it proves comparatively peaceful. And with North Korea, there are many possibilities for conflict to accompany a government collapse.

This report assumes that, at some point in the future, the North Korean government will collapse.[4] Moreover, it assumes that, when the collapse occurs, the Republic of Korea (ROK) will decide to pursue Korean unification, however reluctantly.[5] The presidents of the ROK and the United States established peaceful unification as the objective for Korea in their 2009 and 2013 summit meetings,[6] but unification after a North Korean collapse may be a more likely path to this objective. If these assumptions prove to be true, both the United States and the ROK will want to achieve Korean unification as easily and at as low a cost as possible. But in practice, neither country has prepared much for the unification process and could thus face serious conse-

---

[4] Some view the assumption of a government collapse as extreme, talking instead about a lesser change, associated with the North Korean regime collapsing and leading to a new, likely military, government in North Korea. This report assumes that no replacement government develops but rather that the senior elites divide into factions. This assumption is discussed in more detail in Chapter Two.

[5] Public opinion polls in the ROK vacillate on public interest in Korean unification. Nevertheless, the level of ROK support for unification has fallen over time and while a majority of South Koreans still likely favor unification, this is likely only by a small margin.

[6] In 2009, the "Joint Vision" statement from the U.S.-ROK Presidential Summit said: "Through our Alliance we aim to build a better future for all people on the Korean Peninsula, establishing a durable peace on the Peninsula and leading to peaceful reunification on the principles of free democracy and a market economy" ("Joint Vision for the Alliance of the United States of America and the Republic of Korea," Washington, D.C.: The White House, Office of the Press Secretary, June 16, 2009). The 2013 Summit concluded: "We pledge to continue to build a better and more secure future for all Korean people, working on the basis of the Joint Vision to foster enduring peace and stability on the Korean Peninsula and its peaceful reunification based on the principles of denuclearization, democracy and a free market economy" ("Joint Declaration in Commemoration of the 60th Anniversary of the Alliance Between the Republic of Korea and the United States of America," Washington, D.C.: The White House, Office of the Press Secretary, May 7, 2013).

quences if and when a North Korean government collapse does occur.[7] This report identifies the potential consequences and the challenges that cause or contribute to them. It then proposes actions that could be taken to resolve or at least mitigate the collapse consequences and what must be done before a collapse to prepare for these actions. Many of these same preparations would need to be taken in preparation for a peaceful unification.

Historical Background

North Korea was established as a communist state in 1945 under control of the Soviet Union, the result of the Soviets' late intervention against the Japanese in World War II. The Soviets chose Kim Il-Sung, a Korean partisan leader during World War II, as the head of state. Several key factors of North Korean history help define what a collapse would potentially look like:

- Kim Il-Sung faced many challenges to his leadership, especially through the 1950s. He dealt with them via ruthless purges, brutal repression of dissent, building a personality cult, and heavy use of propaganda with the North Korean people.[8]
- Kim Il-Sung instituted a command economy rather than allowing markets to drive economics. The industrial strength of North Korea peaked in the 1980s. The fall of the Soviet Union and loss of its subsidies were serious blows to the North Korean economy, sending it into serious decline starting around 1990.[9] The North Korean economy performs poorly today. At best, it is on slow

---

[7]   The ROK has found it politically difficult to prepare for collapse because very vocal groups in the ROK strongly oppose even discussing the possibility. Some are reluctant to weaken the stability of North Korea with discussion of collapse, preferring that the North Korean government continue and/or that the ROK avoid the financial consequences of collapse.

[8]   "Kim Il-sung," *New World Encyclopedia*, April 2, 2008.

[9]   See, for example, Andrea Matles Savada, ed., "Industry," *North Korea: A Country Study*, Washington, D.C.: Library of Congress, 1993.

growth; at worst, it is burdened by dilapidated infrastructure that is increasingly failing.

- The North Korean regime has pursued military power as a fundamental requirement, building an active duty force that consumes roughly 5 percent of the North Korean population. The military has been postured to invade South Korea—a second Korean War—and accomplish a militarily imposed reunification. The military has also been a major vehicle for personnel indoctrination.
- North Korea has built nuclear weapons for deterrence and to demonstrate its empowerment, starting at the end of the Korean War. By 2010, North Korea had the nuclear materials for at least five to ten nuclear weapons, although some evidence suggests that imports and uranium enrichment could make the numbers as high as 20 or so.[10] It has also pursued chemical and biological weapons and may have 2,500 to 5,000 tons of chemical weapons.[11]
- Kim Il-Sung chose a hereditary succession, designating his oldest son, Kim Jong-Il, as his successor. Kim Jong-Il was brought up in this system and began participating in purges immediately out of college in 1964. He had 30 years to shape the leadership he inherited in North Korea in 1994 yet still faced assassination attempts in 1994 and 1995.[12] These problems stopped when he gave priority to the North Korean military through the "Military First" politics.[13] This policy gives the military some 25 to 30 percent of North Korea's gross domestic product (GDP).
- Starting in 1995, North Korea experienced a severe famine caused initially by floods but followed by drought in 1997. At least sev-

[10] Bruce W. Bennett, "North Korea's WMD Capability and the Regional Military Balance: A US Perspective," *The Korean Journal of Security Affairs*, Korea National Defense University, December 2009.

[11] ROK Ministry of National Defense (MND), *Defense White Paper,* 2008, pp. 39–40.

[12] "Kim Jong Il," *Biography*, undated; John McCreary, "NightWatch," blog, November 17, 2010.

[13] John McCreary, "NightWatch," blog, January 11, 2010.

eral hundred thousand people died of starvation and perhaps as many as 3 million or so.[14] Starvation has continued, although at lower level, since that time. Overall, starvation has physically and mentally impaired a significant part of the North Korean work-force.[15]

- Kim Jong-Il opposed discussion of his successor for most of his life. After partially recovering from a 2008 stroke, he designated his third son, Kim Jong-Un, as his successor. Since Kim Jong-Il died in December 2011, Kim Jong-Un has appeared to assume control of North Korea, although a group of supporters surrounds him and may actually be making many of the government's decisions.

The Types of Collapse

The question, then, is when and under what circumstances might the Kim Jong-Un regime collapse? Such a collapse could come in one of two forms: regime collapse and government collapse.[16] In a regime collapse, the Kim family regime (and Kim Jong-Un, in particular) is overthrown, and some new leader takes control of North Korea, likely rising from within the military. Under this case, the national control

---

[14] Vaclav Havel, Kjell Magne Bondevik, and Elie Wiesel, *Failure to Protect: A Call for the UN Security Council to Act in North Korea*, Washington, D.C.: U.S. Committee for Human Rights in North Korea, October 30, 2006, p. 22.

[15] According to National Intelligence Council, *Strategic Implications of Global Health*, ICA 2008-10D, December 2008, p. 6:

> Malnutrition-related cognitive disabilities among *North Korean* children and young people likely will impact future economic growth in that country regardless of when Pyongyang opens to the outside world or reunifies with the South. Nationwide malnutrition has compelled Pyongyang to lower minimum height and weight requirements for military service, and an estimated 17 to 29 percent of potential North Korean military conscripts between 2009 and 2013 will have cognitive deficiencies disqualifying them for service.

[16] Similar comparisons are drawn in Andrew Scobell, *Projecting Pyongyang: The Future of North Korea's Kim Jong Il Regime*, Carlisle Barracks, Pa.: Strategic Studies Institute, U.S. Army War College, March 2008, pp. 20–21.

mechanisms and organization could remain largely in place, although the overthrow will certainly disrupt the mechanisms for a period. The new ruler would be prone to purge many of the senior government leaders and replace them with personnel loyal to him.

The alternative kind of collapse would be a government collapse. In this case, the Kim family regime would fail or be overthrown, and no single individual or group would be able to form a new central North Korean government. Most likely, factions would develop, each trying to control parts of the country, with some possibly having very weak control even over their own areas. Many central government functions would fail, including much of the control system.

Note that regime collapse could be a step along the path to government collapse. Indeed, collapse is both a process and an outcome. North Korea has not yet suffered either regime or government collapse, but the collapse process appears to be under way already. Thus, the Kim regime is perhaps best classified as a "failing or eroding totalitarian system."[17]

This report examines the government collapse case. It is in some ways more of a worst case but still quite possible. Moreover, the consequences of such a collapse today would be far worse than they need to be, largely because of a lack of ROK and U.S. preparation. The needed preparation is the focus of this report.

Planning and Preparing for a North Korean Government Collapse

While the focus of this report is North Korean collapse, many of the same preparations would be required to achieve a successful unification whether Korea achieves unification peacefully or through a collapse. A collapse would clearly be the more challenging case, and thus it makes an appropriate focus for planning, to make sure that the approach is adequately robust to cover both cases. But when the preparations are pursued publicly, it will be best to discuss them in terms of prepara-

---

[17] See Scobell, 2008, pp. 5–6, 12.

tion for a peaceful unification, given the political anxieties in the ROK about a North Korean government collapse.

As it was largely impossible to predict the East German and Soviet collapses at the end of the Cold War, so it is impossible to predict a North Korean government collapse other than to say it could happen, perhaps even in the next few years. Many in South Korea feel that such a collapse would provide the best prospect for Korean reunification. But even in the best of cases, South Korea has not adequately prepared the military, economic, and other capabilities that would be needed to handle a North Korean government collapse. South Korea would undoubtedly call on the United States to provide the necessary military and economic support. But the United States is also inadequately prepared for such an event. Any Chinese intervention today could prove to be more of a problem than a help, but preparation could also transform a Chinese intervention to a significant help. Geopolitical reality would limit the ability of other countries to provide any substantial help for weeks to months. In the end, regional stability and economic viability will critically depend on an effective South Korean and U.S. intervention, perhaps with Chinese assistance.

Because South Korea and the United States are inadequately prepared, a collapse today could have dire consequences. Some of the likely consequences would be a humanitarian disaster causing widespread starvation, proliferation of weapons of mass destruction (WMD) to terrorist groups and/or rogue states, civil war in North Korea, the inability to control all of North Korea, military and political damage to South Korea, and vastly expanded black market and criminal activity in North Korea. South Korea–led efforts to intervene and achieve unification could develop into military conflict with North Korean forces, a North Korean insurgency, and military confrontation with China. A failure to establish stability in North Korea, resolve the humanitarian disaster, and control WMD could disrupt the political and economic conditions of Northeast Asia and even leave a serious power vacuum for a decade or more. Such chaotic developments could precipitate serious damage to U.S. interests both regionally and globally while increasing the risk of a terrorist attack against the United States.

Methodology

The top row of Figure 1.1 provides the basic approach of this study. As noted above, it starts with the potential negative consequences of unification, seeks to identify the challenges that could cause these consequences, and proposes responses to the challenges.

For example, one likely consequence of a North Korean collapse would be a humanitarian disaster that would largely be due to inadequate food and medicine in North Korea and the hoarding of what does exist. Hoarding is likely because the government collapse will make the North Korean won of questionable value,[18] forcing people to exchange money for goods and hold them as a means of economic

Figure 1.1
The Study Concept: Backward Planning

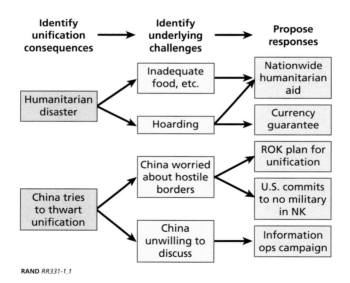

RAND RR331-1.1

---

[18] In practice, many people in North Korea already prefer to do business in foreign currency (such as the Chinese yuan, the U.S. dollar, and the European euro) rather than in the North Korean won. North Korean authorities have repeatedly tried to prevent the use of foreign currency, in part by collecting it, with only modest success. The elites tend to have foreign currency and may use it to hold financial value instead of transferring to goods, reducing some of the causes for a decreased food supply. See Chico Harlan, "In North Korea, Role of Foreign Currency Grows," *Washington Post*, February 15, 2012.

leverage in place of the won. One key action to breaking both these challenges would be nationwide humanitarian aid from the ROK, the United States, and perhaps China. Such an effort would require all three countries to make immense preparations of aid plus transportation and security capabilities needed to deliver that aid. Another response would be for the ROK and the United States to offer a currency guarantee relative to the North Korean won, so that it would continue to be of value and would not have to be replaced by goods such as food.

As another example, China could decide to thwart unification by intervening in North Korea in support of a faction that it identifies as "the legitimate government of North Korea." It could claim that it is intervening to assist the North Korean government in suppressing an insurgency. It might further decide to threaten the ROK and the United States not to intervene, saying that they have no role in North Korea. China could do so because it is worried about having hostile forces (especially from the United States) on its borders. But China has also been largely unwilling to discuss a collapse scenario out of fear of appearing disloyal to its North Korean ally (and potentially destabilizing the North when the North is already in a dangerous condition). To deal with China's concerns, the ROK could explain to China its plans for unification, and the United States could commit to China that U.S. forces would not be based on North Korean territory after unification.[19] The ROK and the United States could use an information operations campaign to communicate this information to China. But note that such an information operations campaign needs to begin now, well before a government collapse, and then be adjusted as circumstances develop.[20]

---

[19] Toward the end of the Cold War, the United States committed to the Soviet Union that it would not base U.S. forces in East Germany if German unification occurred—a similar commitment that helped assuage Soviet fears.

[20] After initiating such a campaign, the ROK and the United States should gradually be able to develop better abilities to discuss North Korean collapse with China and to reassure China that they do not intend to jeopardize Chinese security in responding to a North Korean collapse. Note that the ROK and the United States also need an information operations campaign targeting North Korea, as will be discussed in Chapter Four.

In the course of this research, I recognized that the basic consequences of unification as identified in Figure 1.1 could have higher-order consequences that were more serious. These are shown by additions on the left in Figure 1.2. For example, a humanitarian disaster in North Korea could lead the North Koreans to become disaffected with Korean unification, while Chinese thwarting of unification could lead to a new North Korean government that is, at least for some time, stable. And these consequences could lead to the ROK being unable to unify with North Korea.

The Need for Better Preparation

Both the academic and public policy literature have tended to ignore or significantly underestimate these potential consequences. Mitigating these consequences requires a broader and more explicit understanding of them and of the "challenges" that could exacerbate them. These aggregate challenges include (1) an inadequate overarching strategy to

Figure 1.2
Higher-Order Consequences

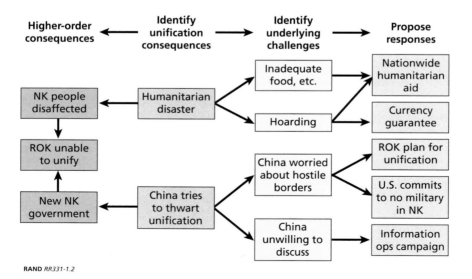

RAND RR331-1.2

deal with collapse; (2) gaps in South Korean and U.S. military and related capabilities; (3) inadequate planning and preparation for such issues as containing WMD, preventing conflict with China, providing humanitarian aid, and establishing economic and social viability; and (4) a failure to secure support for South Korea–led unification from the various North Korean population segments (the elites, the military, the common people, and the black market). Currently, there is also no bilateral, interagency organization to prepare and implement a strategy to address these challenges.

Mitigation of the most dire consequences requires both South Korean and U.S. efforts to overcome these challenges. There is a need to identify (1) potential responses that specify what needs to be done, (2) how these actions need to be timed and sequenced, and (3) how to accomplish them via politically acceptable means. The literature addresses some of these challenges and some possible responses but misses many others and is seldom sufficiently explicit to clarify the package of actions that actually need to be taken.

For example, North Korea's WMD capabilities make WMD proliferation to a terrorist group a potential consequence that could lead to another potential consequence, terrorists using WMD against the United States. The challenges that would exacerbate WMD proliferation include the limited intelligence on the North Korean WMD capabilities and the WMD locations, as well as the lack of ROK and U.S. military capabilities prepared to promptly find, secure, and eliminate that WMD. The decreasing size of ROK military forces, potential commitments of U.S. forces elsewhere, and constraints on ROK reserve call-up and training further complicate any response.

Many of the challenges relate to inadequate military capabilities and plans for dealing with North Korean military forces of reportedly 1.2 million active duty and 7.7 million reserve personnel, vastly more than the United States faced in Iraq. The ROK military has been designed to repel a North Korean invasion, not to deal with a North Korean collapse. Former U.S. Secretary of Defense Robert Gates indicated that he would send primarily air and naval forces to handle Korean contingencies, instead of the U.S. ground forces that would normally be involved in handling a collapse. The mismatch between requirements in specific capability areas and existing capabilities is even more serious and needs to be better characterized so that action can be taken to redress the shortfalls.

Report Outline

The remainder of this report is organized as follows. Chapter Two addresses the possibilities for collapse, recognizing North Korea as a failing state that could collapse and lead to Korean unification. Chapter Three describes the potential consequences of a North Korean government collapse not only to North Korea but also to surrounding countries. Chapter Four talks about how the ROK and the United States need to affect North Korean thinking about government collapse and subsequent unification. Chapter Five discusses the challenges associated with a collapse-induced humanitarian disaster in North Korea, how to respond to it, and the preparations needed to make that response effective. Chapter Six proposes responses to conflict in North Korea, demilitarization of North Korean ground forces, and elimination of North Korean WMD. Chapter Seven recommends how to deal with the North Korean security forces and how to prevent or minimize the human rights disasters that could occur at North Korean political prison camps. Chapter Eight identifies options for dealing with property and business ownership after Korean unification. Chapter Nine addresses Chinese intervention and how to prepare to handle it. Finally, Chapter Ten addresses how two of the prerequisites of preparing for a North Korean government collapse can be handled.

CHAPTER TWO

Possibilities for Collapse

Many sources identify North Korea as a failed or failing state. For example,

> The Fund for Peace and *Foreign Policy* magazine developed the Failed States Index and have measured the degree of failure of states by using 22 quantifiable indicators every year since 2005. North Korea is one of the 20 countries that have been on the list of failed states for the last seven years (2005–11). All these countries are dictatorial, very poor, have experienced civil wars, and all but Ethiopia are former colonies. Excepting North Korea, these former colonies have gone through violent leadership changes since independence.[1]

North Korea is a "former colony" (of Japan) and has also "gone through violent leadership changes" since independence—notably the many purges of senior leaders and others (just not violent changes of the top North Korean leader). Thus, North Korea has much in common with the other states in the failed-state pool.

While North Korea exhibits many aspects of a failed state, its future is highly uncertain. North Korea has created extremely powerful control mechanisms that thus far have been quite sufficient to prevent a government collapse. As a result, Korea experts disagree whether North Korea will actually fail in the short term or whether it will prove to be as resilient as it has been in the past. This is an ongoing debate

---

[1] Park Sang-seek, "What's Behind N. Korea's Survival?" *Korea Herald*, May 1, 2012. See also Fund for Peace, "Failed States Index," 2011.

that only time will resolve. Still, the resilience of the North Korean state does not eliminate the potential for North Korean government collapse. Various factors are evolving in a direction that will render North Korea more susceptible over time to the kinds of system shocks that would eventually cause its government to fail. There is a reasonable probability that North Korean totalitarianism will end in the foreseeable future, with the very strong likelihood that this end will be accompanied by considerable violence and upheaval.[2]

Conceptualizing Government Collapse

A government collapse is inherently a failure of the government to maintain control. Because the actual level of government control can vary significantly over time, collapse is a process rather than a single event. For example, as outside information leaks into North Korea, North Korean indoctrination is gradually eroding, which may eventually facilitate a full collapse of the North Korean government. The cessation of government functions is worse than the mere failure of a particular political party or regime. In the resulting power vacuum, various factions may vie with one another to take control, although they will most often succeed in only limited geographic areas.

In a totalitarian society, such as North Korea's, the government creates a system of controls to remove threats, avert failure, and maintain order. North Korea has implemented one of the most extensive control systems in modern history, including near deification of the Kim family leaders. The North Korean people are thoroughly indoctrinated through ubiquitous propaganda campaigns designed to control their thinking. Citizens are brainwashed to believe that the Kim family leaders are extremely gifted, wise, and benevolent. They are further propagandized to regard their country as the envy of the world (e.g.,

---

[2]   See, for example, Andrew Scobell, "Making Sense of North Korea: Pyongyang and Comparative Communism," *Asian Security,* Vol. 1, No. 3, 2005, pp. 245–266.

North Korea is a "Paradise on Earth"[3]). Their way of life is portrayed as far superior to that of their South Korean brothers; for example, the ROK is portrayed as "a starving U.S. colony, a 'living hell, land of destitution and despair.'"[4] All citizens are enlisted in the fight against "evil" outside powers (mainly the United States) that seek to destroy their near utopia.

The North Korean government sustains this illusion by trying to deny its people access to outside information, thereby preventing them from questioning their indoctrination. The state thwarts the import of books and electronic media. Radios and televisions sold to the North Korean people allow reception only of North Korean state media. The government prevents most of its citizens from acquiring Chinese cell phones because these devices could be used to receive external news near the Chinese border and to transmit to outsiders more realistic accounts of conditions in North Korea. All but the most reliable of North Koreans are restricted from crossing the border because they could bring back information that the regime has not sanitized. And the North Korean closing of the Kaesong Industrial Complex in 2013 may have been heavily motivated by the gradual infiltration of outside information through Kaesong and into the North, a concern apparently significant enough to outweigh the financial benefits to the North of keeping the complex open.

The North Korean state employs at least three different security organizations,[5] with security personnel and other informants interlaced throughout the military and society, to catch and punish any citizens who misbehave or diverge from the party line. These organizations spy on each other as an added safety measure. The punishment for violators is brutal. They are often killed or sent with three generations of their families into an incredibly extreme political prison system:

---

[3]   Kim Hyun Sik, "The Secret History of Kim Jong Il," *Foreign Policy*, September/October 2008.

[4]   Andrei Lankov, "Pyongyang Puts Politics Above Dollars," *Asia Times*, November 26, 2008.

[5]   These three organizations are the Ministry of People's Security, the Ministry of State Security (the National Security Agency), and the Military Security Command.

Most North Koreans are sent to the camps without any judicial process, and many die there without learning the charges against them. They are taken from their homes, usually at night, by the Bowibu, the National Security Agency. Guilt by association is legal in North Korea. A "wrongdoer" is often imprisoned with his/her parents and children. Kim Il Sung laid down the law in 1972: "[E]nemies of class, whoever they are, their seed must be eliminated through three generations."[6]

In large part, North Korean elites sustain the current government, motivated by the belief that collapse could doom them to starvation and perhaps criminal prosecution. The North Korean state has capitalized on the worst news from German unification to sustain this perception:

> German unification completely deprived all East German Communist party and military leaders of their privileges and made them jobless. Kim Jong-il had the plight of former East German leaders photographed and shown to North Korean cadres. And many members of the elite, though they detested Kim Jong-il, thought they had no alternative but to follow him for fear of losing their privileges if the regime collapsed. That is why the regime did not collapse despite the 1990s famine that starved millions to death.[7]

The government also uses a diversionary approach to excuse its failings: "Domestically, it justifies all its policies and denies the existence of any problems through oppression, propaganda and indoctrination. It claims that all its problems are caused by outside enemies, particularly South Korea and the U.S., as a typical person in denial."[8]

To moderate external pressure against the state, North Korea has positioned itself internationally as the ultimate "poison pill." The collapse of the government could spell disaster for China and the ROK

---

[6] Blaine Harden, *Escape from Camp 14*, New York: The Penguin Group, 2012, p. 6.

[7] Kang Chol-hwan, "Power Struggle Looms in N.Korea," *Chosun Ilbo*, May 8, 2009.

[8] Park Sang-seek, 2012.

in terms of refugees, economic demands, stabilization difficulties, and North Korean revenge.[9] China and the ROK might favor the current North Korean system over facing these overwhelming problems. The poison-pill approach has been particularly effective with China, which above all values the prevention of instability in this region.

The North Korean government has effectively implemented the above techniques to maintain control. However, collapse could still be expected if troublesome events overwhelm the government, trigger failure of the control system, and thwart the replacement of national leadership. In all societies, there are events that test the government, varying from economic difficulties to infringement of individual rights to failure to provide promised benefits. As these events become more serious and affect more people, the government relies on its control system to sustain order. When the control system is no longer strong enough to manage dissonance, a collapse occurs. Thus, the likelihood of collapse increases with the prevalence and severity of troublesome events that weaken the control system. And the brutality of that control system will tend to cause a violent and tumultuous period when the North Korean regime and government fail.

North Korea was plagued with severe and ubiquitous challenges during the 1990s, events of the type that would test most governments. The end of the Cold War terminated or significantly reduced Soviet and Chinese subsidies to North Korea, subsidies that were critical to sustaining North Korean economic performance. Figure 2.1 shows data from one source indicating that the North Korean GDP fell precipitously once subsidies ended, particularly in the early 1990s. Markus Noland cites four other sources that document a decline of the North Korean per capita income between 35 to 75 percent of pre-1990s figures, over the same period.[10] These trends had an extreme impact on a

---

[9]   The "poison pill" terminology is mine. China feels that North Korean refugees pose a particular security problem to China. The potential consequences for China of a North Korean collapse are also discussed in Denny Roy, "China and Nuclear Standoff Over N. Korea," *Korea Herald*, August 25, 2009.

[10]   Marcus Noland, "Is the North Korean Economy Growing?" *North Korea: Witness to Transformation*, Washington, D.C.: Peterson Institute for International Economics, March 13, 2012.

Figure 2.1
North Korean Gross Domestic Product

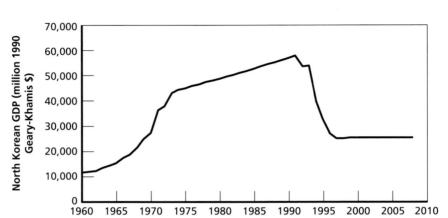

SOURCE: Angus Maddison, "Historical Statistics of the World Economy: 1–2008 AD," Excel workbook, undated.
RAND RR331-2.1

significant proportion of the population; many citizens lost their jobs and quickly became impoverished. The subsequent famine led to the death of at least hundreds of thousands of North Koreans, if not several million. Many of those who survived fled to China, numbering perhaps in the hundreds of thousands. These dramatic national catastrophes occurred during the period of leadership succession from Kim Il-Sung to Kim Jong-Il, a period of inherent challenge to any totalitarian system. This transition was exacerbated by Kim Jong-Il's lack of a warm and empowered personality, rendering his image inconsistent with the personality cult of the regime and the expectations of the citizenry. Despite the predictions of many experts that the North Korean regime would fail under these adverse circumstances, the government did not collapse. Its survival demonstrated the incredible strength of the control system Kim Il-Sung developed.

Since the end of 2011, North Korea has been in the midst of a second hereditary succession, a new period of challenge to the state control system. Many predict the government will again demonstrate its resilience throughout this transition, especially given

Kim Jong-Un's warm and empowered personality, more similar to his popular grandfather than to his father. Moreover, the North Korean economy may be slowly growing as recent Chinese support has made a significant positive difference. Indeed, visitors to Pyongyang describe the city as appearing far wealthier than in the past.[11] Kim Jong-Un has also strengthened his position in the control system through new leadership appointments (e.g., General Kim Won-Hong is the new director of the North Korean National Security Agency) and through countermeasures to bribery. These actions appear to have significantly reduced the refugee flow into China.

On the other hand, the North Korean control system has suffered some erosion. The development of pockets of wealth within an economy where most citizens still have trouble surviving has fundamentally shaken the control system. This dichotomy has created a fertile environment for rampant bribery. Control personnel, who can often afford less than two pounds of rice a month on their official salary, are anxious to augment their income by receiving bribes, and some even extort such payments. Richer citizens possess the means to offer bribes and are motivated to do so to advance their business interests and obtain the lifestyle they desire. Furthermore, outside information is increasingly penetrating into North Korea, belying the North Korean indoctrinations. This is especially true among the richer citizenry, including the elites, who regularly take risks to accumulate wealth and often assume that they can survive discovery through bribery.

---

[11] According to one observer,

> Walking the streets of Pyongyang after an absence of eight years it's easy to be seduced by a superficial optimism that things have changed for the better. Apartment blocks and streets are lit at night. New shops and restaurants catering for local people are thriving. Traffic, including private cars, though hardly at the level of Seoul or Beijing, is a constant on Pyongyang's streets which at last have a traffic light system that works. . . . Even 10 years ago the shops available to the city's 3 million inhabitants could be counted on one hand; the city streets were almost silent and usually pitch black at night, with apartment blocks seldom displaying more than flickering and muted light from torches or candles after dark. Construction had all but stopped in every part of the city.

Hazel Smith, "Don't Expect a Pyongyang Spring Sometime Soon," Washington, D.C.: Center for Strategic and International Studies, PacNet #60, October 28, 2011.

In addition, North Korea is poised to experience further major system shocks in the next few years. The nation's infrastructure is decaying, thereby creating the potential for significant failures in local areas and among individual firms that could ripple throughout the economy. The North Korean energy grid is particularly at risk. Already experiencing many periodic local failures, the grid has degenerated to the point that the distribution of power nationwide is threatened. Bad weather and the lack of chemical treatments to prevent insect infestations and plant disease could lead to the kind of critical agricultural disaster that helped cause the 1995–1998 famine. National inflation could force another currency revaluation, a troubling trend inasmuch as the last revaluation turned into a serious economic disaster. On the international political front, China is exasperated with North Korean provocations and could decide to cut back or terminate its aid, potentially causing an economic fiasco in the North like that of the mid-1990s. Internally, Kim Jong-Un has already purged a significant number of senior North Korean leaders, which could push other senior officials to rebel against him.

At some point, the North Korean control system will fail—but it is very difficult to determine when that might be. Ironically, the slowly improving economic conditions in parts of the North may actually increase the danger to North Korea's governmental system. According to one expert,

> revolutions do not happen when people are really desperate. Most revolutions have occurred at a time of steady improvement in political freedoms and living standards, as the recent Arab Spring has further proved. . . . People start revolutions when they know alternatives to the current system, when they believe things might and should be better.[12]

Currently, such conditions appear to exist in North Korea for selected members of the elite and the merchant class, making challenges to the leadership possible in the future.

---

[12] Andrei Lankov, "Conditions Unripe for North Korea Revolt," *Asia Times*, November 17, 2011b.

The Uncertain North Korean Situation

North Korean leadership excels at denying the outside world most information about its nation. Whenever they cannot deny information, they distort the truth. Consequently, it is almost always difficult to describe reality within North Korea and to predict North Korean events. Some anecdotal information does escape the North, but analysts frequently cannot determine whether this intelligence accurately represents the country as a whole or is purposefully misleading. Although some information can be gathered by outside independent observation, often this evidence is very approximate and uncertain.

Several examples will help illustrate the difficulties of analyzing affairs inside North Korea, given the lack of reliable information:

1. **North Korean leadership.** In December 2011, North Korean leader Kim Jong-Il died. Since his death, official North Korean announcements have proclaimed his third son, Kim Jong-Un, as the new leader of the state, the military, and the Worker's Party. No competing sources have issued statements to the contrary, and there have been no verifiable facts to dispute the truth of the official announcements. Still, it is unclear who is actually making policy decisions and exercising ultimate governmental control. Alternative sources argue varying positions. Some claim that Kim Jong-Un is indeed the leader and the principal decisionmaker,[13] while others postulate that his uncle and "regent" Jang Song-Thaek is in control.[14] Still other analysts contend that a collective leadership group behind Kim Jong-Un is leading the nation.[15] In practice, no outsiders are in any position to verify who actually controls state decisions or to observe what the relative power relationships are.

---

[13] For example, Mok Yong Jae, "Cheong: Jang Has Passed His Peak," *DailyNK*, February 7, 2012b.

[14] Donald Kirk and Clifford Coonan, "Uncle Jang Emerges as Real Power in North Korea," *The Independent*, December 22, 2011.

[15] For example, Benjamin Kang Lim, "N.Korea Military, Uncle to Share Power with Kim's Heir," Reuters, December 21, 2011.

2. **North Korean nuclear weapons**. North Korea apparently tested a nuclear weapon in 2006, 2009, and 2013. Beyond those three weapons, relatively little is known about the number and types of nuclear weapons that North Korea might possess. Typically, estimates are based on the amount of fissile material that North Korea *might have produced* and usually range from perhaps five to 12 plutonium weapons (perhaps somewhat fewer after three were tested).[16] However, this focus on produced fissile material ignores fissile material that North Korea may have acquired from other sources that could augment the weapons it has produced. There is some evidence that it did acquire sufficient plutonium for perhaps another ten nuclear weapons.[17] North Korea might also have produced enough highly enriched uranium for several more weapons. In short, North Korea may have somewhere between zero and 25 nuclear weapons, and the outside world simply does not know the exact number.[18] Lacking verifiable data on this issue, other nations are at a loss because there are significantly different policy implications across that estimated range of nuclear weapons.

3. **Crop yields in the 1990s**. North Korean crop yields can be projected from satellite photographs, direct observation during trips through the countryside, and the relative availability of food after the harvest. The key crops in North Korea are grains, including rice, maize, wheat, and barley. Because North Korea appears to produce insufficient quantities of these grains to sustain its population, the annual estimate of grain production is a key factor in forecasting famine in any given year. Figure 2.2 shows how these estimates compare to the food requirements

---

[16] See, for example, David Albright and Christina Walrond, "North Korea's Estimated Stocks of Plutonium and Weapon-Grade Uranium," Washington, D.C.: Institute for Science and International Security (ISIS), August 16, 2012.

[17] The most consistent claim is that North Korea acquired 56 kg of plutonium from some part of the former Soviet Union. See Bruce W. Bennett, *Uncertainties in the North Korean Nuclear Threat,* Santa Monica, Calif.: RAND Corporation, DB-589-NDU, 2010, especially pp. 15–19.

[18] Albright and Walrond, 2012.

Figure 2.2
North Korean Grain Production: FAO Versus Bank of Korea

SOURCES: United Nations Food and Agriculture Organization, FAO statistical
database, undated, and Bank of Korea, "Economic Statistics System," database, 2010,
item 17.2.1.
RAND RR331-2.2

for this period. The Food and Agricultural Organization (FAO) of the United Nations (UN) provides a long-term historical pattern. The Bank of Korea estimate is more limited, starting only in 1990. A data comparison over the period since 1990 is interesting. Since 1998, the two estimates are fairly similar. But in the period from 1990 to 1994, the estimates differ markedly, with the FAO numbers being roughly twice those from the Bank of Korea. If the Bank of Korea data are accurate, it would be hard to imagine that North Korea experienced a severe famine in the mid- to late-1990s, while the FAO curve paints a much more dire picture. The FAO numbers correlate more closely with anecdotal evidence from that period.

4. **Consequences of famine**. North Korea has been very careful to obscure the famine's toll on human life in the mid- to late-1990s. Independent estimates of those who died during the famine run from many hundred thousands up to 3 million or so, amounting to perhaps 2.5 to 15 percent of the North Korean

population. Reportedly, the most serious losses occurred among the very young and the very old, populations that would naturally have suffered higher death percentages. Yet if one compares the reported population of those who were 0 to 4 years old at the time of the 1993 North Korean census (2,088,508) to the same age cohort at the time of the next census in 2008 (those who were 15 to 19: 2,052,342), it appears that some 98.3 percent survived.[19] Given the death rates by age recorded as part of the 2008 census, one would expect that 97.7 percent of this cohort would have survived in the conditions of 2008. That the conditions in the mid- to late 1990s were much worse suggests that North Korea should have had no more than about 95 percent survival of this age group and perhaps as poor as 83 percent. Therefore, the reported figures suggest that North Korea falsified its 2008 census to obscure the famine effects. This pattern is also reproduced elsewhere. For example, Figure 2.3 shows the North Korean population growth rate over time from the Bank of Korea and the World Bank. Descriptions of the mid- to late-1990s famine would suggest that more people died than were born during this period. Consequently, there should not have been a net population growth, yet both sources report otherwise.

The Background of Collapse and Potential Future Shocks

Today, North Korea has a largely failed economy and agricultural production less than its subsistence requirements.[20] The population survives because of illegal market economy activities that the government

---

[19] In South Korea over this same period, approximately 96.3 percent of the 0–4 age group in 1993 were counted in the 2008 census. This number is likely low because of students overseas in 2008 and is thus not directly comparable. These data were taken from Korean Statistical Information Service, website, undated.

[20] North Korea needs about 5.4 million tons of grain each year to feed its people at subsistence levels. It produced only about 4.1 million tons in 2009. See, for example, "Food Shortage Worsens in N. Korea: Official," *Korea Herald*, February 10, 2010.

Figure 2.3
North Korean Population Change

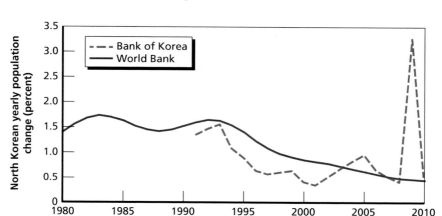

SOURCES: Bank of Korea, 2010, and World Bank, "World Development Indicators,"
December 15, 2011.
RAND RR331-2.3

finds threatening but indispensable and because of substantial foreign
aid, mainly from China in recent years. Even so, a significant number
of citizens are starving to death,[21] while others suffer seriously.[22] North

---

[21] A useful source on North Korean starvation is the Good Friends website. It works in
North Korea and has access to information about what is actually happening, which it regu-
larly posts. The North Korean starvation is described in the site's blog, North Korea Today,
in such issues as 330–335 (February–March 2010), with particular attention to the article,
Good Friends USA, "News of 'Imminent Death from Starvation' Floods the Central Party,"
North Korea Today blog, No. 331, February 2010.

[22] For example,

> [m]alnutrition-related cognitive disabilities among *North Korean* children and young
> people likely will impact future economic growth in that country regardless of when
> Pyongyang opens to the outside world or reunifies with the South. Nationwide malnu-
> trition has compelled Pyongyang to lower minimum height and weight requirements for
> military service, and an estimated 17 to 29 percent of potential North Korean military
> conscripts between 2009 and 2013 will have cognitive deficiencies disqualifying them
> for service.

National Intelligence Council, 2008, p. 6.

Korean economic and agricultural distress is foundational to a society ill prepared to withstand future shocks to its government.

North Korean Economic Difficulties

North Korea's economy is a constant disappointment to the North Korean people and regime. Speaking of the period before 2012,

> [t]he North Korean government often highlights its 2012 goal of becoming a "strong and prosperous" nation and attracting foreign investment, a key factor for improving the overall standard of living. Nevertheless, firm political control remains the government's overriding concern, which likely will inhibit changes to North Korea's current economic system.[23]

When 2012 arrived, North Korea was well short of being "strong and prosperous," although it tried to use ballistic missile tests as a vehicle for claiming success in its economic efforts.

Historically, North Korea was the industrialized part of Korea, whereas the ROK was the agricultural area. But in the 1970s, the ROK economy advanced in a surge of industrialization, and its GDP soon surpassed that of North Korea. In 2011, the ROK per capita GDP was about $31,700, while North Korea's was about $1,800, making the ROK per capita GDP almost 18 times greater than that of North Korea.[24]

In the decades after the Korean War, the North Korean economy appeared to move forward well, subsidized by its Soviet and Chinese allies. Eventually, however, the system began to show signs of distress, until serious levels of erosion became apparent. Today,

---

[23] Central Intelligence Agency (CIA), "Korea, North: Economy—Overview," *World Factbook*, 2012.

[24] Estimates vary; the numbers in the text from CIA, 2012, put the South Korean GDP per capita at about 18 times that of North Korea, while the older Wolf and Akramov puts it somewhere between 8 and 17 times, understandably lower because of the relative growth in ROK GDP since 2005 (Charles Wolf, Jr., and Kamil Akramov, *North Korean Paradoxes: Circumstances, Costs, and Consequences of Korean Unification*, Santa Monica, Calif.: RAND Corporation, MG-333-OSD, 2005, pp. 4–5).

industrial capital stock is nearly beyond repair as a result of years of underinvestment, shortages of spare parts, and poor maintenance. Large-scale military spending draws off resources needed for investment and civilian consumption. Industrial and power output have stagnated for years at a fraction of pre-1990 levels.[25]

Debates have erupted regarding the level of the North Korean economy over the last several decades. In contrast to the GDP pattern shown in Figure 2.1, one expert on the North Korean economy, Marcus Noland, has presented four data sets on North Korean per capita income trends in dollars. These data indicate that, from 1970 to 1990, North Korea maintained fairly constant growth, increasing per capita income between about 30 and 100 percent over the two decades. Then, from roughly 1990 to the mid-1990s, the North Korean per capita income fell by 35 to 75 percent.[26] This downward trend reversed in the late 1990s through 2009, with the North Korean per capita income increasing approximately 25 percent according to most sources[27]—slow but important growth but not nearly enough to return North Korea to its pre-1990s status.

A combination of market economy practices plus Chinese subsidies appears responsible for much of this economic growth. The North Korean black market has always been one form of market activity since the creation of the state. In the early 2000s, the leadership loosened control of economic activity, hoping to offset shortages of food and other goods. After this brief experiment, the government then clamped down on market economy activity during the 2008–2009 time frame, having observed the increased power North Korean merchants were wielding because of their wealth. The negative economic backlash of this reversal forced the North Korean government to reconsider its eco-

[25] CIA, 2012.

[26] Noland, 2012.

[27] Of the four sources, the Bank of Korea data show the most substantial increases, nearly 100 percent from the late-1990s to 2009. The other three sources show roughly 25 percent growth during this period.

nomic policy once again. Eventually, the leadership loosened control on market economy activity, a condition that appears to continue.

According to Peter Hayes and David von Hippel,

> [e]ven for the DPRK [Democratic People's Republic of Korea] economy to remain at its current "subsistence" level, help from other nations has been required. . . . the DPRK receives sufficient crude oil from China to keep one of its two oil refineries running, though at well below full capacity.[28]

Heavy Chinese government investment in the North Korean sectors beyond energy is stimulating some economic activity, especially in the northeast around key ports that China plans to use. Overall, the Chinese provide North Korea support what amounts to a trade gap of approximately $1 billion per year.[29]

Examining GDP by economic sector, as shown in Figure 2.4, provides further insight into the North Korean economy. The Bank of Korea shows major declines in the heavy manufacturing, mining, and construction sectors from 1990 to 1998, key backbones of an industrialized society. These sectors appear to have recovered somewhat since the late-1990s, as have other economic sectors, but they are still well short of their pre-1990 levels.

The actual national industrial capability is in part reflected by North Korean energy use, as shown in Figure 2.5. Energy use declined 40 percent between 1990 and 2000 and has not sustained any real growth since then. Another source shows an even greater decline in energy use—some 60 percent—between 1990 and 2000, with only slight recovery after 2000. Since then,

> the DPRK's energy sector has been sustained primarily by an annual half-million tonnes of crude oil from China, modest

---

[28] Peter Hayes and David von Hippel, "DPRK 'Collapse' Pathways: Implications for the Energy Sector and for Strategies of Redevelopment/Support," Los Angeles: Korean Studies Institute, University of Southern California, and Washington, D.C.: Center for Strategic and International Studies, August 2010, p. 5.

[29] Mark E. Manyin and Mary Beth Nikitin, "Foreign Assistance to North Korea," Washington, D.C.: Congressional Research Service, R-40095, June 1, 2011., p. 22.

Figure 2.4
North Korean GDP, by Economic Sector

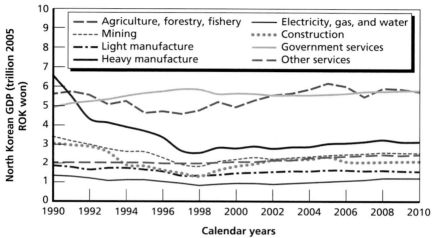

SOURCES: Bank of Korea, 2010.
RAND RR331-2.4

Figure 2.5
North Korean Energy Use

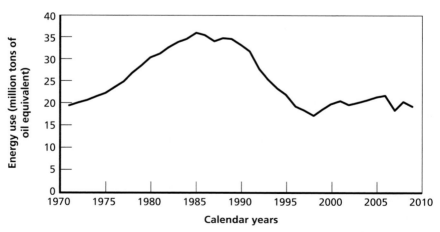

SOURCE: World Bank, 2010.
RAND RR331-2.5

imports of refined oil products, Korean tenacity and ingenuity that have kept some of its coal mines and aging power and coal production infrastructure running, and the substitution of wood and other biomass for subsistence energy use.[30]

During the 1990s, the decline in industrial energy use was roughly 75 percent, with essentially no recovery from 2000 to 2008. In contrast, residential and public and commercial areas have experienced slight growth in energy use. In the future, demand in these sectors may well consume any further growth capacity the North Korean energy sector has, leaving industry with little room for expansion.[31]

In addition, the North Korean energy distribution system is aged and difficult to maintain. Consequently, it likely can no longer operate at a capacity much beyond current levels:

> Since 2000 there have been modest improvements in the DPRK economy and energy sector, with some power plant repairs, new small hydroelectric facilities, and new mining activity underwritten, in large part, by Chinese investment. Still, shortages of power, district heat, and coal persist, with blackouts even in Pyongyang, and much more tenuous power supply in other areas. In effect, the North Korean electricity system, though it is nominally a nationwide transmission and distribution grid, is in effect [a] patchwork of a few regional and some local grids, centered around major and smaller power plants. Most of the large thermal (almost all coal fired) power plants and heating plants are only partially in operation due to damage of various kinds to one or more boilers/generating units, and/or to transformers, substations, or other parts of the transmission and distribution system. This means that even if large amounts of fuel or electricity were suddenly to be available to the DPRK, distribution of that energy would be problematic.[32]

---

[30] David von Hippel, Scott Bruce, and Peter Hayes, "Transforming the DPRK Through Energy Sector Development," *38 North*, Special Report 11-3, March 4, 2011.

[31] Hayes and von Hippel, 2010, pp. 4, 6.

[32] Hayes and von Hippel, 2010, p. 4.

The energy challenges are borne out by anecdotal reporting. In February 2012, NightWatch online reported:

> During the past week, foreign media have reported a worsening of the electric power supply in Pyongyang. Electricity is supplied for three hours a day. . . . Almost all commentators attribute the power outages in mid-winter to the construction surge to make North Korea appear to be a rich and prosperous nation in honor of Kim Il-sung's 100th birthday.[33]

In 2005, Seoul offered to provide North Korea 2 million kW of electricity in exchange for the discontinuation of North Korea's nuclear weapon program. But even at that time, the provision of that electricity to North Korea would have required "extensive modernization of the communist country's power grid system."[34] Major maintenance and modernization of the North Korean power grid is unlikely short of major changes in North Korean political and economic policy.

In short, North Korea's economy is still well below its pre-1990 levels. While it has seen some growth from the mid- to late 1990s, that growth has been modest and may not be sustainable.[35] The growth is fundamentally based on (1) market economy practices (including the black market), (2) Chinese subsidies, and (3) an economic infrastructure that is not being adequately updated and is gradually failing. The instability and unpredictability of these keys to North Korean economic growth make many opportunities for future shocks to the

---

[33] John McCreary, "NightWatch," blog, February 2, 2012.

[34] Lee Joon-seung, "Upgrade of N. Korea's Power Grid Needed for Electricity Aid," Yonhap News Agency, July 13, 2005.

[35] A developing alternative view argues that the North Korean economy really is making sizable growth, based significantly on the value of its trade with China. See, for example, Go Myong-Hyun, "Economic Improvement in North Korea," Seoul: Asan Institute for Policy Studies, Issue Brief 58, June 10, 2013. But Marcus Noland argues that the higher monetary value of North Korean exports to China appears to better reflect inflation in the prices of the goods that North Korea typically sells to China and that physical North Korean exports to China may be fairly constant over time. See Marcus Noland, "North Korea's Vulnerability to a China Shock," *North Korea: Witness to Transformation*, Washington, D.C.: Peterson Institute for International Economics, July 1, 2013.

system possible. Still, North Korea is trying to manage its economic exchange with China by selling the Chinese parts of what may be as much as $6 trillion in minerals in North Korea.[36]

North Korean Agriculture, Food, and Health

North Korean agriculture is in crisis mode, generating a food supply that has tended to be at or below subsistence levels since the turn of the 21st century:

> Frequent weather-related crop failures [have] aggravated chronic food shortages caused by ongoing systemic problems, including a lack of arable land, collective farming practices, poor soil quality, insufficient fertilization, and persistent shortages of tractors and fuel. Large-scale international food aid deliveries have allowed the people of North Korea to escape widespread starvation since famine threatened in 1995, but the population continues to suffer from prolonged malnutrition and poor living conditions.[37]

As a key policy of North Korean socialism, a food "public distribution system" was instituted in the 1950s. The system collected food from farmers and distributed it on a rationed basis to the North Korean citizens, largely to recipients living in urban areas. The program failed in the mid-1990s, when the government was unable to collect adequate food because of the famine. Once the famine ended, the system was partially reinstituted in 2002 but has failed to provide much of the people's requirements since that time, especially outside of Pyongyang.[38] Even in Pyongyang, the public distribution system has struggled, so much so that in 2010, four of the Pyongyang coun-

---

[36] "Economic Gap Between 2 Korea Remains Huge," *Chosun Ilbo*, January 6, 2011.

[37] CIA, 2012.

[38] Some authors claim that public distribution totally failed outside of Pyongyang in 2002. See, for example, Ralph Hassig and Kongdan Oh, *The Hidden People of North Korea*, Lanham, Md.: Rowman & Littlefield Publishers, 2009, p. 114. But the author has seen pictures and heard stories of public distribution operating outside Pyongyang. And some sources say that public distribution has begun in many parts of North Korea in 2013; see "North Korea Resumes Its Distribution of Food Rations," New Focus International, May 3, 2013. This article notes that North Korea appears to be using wartime food reserves and perhaps overseas purchases of food to support public distribution.

ties were transferred to the North Hwanghae Province, apparently to decrease demands on the public distribution system in Pyongyang.[39] Inadequate food production and black market food sales have crippled the public distribution system nationwide. Many farmers have diverted their agricultural products away from the public distribution system because they could earn more selling them on the market.[40]

Charting the difficulties of inadequate food production, Figure 2.6 expands an understanding of the data from Figure 2.2 by adding a rough grain requirement (which increases as the population increases).[41] Grains are a key food source. Given North Korea's limited variety of food sources, about 220 kg of grains per person per year is a subsistence level of food.[42] After the famine, the North Korean government,

> acknowledged that 220,000 North Koreans died of starvation between 1995 and 1998, the height of the catastrophe. At the other end of the spectrum, Hwang Jong Yup, the highest-ranking defector from North Korea, has stated that North Korean agricultural officials estimated internally to the government itself that 2.5 million people perished between 1995 and 1997, including 500,000 in 1995, one million in 1996, and another one million in 1997. Andrew Natsios's review of several independent studies concludes that there is significant evidence to support Hwang Jong Yup's estimates.[43] There have been plausible, fact-based esti-

---

[39] "Pyongyang Now More Than One-Third Smaller; Food Shortage Issues Suspected," *Asahi Shimbun*, July 17, 2010.

[40] Hassig and Oh, 2009, pp. 114–115.

[41] The databases refer to these grains as *cereals*, which is different from breakfast cereals. I therefore speak of grain here.

[42] The FAO/World Food Programme requirement for raw (unmilled) cereals is about 220 kg per person per year. Kisan Gunjalm, Swithun Goodbody, Joyce Kanyangwa Luma, and Rita Bhatia, "FAO/WFP Crop and Food Security Assessment Mission to the Democratic People's Republic of Korea," Rome: Food and Agriculture Organization of the United Nations, Economic and Social Development Department, and World Food Programme, November 16, 2010, p. 16 in the PDF version.

[43] Andrew Natsios, "The Politics of Famine in North Korea," special report, Washington, D.C.: U.S. Institute of Peace, August 2, 1999.

Figure 2.6
North Korean Cereal Production Versus Requirement

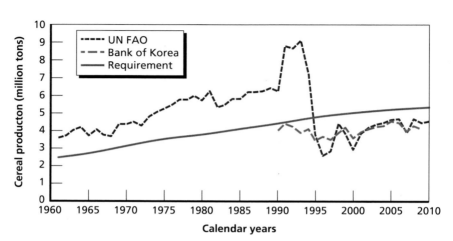

SOURCES: UN FAO, undated, and Bank of Korea, 2010. The "requirement" is also
from UN FAO, undated.
RAND RR331-2.6

mates as high as 3.5 million deaths, although these estimates are
regarded with skepticism by several scholars.[44]

Since available food quantities have not increased above subsistence levels in more recent years, starvation remains a major problem
nationwide. For example, in mid-April 2012, the *DailyNK* reported
that

> [f]ood shortages in the North Korean agricultural heartland of
> Hwanghae Province are leading to starvation deaths . . . A sig-
> nificant percentage of cooperative farm workers are reportedly
> too malnourished to work, and a number are leaving their farms
> to seek help. . . . 20,000 people had died of starvation in three
> counties in South Hwanghae Province; Baechon, Yeonan and
> Chungdan.[45]

---

[44] Havel, Bondevik, and Wiesel, 2006, p. 22.

[45] Choi Song Min and Kim Kwang Jin, "Starvation Deaths Reported in Southern Areas,"
DailyNK, May 20, 2012.

North Korea may be caught in a downward spiral of starving farmers less able to produce food for an overall starving population. Others argue that the food situation is actually improving for now,[46] but it is not clear how much change from year to year is due to variations in the weather and other factors. The North Korean government has been distributing the military's wartime food reserves to the broader population,[47] in contrast to past behavior, and also appears to be purchasing food from foreign sources.[48]

North Koreans who survive on sustenance levels of food suffer from chronic malnutrition, which frequently leads to serious health impairments:

> Even after the widespread famine of the 1990s, prolonged and severe malnutrition persisted; more than half of North Korean children are stunted or underweight, while two-thirds of young adults are malnourished or anemic. The World Food Program currently warns that a new food crisis is in the making as the result of floods and North Korea's refusal to accept food aid from a new South Korean government that is highly critical of Pyongyang.[49]

Malnutrition has a negative impact on mental capabilities. For example, the National Intelligence Council reported that, "[a]s a consequence of early childhood malnutrition, an estimated 17 to 29 percent of poten-

---

[46] For example, University of California San Diego expert Stephan Haggard argues that serious malnutrition is less serious in North Korea in the last couple of years. See Stephan Haggard, "Guns vs. Rice: More on the UNICEF Nutritional Survey," Washington, D.C.: Peterson Institute of International Economics, May 29, 2013, and Stephan Haggard and Alex Melton, "Crisis, Food Prices and Rations," Washington, D.C.: Peterson Institute of International Economics, May 10, 2013. Go Myong-Hyun makes a similar argument. See Go Myong-Hyun, 2013.

[47] North Korean military food reserves are referred to as "Warehouse 2." See "North Korea resumes . . . ," 2013.

[48] Interviews in Seoul, June 2013.

[49] National Intelligence Council, 2008, pp. 46–47.

tial North Korean military conscripts will have cognitive deficiencies severe enough to disqualify them for service by US standards."[50]

Beyond malnutrition, North Korean citizens suffer from a range of other health care problems:

> [L]ack of medicine, equipment, sanitation, and reliable energy supplies make quality healthcare virtually unobtainable outside of Pyongyang. . . . TB [tuberculosis], scarlet fever, and measles [are] particularly prevalent, although Pyongyang's secretiveness makes outbreaks extremely difficult to verify and track. Chronic diseases account for an estimated 40 percent of deaths. . . . North Korean–manufactured illicit drugs—an effort to earn hard currency—[are] increasingly used by citizens of that country as substitutes for scarce medicines or to relieve hunger or boredom.[51]

In short, the North Korean economy is extensively impaired by the dismal state of both its physical and human capital stock: "Widespread malnutrition and accompanying physical and cognitive disabilities among DPRK children and young people [are] likely inhibitors of economic growth—with or without opening to the outside world or reunification with the South."[52] These constraints make substantial improvements unlikely, while raising the potential for significant shocks that could cause catastrophic failures.

Damage to the North Korean Control System

In the past, the North Korean control system has been sufficiently strong to deal with severe threats to the government, as demonstrated by its resilience during the mid-1990s, when famine rocked the nation. However, in more recent years, control has begun to gradually degrade, as has happened in other totalitarian governments that eventually collapsed. Still, North Korean control appears to be very strong. To under-

---

[50] National Intelligence Council, 2008, p. 29.

[51] National Intelligence Council, 2008, pp. 46–47.

[52] National Intelligence Council, 2008, pp. 46–47.

stand the risks of a North Korean government collapse, it is important to examine the nature of the degradations to North Korean control.

Failing Information Control

Since the end of the Korean War, the North Korean government has indoctrinated its population, only allowing them access to state-generated information. But information on the outside is spreading in North Korea, debunking at least some of the North Korean propaganda, and generating the potential for instability: "There is mounting evidence that Kim Jong Il is losing the propaganda war inside North Korea, with more than half the population now listening to foreign news, grass-roots cynicism undercutting state myths and discontent rising even among elites."[53]

Analyzing the results of their survey of North Korean refugees in China and South Korea, Marcus Noland and Stephen Haggard have identified a number of significant shifts in information and resulting North Korean attitudes:

- The survey found that roughly half of North Koreans have access to foreign news or entertainment, a sharp rise from the 1990s, eroding faith in the regime's statements that the United States is causing its woes.[54]
- "Not only is foreign media becoming more widely available, inhibitions on its consumption are declining as well," the report said, referring to broadcasts from South Korea, China and the United States. "The availability of alternative sources of information undermines the heroic image of a workers' paradise and threatens to unleash the information cascade that can be so destabilizing to authoritarian rule."[55]

---

[53] Blaine Harden, "Dear Leader Appears to Be Losing N. Koreans' Hearts and Minds," *Washington Post*, March 24, 2010, p. 11. See also "Millions of N.Koreans Listen to Foreign Radio Broadcasts," *Chosun Ilbo*, April 30, 2010.

[54] Shaun Tandon, "N. Korea Dissent on Rise: US Study," Agence France-Presse, February 1, 2011.

[55] Harden, 2010, p. 11.

- A survey of refugees has found that "everyday forms of resistance" in the North are taking root as large swaths of the population believe that pervasive corruption, rising inequity and chronic food shortages are the fault of the government in Pyongyang—and not of the United States, South Korea or other foreign forces. . . .
- "Evaluations of the regime appear to be getting more negative over time," the report said. "Although those who departed earlier were more willing to entertain the view that the country's problems were due to foreigners, respondents who left later were more likely to hold the government accountable." . . .
- The survey found that cynicism about the government— and willingness to crack jokes about its failures—was higher among refugees who come from elite backgrounds in the government or military. It also found that distaste for the government was strongest among those deeply involved in the markets.[56]

While accepting that individuals dissatisfied enough to risk defection would have a high level of bias against the government, it still appears that the attitudes of the overall population of North Korea are changing. With much more outside information penetrating into the North Korean society, a significant number of citizens likely believe at least parts of that information:

The regime has made desperate and increasingly futile efforts to maintain a stranglehold on information, such as periodic crackdowns by the authorities on mobile phones brought in from China and seizures of widely popular and avidly watched South Korean soap operas recorded on video and DVD.[57]

Even the North Korean military is not exempt:

---

[56] Harden, 2010, p. 11.

[57] "Scenarios—North Korea's Stability Paradox," *Jane's Intelligence Review*, October 1, 2007.

An increasing number of North Korean military officers and soldiers are caught watching South Korean films or soap operas in
barracks, sources say. A Beijing-based source who visits the North
often said Monday, "Several Army officers and soldiers have been
caught watching South Korean movies or TV dramas since last
year, and the military has been providing extensive indoctrination for all officers and soldiers with a view to preventing the cultural infiltration of imperialism."[58]

Corruption in the army has become so widespread that the
government authorized the civilian police (the People's Safety
Agency) to investigate cases of corrupt military personnel. Previously, the military police handled such investigations, but the
government believes the military police have become corrupted,
and can no longer be trusted to find and punish soldiers involved
in criminal acts (stealing, or aiding smugglers to get across the
border). All this reflects poorly on the National Security Agency
(secret police), who are also seen as corrupted.[59]

The Culture of Economic Criminality: Black Markets and Bribery
While the North Korean government desires to control all aspects of
its population's behavior, it has a particular interest in dictating economic activity. By manipulating the availability of income and consumer goods, the government curbs individual freedom and preserves
its artificial system of class distinctions, two keys to perpetuating its
control over its citizenry. However, the current strength of an illegal
black market system and the pervasiveness of bribery have begun to
seriously corrode the government's domination of the economy.

One of North Korea's control mechanisms has been its command
economy. Industry is state directed rather than demand oriented, with
the state using the public distribution system to try to meet people's
needs. But the North Korean regime has generally not been able to
provide enough food and other resources. A survey of North Korean
refugees reported in the *Washington Post* found that

[58] "N.Korean Military's Morale 'Weakening,'" *Chosun Ilbo*, July 5, 2011.

[59] "Survival of the Wickedest," *Strategy Page*, June 26, 2008.

> the ground beneath Kim's government has shifted considerably in the past decade, as private markets have exploded in size and influence—and as most North Koreans are no longer dependent on the dysfunctional central government for food or work. . . . The most striking finding of the survey was the reach of those markets across all strata of North Korean society, with nearly 70 percent of respondents saying that half or more of their income came from private business dealings.[60]

The command economy still has some control on North Korean economics, but the markets are obviously gaining increasing control. A prominent symbol of governmental control failure, the North Korean black market has existed for many years but recently has grown more extensive and influential. In such countries as North Korea, the command economy does not necessarily produce the goods consumers want, and even when it does, these goods are not efficiently distributed. This disconnect may be most distressing to the elites and the growing middle class, who have economic resources but have difficulty getting the products they want. In North Korea, as in many other countries, the black market has stepped in to fill these demands and has done so for decades. This market was necessarily illegal because the North Korean government prohibited market activities—the government claimed to provide whatever North Korean citizens needed.

The black market began to thrive in the 1990s when, as noted above, the North Korean economy suffered many failures, making many goods less accessible. Then, around 2002, the North Korean government conceded to allow some market activity to proceed legally as a means of dealing with shortages of food and other commodities. But the line between legal and illegal market activity was often unclear. Plied with bribes, local officials frequently did not disrupt the market activities. Bribery became a major means of keeping market activity alive and flourishing. Even elites reportedly participated in the illegal markets and other related criminal activities. In 2010, *The Washington Times* recounted:

---

[60] Harden, 2010, p. 11.

A group of offspring of senior North Korean communist and military leaders, including Kim Jong-il's sons, have been linked by Western intelligence authorities to Pyongyang's illicit activities around the world, including distribution of counterfeit $100 bills and drug trafficking.[61]

More recently, *The New York Times* related: "When drugs and counterfeit dollars got too much exposure, the regime shifted toward [counterfeiting] cigarettes and insurance fraud."[62]

Over time, corruption flourished in and around the markets. After all, the merchant class is not supposed to exist in North Korea, but does, largely because of bribery. Bribery has worked in part because of North Korean inflation: "The average monthly salary of a North Korean worker is about 3,000 KPW [Korean People's Won]; however, the monthly expenses for an average family of four hovers around 100,000 KPW."[63] Many government employees make similar wages. The cost of living is so high in part because most families outside Pyongyang need to buy food and other necessities in the market, at market prices. Many families have therefore been forced to send the spouse into the market to make money while the husband maintains his nominal job (as the government often requires). Many public officials can only make ends meet by accepting bribes. Indeed, for lower-level officials (e.g., police and local bureaucrats), bribery is one of the principal ways they avoid starvation:

> According to defectors, it is practically impossible in modern day North Korea for ordinary citizens to survive and participate in the economy without taking part in illegal activities, such as smuggling or secret trade. For this reason, people find it necessary to cultivate close relationships with cadres in the legal system, who become the recipients of bribes in return.[64]

---

[61] Bill Gertz, "N. Korea Elite Linked to Crime," *Washington Times*, May 25, 2010, p. 1.

[62] Sheena Chestnut Greitens, "A North Korean Corleone," *New York Times*, March 3, 2012.

[63] Institute for Far Eastern Studies, "Two Years after the DPRK's Currency Revaluation," Seoul, December 8, 2011. KPW is the North Korean currency.

[64] Mok Yong Jae, "North Korea's Unlikely 'Big 3,'" *DailyNK*, January 28, 2012a.

As bribery has become a more accepted practice in North Korean society, it has become more integral to the North Korean way of life. Those with money can generally continue market activities even in areas or ways that local officials should normally oppose, in keeping with government dogma. Those who provide bribes often get themselves or their colleagues out of trouble that could otherwise lead to imprisonment. In short, they effectively put themselves above the directives of the government because they provide bribe money local officials often need to survive.

The North Korean government has experimented with a number of policies to counter illegal economic practices and to diminish the power of the increasingly wealthy merchant class:

> In late 2007, active antimarket actions were launched in the North when its top leader's ill health became apparent. Kim Jong-il's brother-in-law, Chang Sun-taek, was promoted to the newly created post of first vice director of the ruling Korean Workers' Party and was given responsibility for the police, judiciary and other areas of internal security. He visited the border near China to "clean up" smuggling and speculation, and issued special instructions tightening the regulations relevant to free markets elsewhere in the country.[65]

The government closed many local markets in 2009 and took legal action against the merchants. Then, in December 2009, North Korea instituted a currency revaluation, exchanging 100 old won for 1 new won. The revaluation was particularly devastating because the government also limited the amounts that could be legally exchanged to about $100 at black market exchange rates and required all foreign currency to be promptly exchanged into new won. With these economic reforms, the North Korean government deprived entrepreneurs of the financial capital necessary to provide the bribes that were essential for their business activities. By such means, the government largely succeeded in curbing bribery. To make the revaluation exchange palatable

---

[65] Leonid A. Petrov, "Neo-Cons Rule in Pyongyang," *Asia Times*, December 9, 2008.

to the average population, the government provided all citizens with a new won bonus.

Typical market consequences to these actions ensued. Limits on the currency exchanges caused many merchants to transfer their wealth from money to goods, such as food, which they would then hoard, reducing the available food supply. The extra money provided to all citizens in a hungry country dramatically increased the demand for food. These two extremely powerful changes in supply and demand caused prices to rise drastically. North Korea suffered 1,000 percent inflation in a period of two months (from early December 2009 to early February 2010).

But by 2009, inflation and supply shortages had already made most North Koreans dependent on the markets for many of the goods they acquired, causing the government's market limitations to imperil the survival of much of the population and thereby potentially lead to political disruption. In June 2010, "[b]owing to reality, the North Korean government has lifted all restrictions on private markets—a last-resort option for a leadership desperate to prevent its people from starving."[66] In practice, it took time for merchants to rebuild their capital, but many have now done so; others have entered the markets; and the culture of bribery has expanded beyond its previous status.

Changing key government appointments is another technique the Kim family government employs to reshape the control system in hopes of countering criminality. In April 2011, Kim Jong-Il removed General Ju Sang-Song as the Minister of People's Security, replacing him with General Ri Myong-Su.[67] And in February 2013, Kim Jong-Un replaced General Ri Myong-Su with General Choi Bu-Il.[68] In April 2012, Kim Jong-Un replaced General U Tong-Chuk, first deputy head of the State Security Ministry, with General Kim Won-Hong, the new Minister of

---

[66] Chico Harlan, "N. Korea Reverses Stance on Markets," *Washington Post*, June 19, 2010, p. 8.

[67] Kim Young-jin, "NK Parliament Closes with No Word on Heir's Promotion," *Korea Times*, April 7, 2011.

[68] "N. Korea Appoints New Security Chief," Yonhap News Agency, April 1, 2013.

State Security.[69] By shuffling these assignments, Kim Jong-Un seems to be expressing dissatisfaction with the ineffectiveness of the old leaders and appears to be aiming to reduce bribery and corruption through new leadership. But such changes must raise high anxiety among the very senior North Korean leaders, who must fear the chances and outcomes for themselves and their families of being purged. How these changes will affect government control has yet to be determined.

Other Rebellious Behavior in North Korea

Beyond being tested by rebellious behavior, such as market activities, bribery, corruption, and receipt of outside information, the North Korean government has also been challenged by refugee flows into China and apparently even by assassination attempts against the leadership:

> The famine of the 1990s destroyed absolute state control of food rationing, internal movement of citizens, and information as North Koreans were compelled to defy state restrictions in their struggle for survival—and as those who had escaped to China in search of food and work returned with news of the outside world, according to Human Rights Watch.[70]

In 2009, it was noted that "[t]ens of thousands of North Koreans have crossed the border [into China] seeking a better life. Some 15,000 have successfully defected to the South, while an estimated 100,000 to half a million are in China seeking asylum."[71] By 2012, the number of North Korean refugees in South Korea had grown to about 23,000,[72] an immense increase over refugees who had escaped to the ROK in previous years. Since North Koreans do not legally have freedom of movement, even relocating to the Chinese border is an act of defi-

---

[69] "N. Korea Purged Senior Intelligence Official: Source," *Korea Times*, April 17, 2012.

[70] National Intelligence Council, 2008, pp. 46–47.

[71] Lee Tae-hoon, "NK Regards OPLAN 5029 as Declaration of Warfare,'" *Korea Times*, November 8, 2009.

[72] Bill Keller, "The Day After," *New York Times*, April 29, 2012.

ance, and crossing that border is an act subject to imprisonment or execution for anyone returned to North Korea. By accepting bribes, border guards assigned to prevent people crossing the border without authorization are complicit in this criminal behavior. However, "[s]upplies to border units have been irregular, and as a result many troops have resorted to taking bribes and other economic incentives from defectors—often people they know well—and smugglers. The effect of this has been to undermine crackdowns at the border regions."[73]

In April 2012, the North Korean leadership transferred the border guard force from the Ministry of People's Armed Forces to the National Security Agency:

> These changes have all the hallmarks of Kim Jong Eun desperately trying to restore central government control of the border, which has been blemished in recent years by a procession of civilian defections, smuggling and leaking of information to the outside world. Previous orders to execute would-be defectors on the spot and "exterminate three generations" of defectors' families have also been attributed to Kim Jong Eun, revealing a nasty streak to rival if not overtake that of his father.[74]

While these alterations may reduce defections for a time, the desperate conditions in which the border guards live may eventually doom any system seeking to prevent defections and smuggling.

Of all the North Korean control failures, the most serious are the reported assassination attempts on the North Korean leaders.[75] There are a variety of reports of assassination attempts against Kim Jong-Il. For example,

> [s]imilar irregular activities involving firearms and explosives followed Kim Chong-il's succession in 1994 after his father, Kim Il-sung, died. The regime cracked down hard on protestors over

[73] Kim Kwang Jin and Choi Song Min, "Border Security Goes Back to NSA," *DailyNK*, April 22, 2012.

[74] Kim Kwang Jin and Choi Song Min, 2012.

[75] "Report: Assassins Targeted N Korean Leader's Son," *Irish News*, March 14, 2005.

food and shortages of other necessities. Kim Chong-il survived multiple assassination attempts in his first six months as leader in late 1994 through early 1995.[76]

Later, in 2004, there was an explosion at the Ryongchon train station in North Korea not long after Kim Jong-Il's train had passed through. Given at least one report of some details regarding the parties involved, many have speculated that the explosion was a failed assassination attempt.[77] According to South Korean intelligence sources, in 2005, "there was a family gathering including Kim Jong-il, his second son Kim Jong-chol, Jang Sung-taek's son (Jang is Kim's brother-in-law), during which shots were fired, and fights erupted. In the midst of this chaos, Kim Jong-il also knocked unconscious."[78]

There have been at least two reported assassination attempts against Kim Jong-Un. The first was an apparent internet fabrication, coming out of China.[79] But the second report appears more reliable: "North Korean leader Kim Jong-un faced an assassination attempt in Pyongyang last year during a power struggle in a military bureau, a Seoul-based intelligence source told the *JoongAng Ilbo* Tuesday."[80]

Several accounts of assassination attempts against Kim Jong-Il's oldest son, Kim Jong-Nam, also exist.[81] More recently, these reports have included attacks launched by his brother, Kim Jong-Un, the current leader of North Korea. For example, in 2009,

> North Korean leader Kim Jong-il's first son Kim Jong-nam survived an assassination attempt, according to South Korean news network KBS Monday. KBS reported that the attempt was spear-

[76] John McCreary, "NightWatch," blog, October 19, 2010.

[77] Um Sang-hyun, "N. Korea: Kim Jong-il's Distant Relative Tried to Kill Him With Chinese Blessing," *Shin-Dong-A*, October 2004.

[78] Kim Bumsoo, "N. Korea: Kim Jong-il Was Shot at (and Knocked Unconscious at His Family Compound)," *Future Korea* (in Korean), February 27, 2005.

[79] Adam Cathcart, "How Weibo 'Killed' Kim Jong-un," *The Diplomat*, February 11, 2012.

[80] Chang Se-jeong and Ser Myo-ja, "Attempt to Kill Jong-un Took Place in 2012: Source," *JoongAng Ilbo*, March 14, 2013.

[81] "Report: Assassins Targeted . . . ," 2005.

headed by aides of the North's heir apparent Kim Jeong-un, the 26-year-old third son of Kim who was recently designated to succeed the North's head. However, the plot that was tried out without the knowledge of Kim Jong-il failed as China foiled the attempt. KBS said Kim Jong-nam had maintained a close relationship with senior officials of China.[82]

It is impossible to determine how reliable these reports are. Nevertheless, this apparent pattern suggests that a North Korean leader is not beyond the potential reach of assassination.

The Weakened North Korean Military

For years, the U.S. commanders in Korea have insisted that they can successfully defend South Korea against a North Korean invasion. "General Sharp, the [previous] commander of U.S. military forces in South Korea, says he is certain he can defend against any threat from communist North Korea."[83] In large part, such confidence stems from the fact that the North Korean military has not modernized most of its weapons in several decades. During the same period, the United States and the ROK have made substantial military innovations.

The deterioration of the North Korean food supply and its health-care system have also affected North Korean military personnel: "Poor health is weakening military readiness because capable new recruits are in short supply. Loyalty may also erode over time, according to Eurasia Group; even when soldiers are well fed, they may be concerned about their malnourished family members."[84]

Even with outdated weaponry and malnourished forces, the North Korean military is not powerless; it could cause considerable damage to the ROK in a major conflict. Nevertheless, the North Korean military is poorly resourced and ill prepared for the successful completion of military operations as complicated as a conquest of the ROK.

---

[82] "Kim Jong-nam Survived Assassination Attempt," *Korea Times*, June 15, 2009.

[83] "U.S. General Says Forces Ready to Counter N.Korean Attack," *Chosun Ilbo*, July 15, 2009.

[84] National Intelligence Council, 2008, pp. 46–47.

Concluding Commentary on North Korean Conditions

The immediate past U.S. commander in Korea, GEN Walter Sharp, summarized the situation in North Korea as follows:

> Combined with the country's disastrous centralized economy, dilapidated industrial sector, insufficient agricultural base, malnourished military and populace, and developing nuclear programs, the possibility of a sudden leadership change in the North could be destabilizing and unpredictable.[85]

How Might the North Korean Government Collapse?

It is not the purpose of this report to predict the collapse of the North Korean government. Rather, this report assumes that, at some point, a collapse could happen and seeks to identify ways to mitigate the negative consequences of such a collapse. Still, as I have briefed many audiences, some have asked about how the collapse process might happen. Having a sense of how a collapse could occur then makes it easier to think about the consequences of collapse. I therefore decided to describe one way in which a collapse could occur to provide a background story that some readers will hopefully find useful. A collapse could clearly occur in other ways that might change some of the consequences; the one described here is but one possible course of events.

After years as the leader of North Korea, Kim Jong-Il had a very strong leadership position. He had purged all known opponents and organized the North Korean leadership in ways that made loyalty to him paramount. The death of Kim Jong-Il in December 2011 removed that strong leadership at the top of the North Korean government and set up the conditions for a potential government collapse in North Korea. Kim Jong-Il's designated successor was his 28- or 29-year-old third son, who until September 2010 may not have had any significant visibility or held a major position in North Korea. Indeed, since his mid-teenage years, there had not even been a picture of him avail-

---

[85] "USFK Commander Warns of Possible N.K. Instability," *Korea Herald*, March 26, 2010.

able until late September 2010. He therefore lacked many of the cultural characteristics essential for North Korean leadership, including the appearance of empowerment and acceptance by the North Korean elites and others.

At first blush, the succession after Kim Jong-Il's death appears to have gone quite smoothly. Kim Jong-Un is identified as the successor and commander of the military, the Chairman of the National Defense Commission, and First Secretary of the Workers Party of Korea. He has been depicted as a very personable leader, who, in contrast to his father's lack of public presentations, has made many public speeches. But what is not known is who really rules in North Korea. Is it Kim Jong-Un, his uncle Jang Song-Taek, or some collective leadership? Who makes what decisions?

This report postulates that one path to a North Korean government collapse could involve the assassination of Kim Jong-Un. The loss of this new leader before his successor has been identified would create a difficult situation in North Korea. Kim Jong-Il always encouraged competition in the second tier of national leadership, purging or moving aside anyone who appeared to get too powerful (including, for awhile, his brother-in-law, Jang Song-Taek). Two or more factions may therefore develop as the result of the elimination of the central leader.[86] Each faction would control some North Korean territory, although, at least initially, that territory may not be entirely contiguous. And some territory may sink into anarchy. Figure 2.7 notionally captures how these factions would absorb elites and others from all groups in North Korea.

As the factions develop, the central North Korean government breaks down, with some of its functions being taken over by the factions in their territory. In particular, food distribution may largely cease in many areas. The failure of central control would also raise questions about the value of North Korean money, with many of the

---

[86] Some postulate that, while the Kim family regime may fail, a new central leadership (likely military) would take control. We do not reject that possibility but treat it as beyond the scope of this report, which is examining government failure as opposed to just regime failure.

Figure 2.7
The Potential Nature of Sudden Change

Tier 1: Kim Jong-Un assassinated		
Faction A	Tier 2: Possible successors	**Faction B**
	Tier 3: Other senior elites	
	Tier 4: North Korean professional military	
	Tier 5: Other North Korean elites	
	Tier 6: Military conscripts	
Division into more factions?	Tier 7: Common people	

RAND RR331-2.7

richer North Korean people hoarding food as a way of holding wealth (this happened after the December 2009 currency revaluation). As a result, food could become difficult to find, creating a humanitarian disaster far more serious than usual in North Korea.

To understand the challenges such a government collapse would pose, it is important to note that the North Korean active duty military is about three times larger than the Iraqi military was in 2003 and that the North Korean forces can be expected to be both more determined and more capable. Moreover, the North Korean reserves are reportedly more than ten times the size of the Iraqi reserves in 2003. And North Korea apparently does have WMD. Civil war could develop between the factions fighting to gain control of the country and to secure the limited food and other resources available in the North.

Getting a ROK Decision to Intervene and Seek Unification

As noted earlier, opinion polls in the ROK are split over the importance of unification, especially given its likely cost. Therefore, if the

North Korean government were to collapse, it is not entirely clear that the ROK would decide to intervene in the North and seek unification. Indeed, during the mid- to late 1990s, when famine in the North caused a serious humanitarian problem and hundreds of thousands of deaths, the ROK did not intervene. Of course, many in the ROK and the United States were projecting the imminent collapse of the North Korean regime at the time, and the ROK may therefore have waited to act until the regime failed. A humanitarian disaster in the North after a North Korean government collapse would put some pressure on the ROK to intervene, although the ROK government may take some time to decide to intervene because of the risks and likely long-term costs of that action.[87]

This report assumes that the ROK would intervene and would seek Korean unification. Chapter Three will discuss the ROK intervention decisionmaking process in more detail.

Two Key Assumptions

This report pays particular attention to two key issues that will affect the course of any unification effort. The first is whether North Koreans, especially the North Korean elites, will accept or fight a ROK-led unification. Today, the North Korean elites would be more likely to fight against unification; thus, one objective of preparing for sudden unification would be to help North Koreans recognize the advantages of ROK-led unification, seeking to co-opt especially the North Korean elites. It is also important to remember that, if the unification process is handled poorly (e.g., inadequate humanitarian aid and/or security problems), North Koreans can be expected to become disaffected and move even more in the direction of opposing ROK-led unification. This issue is discussed in Chapter Four.

The other key issue is how China will act if it decides to intervene in North Korea. At one extreme, China might be very supportive of the

---

[87] The ROK has closely studied the costs of German unification, and many in the ROK are anxious to avoid such costs.

ROK and U.S. intervention and collaborate on achieving key objectives. At the other extreme, China could preemptively identify one of the factions as the legitimate government of North Korea, claim that it was intervening to counter the insurgency being waged against that legitimate government, and argue that the ROK and the United States are not welcome on North Korean territory. It is difficult to project where along this spectrum China would respond.

Both these issues would make a huge difference in both the potential consequences of unification and what must be done to mitigate those consequences.

CHAPTER THREE

The Potential Consequences of Collapse

The collapse of the North Korean government could have global consequences, certainly for any country tied economically to Northeast Asia. This point was illustrated by the Japanese earthquake, tsunami, and nuclear disaster in early 2011, which affected the availability and costs of Japanese goods around the world. Of course, the consequences will likely be most serious in North Korea, where a humanitarian disaster, potentially complicated by civil war and related consequences, could seriously hurt much of the population. North Korea's neighboring countries could also be physically affected by refugees, criminal activity, and the actions of some North Korean factions that could launch attacks at targets beyond the North Korean borders. Many of these consequences could have second- and third-order effects, for example, forcing the ROK and/or China to intervene in North Korea, potentially leading to conflict between ROK and Chinese forces if both intervene. The United States would likely support ROK intervention, creating a potential for conflict between China and the United States as well.

This report limits its examination of the collapse consequences in two ways. First, it addresses only the negative consequences—likely the most prevalent consequences—in an effort to identify how to avoid or minimize them. For example, while unification could eventually make the combined Korea an economic powerhouse that would be a great boon to the Korean people, it is not a consequence considered. Second, this project focuses primarily on the Korean consequences of collapse, the consequences to North and South Korea. It also considers some potential consequences for the United States and Japan. But this report does not address in any detail the consequences to China and/or Russia, looking primarily at whether either country would conclude that it must intervene and potentially complicate the situation for the United States and its allies.

This chapter describes the potential consequences of collapse. It notes some of the literature on the potential consequences of a government collapse,[1] although this literature usually fails to define how serious they could be.[2] It begins with an overview of the consequences, describing some of the interactions between them. It then examines the consequences in more detail.

The Potential Consequences

Much of the literature on North Korean futures focuses on alternative evolutions of the Kim family regime, offering scenarios that generally include a government collapse as defined here. This literature tends to focus more on comparing the alternative evolutions, often on the signs and indicators of each.[3]

---

[1] Many of the specific consequences described in this chapter are found in Paul B. Stares and Joel S. Wit, "Preparing for Sudden Change in North Korea," Washington, D.C.: Council on Foreign Relations, Council Special Report No. 42, January 2009, pp. 16–28. See also Moo Bong Ryoo, *The ROK Army's Role When North Korea Collapses Without a War with the ROK*, Ft. Leavenworth, Kan.: School of Advanced Military Studies, U.S. Army Command and General Staff College, January 2001, p. 21.

[2] Ironically, the strenuous Chinese efforts to avoid weakening the North Korean regime suggest that the Chinese understand much better than the United States and South Korea how serious the consequences of North Korean collapse could be. Even when China has had to hurt its relationship with South Korea, a major trading partner, undermining the Chinese image of being a responsible great power, China has significantly limited destabilizing criticism of such North Korean actions as the 2010 artillery shelling of Yeonpyeong Island.

[3] See, for example, Scobell, 2008; Jonathan D. Pollack and Chung Min Lee, *Preparing for Korean Unification: Scenarios and Implications*, Santa Monica, Calif.: RAND Corporation, MR-1040-A, 1999; and Yoo Ho-Yeol, "Current State of North Korea and Types of Its Contingencies," Seoul: Ilmin International Relations Institute, Background Paper Series No. 2, August 2010. Some of this literature identifies not only alternative scenarios for the North Korean future but also a brief description of some of the consequences of each scenario. See, for example, Han Yong-Sup, "Politico-Military Repercussions of North Korean Crisis," Seoul: Ilmin International Relations Institute, Working Paper Series No. 4, September 2010.

Figure 3.1 summarizes many of the potential consequences of a North Korean government collapse, focusing on the Korean perspective. It also identifies expected interactions between them. It starts by recognizing that a North Korean government collapse would likely lead to a humanitarian disaster in North Korea (bottom left), for reasons discussed earlier. Collapse could also lead to warfare in the North, probably starting as a civil war but potentially spilling over the borders into other countries. A collapse could lead to WMD and other weapons being out of state control, threatening both WMD use and WMD proliferation to third parties. The risks of WMD use and proliferation would be increased by warfare in the North. Warfare could cause considerable damage to North Korea, create great instability in the North, and worsen the humanitarian disaster, which could in turn cause many North Koreans to displace from their homes and seek to cross into China and the ROK as refugees.

Figure 3.1
Potential Consequences and Ties Among Them

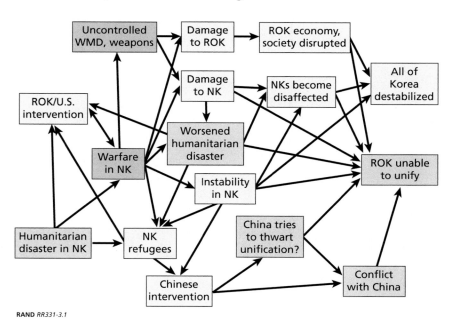

RAND RR331-3.1

As noted in the previous chapter, these consequences and the potential for Korean unification could lead to ROK and U.S. intervention. The rest of this report will generally speak of ROK and U.S. actions in the belief that the ROK-U.S. alliance would lead the two countries to take combined action.[4] This is not to say that each country would view all the consequences as of equal magnitude, but both would feel strongly pressured to intervene. Note also that, to keep Figure 3.1 intelligible, many of the consequences that would cause ROK and U.S. intervention do not have arrows back to this intervention. Thus, uncontrolled WMD would be a major factor causing U.S. and likely ROK intervention, and damage to the ROK would strongly affect ROK and likely U.S. intervention. Unless ROK and U.S. intervention is handled extremely well, many North Koreans—and especially the elites—could become disaffected with the ROK leadership, the North Koreans feeling that they had been cheated, abused, and/or exploited. If a large number of North Koreans become disaffected, true unification could become very difficult to achieve.

A civil war in North Korea and especially the use of WMD could spill over into the ROK and cause serious damage. Factional forces could cause considerable damage with artillery and special forces attacks on the ROK, especially if nuclear and/or biological weapons are used. In addition, one or more North Korean factions could purposefully attack the ROK, potentially as a form of revenge if they perceive themselves unlikely to survive. Thus, ballistic missile attacks against ROK cities—especially ones using nuclear weapons or even chemical or biological weapons—could cause damage across the ROK. Besides the physical damage done, the ROK economy and society could be significantly affected. All these consequences could make it difficult for the ROK to pay for and manage unification. From a ROK perspective, the worst outcome could be destabilization of all of Korea, including the ROK, as crime and insurgency spread, if the ROK is unable to contain and defeat them.

---

[4]   The discussion of the ROK Defense Reform Plan (DRP) in Chapter Six will note that by 2020 or so, the ROK military may become too small to support a viable intervention on its own and would definitely need augmentation with U.S. military forces.

In addition, China could intervene; indeed, some say that China would be likely to intervene. In doing so, China could try to thwart unification, as discussed above. As ROK, U.S., and Chinese forces advance, conflict could develop between the ROK–United States and China. Both Chinese efforts to thwart unification and conflict with China could further jeopardize Korean unification.

Figure 3.2 provides initial estimates of the potential consequences. The subsequent sections will address these in more detail. However, it is important to note that the consequences are highly uncertain. The consequences noted in Figure 3.2 tend to be on the high side, but are all possible. For example, if even 10 to 20 percent of the North Korean military decided to become insurgents or criminals, the subsequent security situation in North Korea could be far worse than ever experienced in Iraq, raising serious questions about whether North Korea could really become part of a unified Korea.

Figure 3.2
Potential Consequences

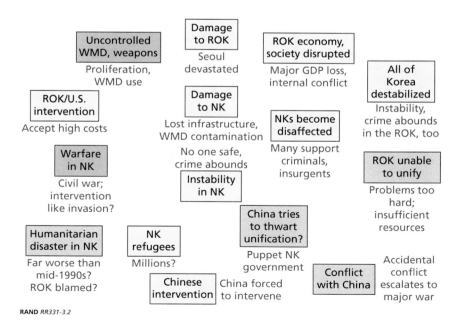

RAND *RR331-3.2*

Other consequences are also possible. For example, a North Korean faction could launch one or more nuclear weapon–tipped intercontinental ballistic missiles (ICBMs) at the United States. A worst-case outcome could see the nuclear weapon functioning reliably, penetrating U.S. missile defenses, hitting a U.S. city, and killing or seriously injuring tens of thousands of Americans.[5]

Consequences in North Korea

This section looks at the likely consequences in North Korea in more detail.

The Failure of Government Functions

When the central government fails in North Korea, the services the central government provides would also largely fail. This will be less true of the North Korean military because most of the factions would likely be led by military commanders, personnel with the power to impose order within some parts of North Korea. The military forces under command of the faction leaders would likely become the backbone of the new security apparatus in these areas, with many of the flaws associated with military control in other countries where the military has not previously had the role of controlling the population. Some faction leaders would seek the loyalty of the former security forces, and especially forces of the Ministry of State Security and/or the Ministry of People's Security. Because the latter personnel are more accustomed to keeping the civilian population under control, they would likely do a better job with the civilians. To the extent that faction leaders and their supporters were politically knowledgeable and adroit, they may recover some of the other government functions and the associated personnel in the geographic areas that they control, but in other areas, government supported functions would largely fail.

The stability of many of the factions is unlikely to be high. Weaker factions would probably seek deals with stronger factions to

---

[5] It is for exactly this reason that the United States has deployed missile defenses in Alaska and California that could hopefully avert such an outcome.

survive, but the leaders of the weaker factions may then be subject to purges as the stronger factions consolidate. Even within factions, the faction leaders would have not purged and shaped the leadership supporting them, having not had full authority to do so previously. So the loyalties of many officials may not be with the faction leaders, causing some potential for dissonance, especially at first, and some motivation for faction leaders to purge personnel they fear could be disloyal. This dissonance and these purges would cause a degree of instability within the factions and in the areas they control. Thus, uprisings against the faction leaders may also develop.

A serious degradation in personal security can also be expected. Local police and related security functions may also fail, leading to a higher degree of lawlessness than exists even in the current North Korea: "North Korean society is plagued by severe conflict between cadres and ordinary people. In that vein, public disorder, for example, such crimes as plundering and arson, will emerge as the biggest downside of incapacitated governmental powers in North Korea."[6]

In addition, within faction areas, the faction leaders may be very brutal in eliminating perceived dissent and purging individuals believed to be disloyal. Some already corrupt military and security personnel may also take advantage of these circumstances to eliminate opponents, to extort resources from those with means in the civilian population, and to treat other people poorly. As one author postulates, a North Korean government collapse could lead to conditions in which,

> [d]ue to the collapse of the distribution system, some soldiers attack civilians to procure food, leading to small gunfights between the military and civilians. The military opens fire on some North Korean defectors, and the people's discontent with the military grows. The people increasingly raid military units and seize firearms.[7]

---

[6] Suh Jae Jean, "Social Consequences of North Korean Contingency," Seoul: Ilmin International Relations Institute, Working Paper Series No. 2, June 2010, p. 8.

[7] Han Yong-Sup, 2010, p. 9.

The criminal elements of the black market may also attempt to exert increased control in some areas and remove competitors while also using extortion. In some areas, the overall security situation could deteriorate into anarchy, and even where it does not, instability can be expected to increase.

In theory, some North Korean faction leaders could decide to seek the welfare of the population in the area that they control. But the persistent North Korean culture of criminality has likely poisoned the approach of many North Korean leaders. They have advanced in a society that practices "the survival of the fittest," and they have normally achieved their positions by winning such struggles. The faction leaders are more likely to be brutal than benevolent, more likely to be devious than open and fair, and more likely to be exploitative than generous.

Conflict

As the regime sees a collapse coming, it may attempt to start a "diversionary war"[8] by invading the ROK:

> The impetus would be a sense in Pyongyang that the regime was in an extremely dire position that could only be saved by some kind of military operation either to reestablish the status quo or achieve unification. In either case, North Korean logic would be that, without some kind of proactive military strike, the regime would collapse.[9]

North Korea already uses provocations to try to manage its internal political challenges; North Korea could invade the ROK as an escalation of the provocations in response to escalating threats to the regime. This threat has not changed in almost two decades: In 1996 another expert argued that the

> most serious question to be answered is: Based on the DPRK situation laid out above, will the north attack the ROK in an

---

[8] See, for example, Jack S. Levy, "The Diversionary Theory of War: A Critique," in Manus I. Midlarsky, ed., *The Handbook of War Studies*, Ann Arbor: The University of Michigan Press, 1989.

[9] Scobell, 2008, pp. 20–21.

attempt to shoot its way out of its internal problems? Many people, including the CINCUNC [Commander in Chief, United Nations Command] and the Director of the Defense Intelligence Agency (DIA) worry that this may be the case and rightly so, as this would cause tremendous casualties and destruction in both the north and south.[10]

Eventually, the North Korean military would almost certainly be defeated despite horrendous damage to the ROK,[11] especially to the Seoul area. On the defeat of the North Korean attack, ROK and U.S. forces would likely be compelled to intervene in the North to complete the defeat or surrender of the North Korean forces, remove the North Korean government that had caused so much damage to the South, and reunify the peninsula to achieve security in the medium to long term.

Whether or not North Korea invades the ROK in desperation, ROK and U.S. forces would likely enter North Korea at some point to help deliver humanitarian aid to the North Korean people in response to the government collapse. As they and perhaps China and Russia intervene,[12] most of the faction leaders would likely feel that outside control of their area would not be in their interest unless serious work is done to co-opt them. And even if the faction leaders are satisfied, some of their subordinates—especially hardline individuals—could decide to fight with those intervening, precipitating broader battles:

> "The regime in Pyongyang could collapse without necessarily its army corps and brigades collapsing," Maxwell says. "So we

---

[10] David S. Maxwell, *Catastrophic Collapse of North Korea: Implications for the United States Military*, Ft. Leavenworth, Kan.: School of Advanced Military Studies, United States Army Command and General Staff College, May 1996, p. 13. The CINCUNC was a title given to the U.S. commander in Korea, who would also have commanded all U.S. and ROK forces if war had occurred.

[11] General Sharp, the previous U.S. commander in Korea, said, "They would cause huge damage in the Republic of Korea, but I'm confident that we have the capabilities . . . to defeat them." As quoted in "U.S. General Concerned by Threat to Seoul Posed by N. Korea's 800-Missile Arsenal," East-Asia-Intel.com, October 17, 2008.

[12] Russia may well decide not to intervene, and even if it did decide to intervene, the forces available in the Russian Eastern Military District would be limited.

might have to mount a relief operation at the same time that we'd be conducting combat ops. If there is anybody in the UN who thinks it will just be a matter of feeding people, they're smoking dope."[13]

Even if North Korean military opposition does not develop immediately, it could develop over time. Thus, to stabilize North Korea, ROK and U.S. forces will need to stop any ongoing conflict and seek to demilitarize the North Korean military and security forces.

Internal conflict within North Korea can also be expected. To secure needed food, energy, and other resources, the faction leaders may be forced to carry out raids or more significant combat with neighboring factions. Moreover, some of the faction leaders may believe that they would be able to establish control over all of North Korea if they can defeat the neighboring factions. The result could well be a civil war in North Korea that causes many casualties and a further deterioration of the already disastrous humanitarian conditions. As conflict develops, faction leaders can be expected to mobilize reserve forces in the areas they control (potentially leading to as many as 9 million North Koreans being under arms), further reducing the economic production in these areas and pulling families apart. The involvement of so many reserves could create circumstances in which the factions perceive that everyone could be a combatant; they may therefore fail to differentiate and spare noncombatants whose loyalty they cannot count on.

While mobilization might be expected to improve security in some areas, the mobilized forces would be unlikely in practice to have the food and other resources they need. They would have little choice but to take these resources from the local people. Especially in areas where the local commanders are also criminal bosses associated with the black market (as at least some are likely even now), these local commanders can be expected to steal from and otherwise abuse the population in their immediate areas, seeking to enrich themselves. In doing so, they would probably take a short-term perspective, stripping factories and other infrastructure to make short-term sales and oth-

---

[13] Robert D. Kaplan, "When North Korea Falls," *The Atlantic*, October 2006.

erwise abusing or even selling the people in their areas. While some faction leaders may stop this abusive behavior initially, unresolved civil war conditions would likely divert their attention over time; the longer the collapse goes on, the higher the potential for abusive behavior to spread.

If a civil war develops, the conflict would pose total-war consequences for the faction leaders: They would achieve victory or likely be killed. Under such extreme circumstances, the employment of WMD would be expected. Since many North Korean active duty soldiers and more reservists apparently lack masks and other equipment to protect them from WMD effects, these soldiers would be very vulnerable to the effects of WMD. Thus, chemical weapon use may be quite effective against opposing forces in either an offensive or defensive mode. Nuclear weapons may be used for coercive purposes, while biological weapons may be used to cause massive damage (among starving people suffering from degraded health conditions) in opposing areas. The factions may also sell some WMD and related assets (such as experts) to third parties to provide needed funds for faction survival and conflict. The North Korean government already makes some such sales to such countries as Iran and Syria; in these more extreme conditions of civil war, the faction leaders may well be prepared to provide WMD and/or related assets to terrorist groups or anyone else with sufficient financial resources.[14]

---

[14] As will be discussed later, the United States and its allies can be expected to establish a naval quarantine of North Korea if such conditions develop, probably under the auspices of the Proliferation Security Initiative (PSI). Still, thousands of fishing ships and other boats could carry some WMD assets, overwhelming any effort to stop and search them all. Dealing with aircraft that leave North Korea will be more difficult; at some point, the United States and its allies will need to decide whether or not to shoot such aircraft down if they refuse to land and be inspected (although a failure of the radio communications on some aircraft can also be expected). Stopping aircraft would be complicated if the aircraft were flying out of North Korea into China or into the northern part of the Yellow/West Sea, including a lack of places for imposing landings. Even more troubling would be proliferation across the North Korea–China or North Korea–Russia borders, likely with criminal organizations in North Korea trading with criminals in the neighboring countries. The North Korea–China border is some 1,400 km long, and a major area for trade and other activities. The North Korea–Russia border is only about 18 km long and has only one or two bridges across it, constraining the proliferation threat.

Severe Famine, Starvation, and Other Health Consequences

Because North Korea already has difficulty feeding its population, a government collapse would likely plunge the North into starvation. Those with money would be motivated to hoard food to guarantee their access to it and because the price of food could well skyrocket in the postcollapse environment. As food disappears, the military and others with arms would likely increase their raids on those who potentially have food, stealing what little remains. The humanitarian aid organizations helping in North Korea would probably reduce their assistance as the security in North Korea deteriorates and could curtail their assistance if security decays to the point that their personnel are seriously threatened. The currently inadequate food supplies could be reduced below the starvation level for many people in North Korea.

Many factors could affect the severity of starvation. These include how poor the crops were in the year immediately before the collapse, the time of year in which the collapse occurs,[15] the degree to which the collapse further disrupts agricultural activity in North Korea, and the duration of the collapse before significant outside humanitarian assistance arrives. Still, conditions like those of the 1995 to 1998 famine, and quite possibly worse, can be expected.[16] As the conditions of starvation develop, many people will be too weak to work, further undermining the economic viability of North Korea. North Korea would likely fall into a downward spiral in terms of nourishment and economic viability.

A decaying food situation will also have broader health effects. North Korea already suffers from serious diseases due to poor health conditions, including "scarlet fever, measles, typhoid, paratyphoid, and typhus."[17] As the North Korean government fails, its effort to sustain national health will also be impaired. These diseases will only be exac-

---

[15] Famine in North Korea is often worst in the spring, when the food supply from the previous year runs low and the spring crops have not yet become available.

[16] Hopefully, humanitarian aid would arrive in months, not years, although a degradation in the security environment could prevent aid receipt.

[17] Jonathan Stafford, "Finding America's Role in a Collapsed North Korean State," *Military Review*, January–February 2008, p. 101.

erbated in the aftermath of a collapse and especially if large refugee flows begin.

An intense food shortage coupled with disease could further cripple any residual government functions:

> Defunct state activities result in abnormal market functions. Hence, it is highly likely that market functions will be paralyzed and the national economy as a whole will not operate normally. The scarcity of goods will cause prices to soar; a lack of consumer goods may drive the people to anxiety and fear. Yet, it is none other than cadres, who have relied on rations, that will suffer the most in a contingency. Ordinary North Koreans have managed to make a living on their own, in markets. Thus they have the ability to survive in crisis situations. On the contrary, cadres do not. In fact, they can degenerate into the most vulnerable class following a contingency. This is why a contingency could very quickly destroy state functions in North Korea.[18]

While the most senior North Korean government personnel often have substantial stashes of foreign currency that could help them weather such circumstances,[19] many government employees, especially in the Pyongyang area, depend on the public distribution system for survival, given their paltry official salaries. The loss of the public distribution system would be a disaster for them, at least diverting them from their government jobs to survive and accelerating government failure.

Moreover, the failure of the central government will raise concerns about the degree to which the North Korean currency retains any value. If the currency is questionable, those with money may exchange North Korean won for foreign currencies. Fortunately, the North Korean economy is already infiltrated with foreign currency, especially

[18] Suh Jae Jean, 2010, p. 8.

[19] According to the *Washington Times*, "[p]arty officials have been keeping massive sums of dollars close to hand—$500,000 to $1 million in their homes" (Andrew Salmon, "North Korean Reforms Are Smokescreen, Say Senior Defectors," *Washington Times*, August 28, 2012).

in the Pyongyang area.[20] So the use of foreign currency will become a means of holding wealth in some areas. Even in these areas, however, those seeking to hold wealth may prefer to hoard food because of the inflation in food prices that can be expected. Such hoarding would further reduce the food supply.

Some in North Korea would likely hope that collapse would bring a prompt unification and betterment of conditions in North Korea. If a ROK intervention and unification were delayed, many in the North could blame the ROK for the deterioration of conditions over time. The North Korean people would likely become disaffected with unification and the ROK government. And even if disaffection is not serious early in the unification process, North Koreans could develop negative feelings as unification proceeds because it does not live up to their expectations, leading to fairly serious opposition to the ROK in North Korea. Some North Koreans could even hope for a return to the conditions of the Kim family regime. A yearning to return to North Korea has developed among North Korean refugees in South Korea, and some have even tried to return, because they have not perceived that they received good treatment in the South. Many Russians have similarly yearned for a return to the Soviet system, in which they felt they were part of a great power (and where their memories are often biased in favor of the good they remember as opposed to the offsetting bad).

Human Rights Consequences

When any extreme dictatorship fails, the potential for human rights consequences is extremely high. This can come in the form of revenge, with the formerly oppressed people attacking the former security personnel who killed or otherwise abused their neighbors. Security personnel may act to kill people they have abused before the victims can testify against the security personnel.

In the latter category, "[i]nternational organizations estimate that North Korea holds about 200,000 political prisoners."[21] The prison

---

[20] Interview with an individual who lived in Pyongyang for five years until recently.

[21] Jiyeon Lee, "North Korea Plans Prisoner Release to Mark Dead Leaders' Birthdays," CNN, January 10, 2012. The article concludes by stating that "[i]nternational organizations

guards at these facilities are security personnel, members of the Ministry of State Security. The guards in these camps practice such extreme brutality against the prisoners that they would be subject to criminal prosecution in most countries in the world. One author speaks of the view of a one former inmate, Shin Dong-Hyuk:

> If North Korea does collapse, Shin may be correct in predicting that its leaders, fearing war crimes trials, will demolish the camps before investigators can get to them. As Kim Jong Il explained, "We must envelope our environment in a dense fog to prevent our enemies from learning anything about us."[22]

Potentially tens of thousands of North Korean prisoners could be executed—a massive abuse of human rights. Indeed, uncertain of the course of ROK-U.S. or Chinese intervention, the North Korean guards and their bosses in the Ministry of State Security may attempt to exterminate the prisoners very quickly to prevent the survival of any human witnesses and to give the guards time to disappear, likely in the refugee flow.

Internally Displaced People and Refugees

Despite the security forces deployed to stop them, the North Korean population demonstrated a serious willingness to flee their homes in search of food during the mid-1990s famine in North Korea. Many of these people eventually became refugees, crossing the Chinese border. China was not pleased with this development: It already had some 2 million ethnic Koreans in Manchuria,[23] whom the Chinese leadership viewed as a potentially troublesome minority. China therefore refused to consider North Koreans as refugees, which would have

---

estimate that North Korea holds about 200,000 political prisoners. Park said that he believed the overall prison population to be between 300,000 and 400,000." Subtracting 200,000 political prisoners from 300,000 to 400,000 total prisoners implies that North Korea has an actual criminal population of between 100,000 and 200,000 people.

[22] Harden, 2012, p. 11. Shin was born as a prisoner in a North Korean prison camp and likely has a relatively accurate view of the guards and their bosses.

[23] Jason Lim, "If North Korea Collapses," *Washington Times*, December 17, 2004.

given them UN-sanctioned rights, and instead returned many of them to North Korea and most unpleasant fates. This procedure continues today.

With a North Korean government collapse, food and security will both become problems for the North Korean people. These two problems are powerful motivations for people to displace from their homes, seeking food and security elsewhere before they are unable to. But since there would not likely be a place with ample food supplies in North Korea, many of these people could flee toward either China or the ROK. The breakdown of the North Korean internal security system would reduce the restrictions on such movements of people:

> The most commonly feared spillover effect of a violent or prolonged succession struggle that causes a catastrophic breakdown in the food distribution system and public order is a large exodus of refugees. China would be the most logical destination given the formidable obstacle that the heavily mined and guarded demilitarized zone (DMZ) poses to reaching South Korea.[24]

Official ROK projections of refugee flows toward the ROK amount to 3 million or so people.[25] Of particular concern would be the fact that, once these people displace from their homes, their humanitarian needs burgeon, and they are exposed in ways that make death or injury far more likely, especially during the colder parts of the year.

Potential Consequences in South Korea

A North Korean government collapse could cause various consequences in the ROK. The most serious consequences would likely be associated

---

[24] Stares and Wit, 2009, p. 18.

[25] Na Jeong-ju, "3 million NK Refugees Expected in Crisis: BOK," *Korea Times*, January 26, 2007. In addition to the DMZ problems just mentioned, about 80 percent of the North Korean population lives in areas around Pyongyang or further north, many of them closer to China than the ROK. Therefore, even more displaced persons would likely move toward China. See the 2008 North Korean census (which is troubled with falsifications): Central Bureau of Statistics, *2008 Population Census: National Report*, Pyongyang, DPR Korea, 2009.

with threats to ROK security. But various other consequences are also possible.

North Korean Military Threats to the ROK as a Collapse Develops

As the conditions for a collapse mature, the North Korean regime could try to invade the ROK as a diversionary war to prevent a North Korean collapse. While the invasion would not be a consequence of collapse, per se, it could cause serious conditions in the ROK that would impede a ROK response to an eventual North Korean government collapse. Given the conditions in North Korea, the ROK should consider any invasion to be diversionary and should seek to precipitate a collapse of the North Korean government as part of its defense. Indeed, the most effective means for the ROK to limit damage may be to cause the attack to fail because of government failure rather than military failure.

That said, a North Korean invasion of the ROK could cause considerable damage to the ROK, especially the area from Seoul northward. For example, North Korean artillery could cause substantial devastation in Seoul and elsewhere along the DMZ. North Korean forces advancing into the ROK could also cause many casualties to ROK military personnel and significant damage to the ROK land over which the conflict is fought, and ROK industry and other parts of its economy in the area of the conflict. Political, human rights, and other damage would almost certainly occur in areas the North occupies for any length of time. An eventual ROK counterattack to drive North Korean forces out of ROK territory and reestablish the ROK border would cause further damage. To provide a rough estimate of the damage from such a conflict, GEN Gary Luck, the U.S. commander in Korea at the time, said in his 1994 testimony to Congress that casualties in a future Korean war could equal the casualties of the first Korean War; just the military casualties were 36,000 U.S. dead and 400,000 ROK dead.[26] General Luck's accounting apparently assumed that only conventional weapons would be used. Economic losses could amount to 10 to 20 percent of ROK GDP over the first year of conflict simply due to military mobilization of civilian personnel and resources;

---

[26] Kirk Spitzer, "Isles Key in S. Korea Defense," *Honolulu Advertiser*, March 3, 1994, p. 1.

the physical damage of an invasion could raise the economic losses much higher—perhaps as much as a 50 percent loss of ROK GDP the first year.

All this damage would be far worse if North Korea used WMD as part of an attack, which it could decide to do. In particular, once a North Korean offensive were stopped and ROK and U.S. forces began a counteroffensive, the North Korean leaders would know that, unless the ROK and U.S. forces were stopped, the North Korean regime would probably be destroyed over time. Thus, the leaders could decide to use WMD to stop the ROK and U.S. advance as an act of desperation, using artillery to fire chemical weapons, ballistic missiles to deliver all forms of WMD, and improvised explosive devices with any form of WMD on North Korean territory and captured ROK territory. Depending on the scope and magnitude of WMD used, ROK personnel losses in the Seoul area alone could easily double the historical losses from conventional conflict and leave the ROK economy in shambles for years. Just a single North Korean nuclear weapon detonated in Seoul with a 10 kiloton yield could cause 200,000 or so fatalities, a similar number of serious injuries, and a financial cost of some $1.5 trillion.[27]

While the damage from such an invasion would not be a direct consequence of North Korean government collapse, it would surely be related. Therefore, this report will consider actions that the ROK could take to make a North Korean invasion short lived and to reduce the damage that an invasion could cause.

North Korean Military Threats to the ROK Postcollapse
North Korean military forces could pose a threat to the ROK after a collapse either as a continuation of an invasion or in terms of new military actions against the ROK.

The Effect of Collapse on a North Korean Invasion of the ROK
The previous subsection described the potential nature of a North Korean diversionary invasion of the ROK. Just because the North

---

[27] See Bennett, 2010, especially pp. 53, 57.

Korean government collapses does not necessarily mean that the invasion will stop. Some sectors of the invasion, in particular where military operations remain coherent, may continue seeking to advance and causing significant damage. Considerable fire support might also continue as part of the continuing invasion, including the use of artillery and ballistic missiles and the potential use of WMD. But as the various postcollapse factions divide, they are more likely to withdraw forces from the ROK to use as part of the likely military confrontation in North Korea. The forces to be withdrawn would likely lack coherent military support and may therefore turn to significant use of WMD to cover their withdrawal and repulse the pursuing ROK forces. This WMD use may not be limited to countermilitary attacks and may also involve WMD coercion to achieve safe return of the North Korean forces or even diversionary attacks against civilian targets to provide North Korean forces the ability to disengage and withdraw. As noted previously, some may argue that many of these North Korean military efforts would not be a direct consequence of collapse, but they would nevertheless be related, and ROK preparation could reduce the damage that would be done.

North Korean Military Action Against the ROK Initiated After a Collapse

Even if North Korea does not invade the ROK during the collapse process, one or more North Korean Army groups along the DMZ may decide to take military action against the ROK after a collapse, as could North Korean missile, air, or naval units. In some cases, this action may be coercive, demonstrating their capability and will to cause damage to the ROK if ROK military forces advance into the North. Some North Korean commanders may also demonstrate the use of military force to coerce aid from the ROK. In other cases, North Korean military attacks on the ROK could be accidental, potentially reflecting mistakes by North Korean soldiers during an exceptionally tense time and reflecting a partial breakdown in discipline. In a North Korean civil war, the units of some factions could seek "safety" in the ROK, and a pursuing faction could decide to continue armed pursuit into the ROK.[28] Moreover, factions may feel that the ROK is assisting their adversaries and may thus launch attacks against ROK lines of communication and the forward bases that could be used to support their adversaries.[29] One or more North Korean factions could try to provoke or punish the ROK as engagements of the civil war spill over into the ROK.

The Implications of North Korean Military Attacks

While North Korean military attacks would tend to cause less damage after a collapse, some factions could still fire one or more nuclear-tipped ballistic missiles into Seoul or other ROK cities or military facilities, raising the damage substantially. Even if the direct damage is much less, the indirect damage could be significant as foreign capital is withdrawn from the ROK markets because of the risks to the ROK economy. Moreover, if some North Koreans were to use a contagious biological weapon, such as smallpox or plague, even in small amounts, ROK goods and services could become stigmatized to the point that the lucrative ROK export market largely dried up even after the infection was resolved.

For example, "North Korea would use 'human bombs' on South Korean and Japanese targets. North Korea's 100,000+ Special Forces are trained to attack nuclear reactors, dams, missile sites and other targets in Japan, Okinawa and South Korea."[30] North Korean special forces could cause particularly large amounts of damage using WMD; they may be the ideal means of delivering biological weapons against the ROK.

North Korean experimentation with cyber attacks and Global Positioning System (GPS) jamming illustrate other forms of "military"

---

[28] Stares and Wit, 2009, p. 17.

[29] According to one observer, "[t]hat a civil war beyond imagination could break out and spillover into neighboring countries is likely as those 1.2 million armed men take sides and fight for survival. Again, there will be massive migration of the population searching not only for a better life but also to escape the devastation caused by the civil war" (Maxwell, 1996, p. 16).

[30] Lee Wha Rang, "Wagging the Dog—The Korean Style," Kimsoft website, December 25, 1998.

damage that could be done to the ROK. North Korea has apparently been responsible for a range of cyber attacks on the ROK, causing major financial implications and other effects.[31] North Korea has jammed GPS signals along the DMZ on several occasions, including affecting GPS reception for aircraft landing at Incheon airport.[32] North Korea was likely testing its capabilities in these attacks. In the aftermath of a government collapse, one or more factions could use these capabilities to potentially cause far more extensive cyber and electronic jamming effects in the ROK. This would be especially true for any faction seeking to repel a ROK and U.S. intervention in the North.

Some of the North Korean factions, likely regime loyalists, may even take more extreme action. It is reported that Kim Jong-Il told his father that if North Korea lost a war, "I will be sure to destroy the Earth! What good is this Earth without North Korea?"[33] North Korean factions that fear defeat may pursue a similar spoiler approach, potentially using WMD and perhaps even nuclear weapons against the ROK and other countries. Alternatively, as the government fails, it may order such attacks, feeling that it has nothing to lose.

Other North Korean Security Threats to the ROK Postcollapse
There is some worry in the ROK about North Korean refugees entering the ROK, including North Korean criminal or insurgent elements.

A North Korean Refugee Flood Toward the ROK Border
Estimates vary on the number of North Korean refugees who might attempt to enter the ROK after a North Korean collapse. At the high end,

> [a] report by the Korea Employers Federation (KEF) predicted that if the North Korean regime collapsed suddenly, up to 3.65 million people from the communist country may cross over

---

[31] The most serious was apparently the disruption of the Nonghyup Bank starting on April 12, 2011 ("Evidence Points to N.Korea in Hacker Attack on Bank," *Chosun Ilbo*, May 4, 2011).

[32] "N.K. Jamming Affects Flights: Seoul," *Korea Herald*, May 2, 2012.

[33] As quoted in Hyun Sik Kim, 2008.

into capitalist South Korea. "Even under a conservative estimate, up to 1.61 million North Koreans may move to South Korea, mainly because of the huge difference in wages and employment opportunities," the KEF said. It said such a wholesale movement of people could seriously disrupt the local labor market and cause other social problems.[34]

A flood of refugees seeking to cross the DMZ, with many being hurt by mines or North Korean military action against them, would be particularly serious and compel ROK action of some form.

A major refugee flow toward the ROK could leave it with a difficult decision: Allow the North Koreans into the ROK or hold them in refugee camps north of the DMZ? Practically, the ROK would prefer not to have this flood come into the ROK, but legally, all North Koreans are Korean citizens with the same rights as those who have been living in the South. So it may be difficult to keep them in refugee camps north of the DMZ. Whichever option is chosen, taking care of all of the needs of hundreds of thousands of North Koreans will be challenging. That is, whether the North Korean refugees are kept in North Korea or the ROK, the ROK government will need to find housing, food, water, clothing, medical care, jobs, and other items for them, and ROK authorities are unlikely to find spare housing or other assistance that would be adequate for such a large refugee flow.

If a massive flow of North Koreans were allowed to enter the ROK, they would probably have a worse experience than current North Korean refugees who receive training and preparation for the ROK culture and yet still often fail. Desperate to find employment, many North Koreans would likely be prepared to underbid South Koreans or foreign workers to perform basic jobs. Working for lower salaries, they could have a union-busting effect that the unions would fight against. And if the North Koreans fail to find jobs, they could turn toward crime or begging to sustain their needs. As a result, animosity could develop between the North Korean refugees and people already living in South Korea, leading to demonstrations and potentially to violence.

---

[34] "Sudden Unification Could Cause 3.65 Mln N. Koreans to Enter S. Korea: Report," Yonhap News Agency, January 24, 2012.

In addition, many of the North Korean refugees will be in great need of medical and other care:

> Even after the widespread famine of the 1990s, prolonged and severe malnutrition persisted; more than half of North Korean children are stunted or underweight, while two-thirds of young adults are malnourished or anemic. . . . Widespread malnutrition and accompanying physical and cognitive disabilities among DPRK children and young people [would be] likely inhibitors of economic growth—with or without opening to the outside world or reunification with the South. If reunification occurs, South Korea will face costs not only of incorporating an economic void, but also those of a huge health-care burden. Seoul could look to other countries or to multilateral organizations to help defray expenses.[35]

These health care problems would have both immediate and long-term consequences. The immediate consequences would include a substantial increase in the demand for ROK medical services without a significant increase in supply, making health care less accessible to everyone in the ROK and potentially increasing health care costs.[36] There would also be the possibility of spreading disease, both because of the impaired health of the North Koreans and because different forms of disease will have developed in North and South Korea, potentially overcoming the immunities previously established in each country.

North Korean Instability and Criminal Threats

As central control breaks down in North Korea, security will also break down. North Korea is already plagued by black market activity, bribery, and other criminal activity; criminal and lawless behavior

---

[35] National Intelligence Council, 2008, pp. 46–47.

[36] The ROK has a government-funded health care system. That system usually pays for most health care. To this point, the ROK supply of health services generally meets the demand. But if a period develops when demand vastly exceeds supply, it is not clear how the system would work—it would at least have to ration care in some manner and would have to provide incentives to entrepreneurial health care providers to accept payments to provide "extra" care.

would increase and likely spill over into the ROK and China, especially if refugees begin pouring across the borders. In addition, as government control fails in the North, the North Korean prisons holding true criminals will likely empty,[37] leading to these criminals intermixing in the refugee flow. After all, many of the true criminals would either not have family ties in North Korea or may fear being identified as criminals, and conclude that their fortunes would likely be better in the South.

In addition to the spread of individuals who had been criminals, many in the North Korean military may conclude that the ROK provides a rich source of money for their entry into criminal activity. North Korean special forces, in particular, may seek revenge against the ROK in these actions, potentially targeting the rich in the ROK with extortion and other crimes. They may also seek to assassinate government leaders, including police and others seeking to maintain security, much as has happened in Afghanistan and Iraq. They may be joined in such activities by the established criminals, likely leading to conflict between different criminal groups in the ROK.

This North Korean criminal activity could have a significant destabilizing effect on the ROK. Criminal groups could steal the profits of ROK firms, undercutting investment in ways that would gradually reduce the competitiveness of ROK firms. The criminals could also establish control over some parts of the ROK economy. These activities would almost certainly lead to criminal bribery and subversion of political officials in the ROK, leading to serious instability and negative national consequences.

Ironically, the spread of criminal activity into the ROK may be worse if the ROK decides not to intervene in North Korea. In such circumstances, North Korean refugees with criminal intent may be more able to enter the ROK: ROK intervention would allow the ROK to establish refugee camps in North Korea and give ROK personnel some time to identify potential criminals before allowing refugees access to the ROK. ROK efforts to stabilize the North may reduce the number

---

[37] As noted earlier, North Korean prisons apparently hold as many as 200,000 political prisoners and another 200,000 true criminals. The latter are being referred to here.

of North Koreans who decide to pursue crime, both by providing alternative employment and by identifying and detaining criminals while still in the North.

In addition, the ROK government should recognize that the stronger the hold that criminal organizations establish in North Korea, the more difficult it will be to stabilize the North at some future time. Thus, expeditious intervention may be prompted by more than just a humanitarian crisis.

The Potential Implications of Chinese Intervention
China would face threats across its border with North Korea similar to those the ROK would face. While a North Korean invasion into China would not happen, limited North Korean attacks, North Korean spoiler attacks, refugees, and instability or criminality are all possibilities. China wants none of these problems on or across its borders and may see little ability to resolve them short of intervening in the North. Whether China would intervene is discussed later in this chapter, along with the resulting consequences for the ROK (and the United States).

Implications for the United States

As with the ROK, the United States faces potential military damage and other consequences from a North Korean government collapse.

Military Damage
A North Korean government collapse would still leave North Korean weapons intact but potentially under the control of various factions or groups. Few of these weapons have the range to reach the United States and cause direct damage, but some could have the range. The most serious threat would come from North Korean ICBMs, which could carry nuclear weapons to U.S. targets. North Korea has yet to master the ICBM technology, but it is working to do so. In June 2011, then–Secretary of Defense Robert Gates said: "And with the continued development of long-range missiles and potentially a road-mobile intercontinental ballistic missile and their continuing development of

nuclear weapons, North Korea is in the process of becoming a direct threat to the United States."[38]

North Korea could also put short-range missiles, which it has mastered, onto ships that could launch the missiles against the United States from international waters off the U.S. coastline. At least one North Korean sympathizer has proposed such attacks:

> North Korea is expected to concentrate on destroying civilian targets in South Korea, Japan and America. The North Koreans are expected to use every means for this purpose. They have ample supplies of biochemical weapons and 20–30 nuclear devices. In addition, North Korea has tons of radioactive substances, which can be sprayed, over population centers. North Korean missiles could explode miles away from their targets and yet cause catastrophic damages by contaminating rain clouds and air mass with ABC [atomic, biological, and chemical] substances. . . . North Korea has spent billions on developing "stealth" submarine and surface vessels. . . . One may assume that these vessels are designed to carry ABC weapons . . . Some ships would launch short-range Scud missiles, which North Korea has been mass-producing since 1970's.[39]

While one always needs to question such assertions, the threat of ship-based short-range missiles is supported by other evidence:

> North Korea reportedly purchased 12 decommissioned Russian Foxtrot and Golf-II class submarines for scrap metal from a Japanese company. "The Golf-IIs, which are capable of carrying three SS-N-5 SLBMs [submarine-launched ballistic missiles], did not have their missiles or electronic firing systems when they were sold to the North Koreans, but they did allegedly retain significant launch sub-systems including launch tubes and sta-

---

[38] Robert M. Gates, "Remarks by Secretary Gates at the Shangri-La Dialogue, International Institute for Strategic Studies (IISS), Singapore," Washington, D.C.: U.S. Department of Defense, June 3, 2011

[39] Lee Wha Rang, 1998. Lee exaggerates North Korean capabilities in some ways, but the use of ballistic missiles from ships off the U.S. coast seems relatively possible.

bilization systems," . . . Some experts believe that "this technology, in conjunction with the R-27's well-understood design, gives North Korea the capability to develop either a submarine or ship-mounted ballistic missile," the report said. "It is also possible, according to some observers, that North Korea might attempt to incorporate this launch technology into a merchant ship."[40]

North Korean factions or groups in control of these weapons could cause damage to the United States in two ways. First, they could launch these weapons directly against the United States, and some may have reason to do so, believing the North Korean propaganda that the United States is the ultimate enemy of North Korea and possibly perceiving that the United States is therefore responsible for the North Korean government collapse. Second, they could sell these weapons or other WMD to third parties, such as terrorist groups:

> Whatever the humanitarian imperatives, a possible breakdown of internal controls over North Korea's stockpile of weapons of mass destruction (WMDs) would likely provide even stronger pressures to intervene. There is little or no information on what those controls are today, but the stockpiles are almost certainly the responsibility of the North Korean military. If the cohesion of the military were to begin to fray, preventing leakage of WMDs, materials, and technologies beyond the North's borders would become an urgent priority. Although neighboring states share a common interest in preventing such a leakage, serious differences could still arise over the necessity and execution of any military operation designed to secure WMDs.[41]

---

[40] "N. Korea May Have Sea-Based Missile System: Report," *Korea Herald*, March 17, 2009; Steven A. Hildreth, *North Korean Ballistic Missile Threat to the United States*, Washington, D.C.: Congressional Research Service, February 24, 2009, p. 5. The R-27 missile is better known in the United States as the Soviet SS-N-6 missile used on Soviet *Yankee*-class ballistic missile submarines during the Cold War. The North Korean variant of this missile is known as the Musudan.

[41] Stares and Wit, 2009, pp. 18–19.

North Korean cyber attack capabilities would also not be limited by geography. Operating over the Internet, North Korean hackers could easily reach U.S. websites and then deliver cyber attacks against them. Indeed, in some cases, they may have already inserted the means for such attacks into U.S. computer systems and are only waiting for the appropriate situation to launch the attacks.

Other Costs

Northeast Asia is an extremely important market for U.S. economic activity. A North Korean collapse that destabilizes the region and increases criminal activity could disrupt U.S. trade with the region and could also have serious political implications: The U.S.-allied ROK could transform into a country against the United States in such circumstances.

ROK and U.S. Decisions to Intervene

In the aftermath of a North Korean government collapse, the ROK and United States may be reluctant to intervene, afraid that they do not understand the situation, that they are not prepared to deal with the consequences, and that the cost of unification will be too high. There will be less recognition of the consequences described above, consequences that could be most severe.

In practice, a trade-off between the consequences of intervening and the consequences of not intervening should determine whether or not to intervene. For example, if an intervention in North Korea allowed the United States and the ROK to eliminate many of the North Korean nuclear weapons, preventing a nuclear attack against two ROK cities and one U.S. city, the damage averted may outweigh the costs of intervening in terms of either financial costs or lives lost. But the costs of an intervention are more easily foreseeable than the consequences averted by intervening. In particular, the costs of sending forces into North Korea are less uncertain than predicting how many nuclear attacks against U.S. and ROK cities an intervention can avert. Similarly, it is also difficult to estimate the positive consequences of intervening: the unification of Korea and thereby the creation of a stronger state. As a result, there will tend to be a bias favoring not intervening in the North.

Many in the ROK would still probably conclude that a collapse is a unique opportunity to achieve unification with North Korea; they could pursue efforts to unify under South Korean control and seek U.S. support for such an intervention.[42] The ROK and U.S. could seek UN Security Council sanction before intervening, which China may also seek, although obtaining UN sanction for intervention would delay the intervention process.[43]

Military Implications of a ROK and U.S. Intervention in North Korea

The North Korean missile and WMD threats may particularly motivate the United States and the ROK to intervene, despite their likely reluctance, given the U.S. experiences in Iraq and Afghanistan and the potential challenges of North Korea. The emergence of a North Korean mobile ICBM would be particularly strong motivation for U.S. intervention, as the United States would be the likely target of such missiles.[44] In addition, the United States has long worried that North Korea may proliferate its WMD, which becomes more likely when central government control is lost. If WMD is transferred to terrorist organizations, many of them will want to use that WMD against the United States, and it is very hard to deter terrorist groups. In particular, if nuclear weapons, fissile materials, or nuclear experts are being proliferated, the United States may decide that it must intervene to stop the threat to the United States. But U.S. and ROK intervention will not necessarily stop all WMD use or proliferation and may indeed precipitate some WMD use.

---

[42] While the opportunity would be unique, some in the ROK will view it as too costly. "What is important is that, if Seoul were to view a North Korean contingency as an opportunity for unification and attempt to expedite unification, the burden and confusion that our society will face will indeed be serious" (Suh Jae Jean, 2010, p. 2).

[43] See, for example, Maxwell, 1996, pp. 32–33.

[44] Bill Gertz, "Inside the Ring: North Korea's ICBM," *Washington Times*, March 7, 2012.

If the ROK and the United States decided to intervene in North Korea, one or more North Korean factions could oppose their intervention and could create a serious conflict situation. Many ROK and U.S. soldiers could be injured or lose their lives. The faction(s) could also launch attacks against the ROK and cause severe damage, especially if they use WMD:

> The most worrisome scenario would be the North Korean military, which has seized control of nuclear weapons, declaring that it is entitled to use its nuclear deterrent and launch other forms of military attack against those foreign powers intervening in North Korea's civil war.[45]

Thus, even if all the ground combat associated with achieving unification occurs on North Korean territory, the ROK could still suffer substantial damage from artillery, missiles, and other forms of attack (e.g., cyber attacks).

In any intervention, ROK and U.S. forces would seek to rapidly defeat major North Korean military threats, such as those just described. Thus, North Korean missiles and WMD would be a major focus for capture and/or destruction, as would North Korean artillery. These military actions would need to be carried out promptly because any attack on such weapons is likely to push the North Korean factions into a "use them or lose them" situation.

In the end, unification will be successful only if ROK and U.S. forces are able to stabilize North Korea. The U.S. experience with stabilization in both Iraq and Afghanistan suggests that this effort could be extremely challenging. The North Korean active duty forces are three or so times larger than were the Iraqi active duty military forces, and North Korean reserve forces may be as much as 10 times larger. Today, with only 24 ROK active duty ground force divisions and perhaps several U.S. divisions,[46] the ROK and U.S. forces must plan to co-opt many of the North Korean military personnel for stabilization to suc-

---

[45] Han Yong-Sup, 2010, pp. 15–16.

[46] Today, the ROK Army has 22 active duty divisions, and the ROK Marine Corps has two.

ceed promptly.[47] By 2022, when the ROK may have only about 14 to 16 active duty divisions,[48] stabilization of North Korea will likely be impossible without co-opting North Korean military personnel, and even then, Chinese assistance may also be required. If stabilization fails, insurgency, crime, and disorder could spread even into the current South Korea, creating most disastrous consequences.

Even if stabilization of the North succeeds, ROK and U.S. forces could suffer tens of thousands of fatalities and far more casualties. In addition, the ROK population could suffer the consequences of stand-off North Korean attacks, as could some of the roughly 100,000 U.S. citizens living in the ROK or visiting it. But the ROK population and U.S. citizens in the ROK could also be threatened by North Korean military attacks if the ROK and the United States do not intervene in the North.

Finally, if intervention into North Korea eventually led to a conflict between China and the ROK-U.S. alliance, the damage done to the U.S. military would almost certainly be extensive. The damage done to the United States could also be immense, as discussed later, under Chinese intervention.

The Financial Costs of Intervention

Should the ROK decide to intervene in North Korea, it can expect to incur major financial costs for doing so. Simply providing the humanitarian aid required in North Korea and stabilizing the country will be very expensive. A recent estimate of the U.S. costs of the campaigns in Iraq and Afghanistan put the total costs at $3.2 to $4 trillion to date.[49] Much of these costs were for the U.S. military; the ROK military has lower unit costs, but even so, the ROK military's costs to achieve uni-

---

[47] The U.S. successes in stabilizing Iraq were heavily due to co-opting various Iraqi factions that had previously supported the insurgency.

[48] The ROK Army is being reduced by more than 100,000 personnel over the next ten years because of demographic challenges. Current plans call for 12 or so active duty army divisions and two marine divisions. The available manpower will continue to decline through 2030, almost certainly reducing the number of ROK active duty divisions even further. See the discussion of ROK Defense Reform in Chapter Six.

[49] Brown University, "Costs of War," August 2012.

fication could easily be $500 billion before dealing with the costs of developing North Korea. There are widely different estimates of these developmental costs; they differ in part by the end point identified as being needed:

> A cursory look at the recent estimates of the costs of unification indicates that these estimates cluster around two points. The pessimists usually expect the cost to amount to U.S.$2 trillion, give or take $1 trillion, while optimists think it could be as low as $200 billion. . . . So far the most pessimistic observer of them all has been Peter Beck, who back in 2010, whilst at Stanford University, predicted that it would cost between $2–5 trillion to bring the income of the average northerner to 80% of South Korean levels.[50]

To put these costs into context, the ROK government budget runs about $250 billion per year.[51] If unification were to cost $2 trillion ($500 billion for military operations, $500 billion for damage suffered in the ROK and North Korea,[52] and $1 trillion for economic development of the North), that would be about eight times the annual ROK government budget. Paying for unification in ten years would require the government budget to increase significantly, potentially causing up to a doubling of the ROK tax rates[53]—something few ROK citizens would desire. And this estimate ignores the humanitarian aid, health care, and other costs that would be associated with unification.

Because the costs of ROK intervention and unification could be so high over time, the ROK would likely seek financial assistance from

---

[50] Andrei Lankov, "Costs Stir Korean Unification Dreamers," *Asia Times*, August 9, 2012.

[51] See CIA, 2012.

[52] While North Korea has a very limited economic infrastructure and GDP to be damaged, much of the "damage" to the North could occur as the result of the use of WMD, leaving radiation, disease, and contamination residuals that would be quite expensive to ameliorate.

[53] This is obviously a very simple calculation, assuming no damage to the ROK economy, ignoring the other anticipated growths in government spending, and assuming that unification would be paid for in ten years, which would be sooner than the North Korean per capita GDP could come close to ROK levels, a usual criterion for completing unification.

the United States and other countries. It is difficult to predict how large a commitment the U.S. government would make to assisting the ROK over time, but it would likely amount to at least a few billion dollars, and perhaps tens of billion dollars or more. These numbers would include humanitarian and other aid for North Korea.

The United States would also need to consider the implications for the U.S. economy of a North Korean government collapse and the subsequent chaos that ROK and U.S. intervention would cause. Damage to the ROK could significantly reduce ROK exports, affecting some U.S. markets significantly.

Some Political Costs

In the period before the ROK decides to intervene in a North Korean collapse, there would likely be a heated political argument in the ROK over whether intervention would be appropriate. The cost of intervention would be an important issue here, with many in the ROK fearing the price they would need to pay to unify with North Korea. There would also be other fears about North Koreans coming into the ROK and engaging in criminal activities or taking away jobs. It is difficult to predict how serious such debates would become, but it is certainly possible that they could become far more serious than the "U.S. beef" disturbances of 2008; indeed, the intensity of these debates could be so great as to become violent. These political debates could continue after intervention, with opponents of intervention seeking to limit the intervention and perhaps to leave North Korea as an independent state to avoid unification costs.

Arranging an Intervention in North Korea

If the situation in the North becomes serious, the neighboring states may decide to act very quickly to intervene:

> If deemed necessary, PLA [People's Liberation Army] troops would be dispatched into North Korea. China's strong preference is to receive formal authorization and coordinate closely with the UN in such an endeavor. However, if the international community did not react in a timely manner as the internal order in

North Korea deteriorated rapidly, China would seek to take the initiative in restoring stability.[54]

Such unilateral action seems most likely because crafting a Security Council resolution will likely take time, especially if a North Korean representative at the UN opposes outside intervention and also if the ROK wants to seek unification and China decides to oppose or limit unification. If China does intervene first, the domestic politics in the ROK are likely to drive immediate ROK intervention. The ROK population would perceive a Chinese intervention in North Korea as a major violation of Korean autonomy and an affront to the Korean people; the ROK would need to intervene to prevent China from taking control of North Korea, an entirely unacceptable outcome (see the later section on "Forcing ROK and US Intervention").

There would also be other pressures on the ROK and the United States to intervene. Many in the ROK would feel obligated to help their Korean brethren in the North during a serious humanitarian disaster there. The ROK may also need to handle the North Korean refugee flow and would prefer not to build refugee camps on ROK territory. The ROK would also be concerned about violence spilling across the ROK border, including artillery or missile attacks on the ROK. The United States would worry about all of these conditions but in particular about WMD and other weapons leaking out to terrorist groups and eventually being used on the United States.

If China does not decide to intervene first, it will almost certainly insist on its right to intervene at the same time as the ROK to deal with its concerns. The ROK is likely to oppose Chinese intervention.[55] But

---

[54] Bonnie Glaser, Scott Snyder, and John S. Park, "Keeping an Eye on an Unruly Neighbor: Chinese Views of Economic Reform and Stability in North Korea," Washington, D.C.: Center for Strategic and International Studies and the U.S. Institute of Peace, January 3, 2008, p. 19.

[55] In 2002, China launched a "Northeast Project" designed to justify its historical claims to Manchuria and potentially North Korea. This project has generated considerable anger in South Korea and even in North Korea:

> China wants to safeguard her interests and extend her influence in northeast Asia. Most assume that the two Koreas will be unified once North Korea collapses. However, a more likely possibility is for North Korea to be absorbed by China. With North

if both do decide to intervene, they may require the establishment of zones of control with a separation line, as applied to Germany after World War II. This approach would effectively cede certain Korean territory to China, at least in the short term.

As the situation deteriorates, unilateral action by the key players becomes more likely, as does a willingness to make compromises in the Security Council. Intervention by at least one country seems almost certain to occur eventually, especially as the deteriorating situation worsens the consequences of collapse.

Chinese Involvement

As noted above, this report does not directly consider the potential consequences for China of a North Korean government collapse. Rather, it examines the pressures on China to intervene after a collapse and the potential consequences if it does or does not.

Would China Intervene?

China would likely decide to intervene in North Korea for both security and economic reasons.[56] According to one expert, China has sought buffer states around its periphery to reduce foreign and especially U.S. threats to China. The collapse of North Korea, followed by ROK and likely U.S. intervention and the ROK seeking Korean unification, would remove this buffer and leave China very vulnerable. China fears that ROK and especially U.S. intervention into North

---

Korea currently dependent on China for many of its basic necessities including fuel, the absorption process could actually be very smooth and natural. Further, in order to justify a full absorption, China can conveniently point to the "academic" research by the Northeast Project team that purports to prove that Manchuria and North Korea were originally Chinese to begin with.

Lim, 2004.

[56] One author argues that South Koreans are afraid that China will at some time support a coup against the Kim family regime. He also argues that China is likely to use an initial ROK and U.S. intervention as justification for a Chinese intervention into North Korea after a collapse. See Timothy Savage, "Big Brother Watching: China's Intentions in the DPRK," *China Security*, Autumn 2008, p. 56.

Korea would cause shockwaves throughout China, raising concerns about a broader U.S. campaign against Chinese control throughout its territory (especially in areas where ethnic groups oppose Chinese control). This would be an unacceptable outcome for China and would therefore force China to intervene.[57] China would likely claim that it is supporting the legitimate North Korean government (one of the factions), consistent with its alliance with the North, and therefore does not require UN approval (although it might still seek ex post facto UN backing).

North Korean refuges could also compel Chinese intervention, although this issue is also tied to the Chinese desire for a buffer zone and Chinese fear of U.S. interference:

> One reason is the border security issue: a massive number of North Korean refugees streaming across the Yalu River would create difficult socioeconomic disruptions in the region. A more important reason can be found in the 2 million ethnic Koreans living in Manchuria. In fact, the Yanbian Korean Autonomous Prefecture borders on North Korea. If the two Koreas were to be unified under South Korea's leadership, then a unified Korea that shares America's democratic values and entrepreneurial spirit would exert a strong sociocultural influence in large parts of Manchuria through its common ethnic ties just across the border. It would necessarily compete with Chinese political control. The Chinese absorption of North Korea, therefore, would provide China with a buffer zone against American influence.[58]

Serious instability in North Korea could thus ignite instability in the ethnic Korean regions of northeast China, and that instability in China would only be heightened by ROK and U.S. intervention in North Korea.

The potentially several million North Korean refugees would strengthen the already significant numbers of the ethnic Korean popu-

---

[57] Andrew Scobell, "The View from China," in Gilbert Rozman, ed., *Asia at a Tipping Point: Korea, the Rise of China, and the Impact of Leadership Transitions*, Washington, D.C.: Korea Economic Institute, 2012, pp. 69–81.

[58] Lim, 2004.

lation in Manchuria and would likely raise concerns about the "rust-belt" character of the Chinese economy in the region. Some of the North Koreans would also be lawless, stealing to meet their needs and potentially hurting Chinese citizens. Thus, China does not want these refugees in China. Its only way to achieve such an objective would be to intervene promptly after a North Korean government collapse—before major refugee flows could begin[59]—and take control of a substantial buffer zone in which to create refugee camps in North Korea and build barriers to prevent penetration into China.[60] Because of the rugged North Korean terrain near the Chinese border, the Chinese would likely need to advance 50 to 100 km or so to have the land for creating refugee camps far enough inside North Korea, with appropriate barriers against evasive refugee flows between the camps and the Chinese border. China's combined concerns about U.S. interference and the refugee threat could motivate it to intervene even before the ROK would intervene (forcing a ROK decision, as noted above).

China would also be concerned about North Korean attacks on China.[61] North Korean missiles are not limited to flying south toward the ROK or east toward Japan—the missiles could also be launched at Chinese targets to the west and north. And those missiles could carry WMD, including nuclear weapons. China could secure at least many of those missiles and weapons within the 100 km or so needed to deal with refugees.[62] For example, the Yongbyon nuclear facility is

---

[59] If conditions in North Korea deteriorate toward a North Korean government collapse, the flow of refugees could actually begin well before the collapse.

[60] In theory, the Chinese government could take far more extreme action, such as shooting all North Korean refugees trying to cross into China. But such Chinese actions would be promptly shown in the world media and so undercut Chinese global influence as to be unacceptable to all but the most brutal of Chinese governments. The current and anticipated Chinese governments would be unlikely to take such action.

[61] See the earlier discussion of Kim Jong-Il's approach to losing a war under the section on military threats to the ROK.

[62] The concept of a Chinese intervention in North Korea to stop refugee flows is well established. For example, "given its past attitudes toward North Korean refugees, as well as fears of the negative political and economic consequences of accepting increasing numbers onto its territory, Beijing might opt for seizing a narrow strip of land inside the North to prevent any influx" (Stares and Wit, 2009, p. 18). In practice, it would be impossible to accom-

only 130 km by road from the Chinese border and may thus motivate a deeper Chinese intervention in that sector. China might also be interested in reaching such facilities because evidence of Chinese assistance to the North Korean WMD program might be found there, evidence that could taint China's global image.[63]

China might decide to go further and race the ROK and the United States to Pyongyang. Control of Pyongyang would give China a strong bargaining position for postcollapse negotiations, should it decide to leave North Korea.[64] Alternatively, if China decides to sustain a North Korean government and abort Korean unification, control of Pyongyang would give it a means of legitimizing the North Korean puppet government it could decide to install. Chinese control of North Korean territory north of Pyongyang would give it free access to ports on the East Sea/Sea of Japan and the ability to exploit most of the North Korean mineral resources, resources that are now expected to be substantial.[65] According to one observer, "unencumbered Chinese access to North Korea's minerals, labor and ports would fuel China's ever-growing economy. Through the calculated distortion of history, China is therefore being proactive against scenarios on the Korean peninsula it dislikes."[66] According to another,

---

modate hundreds of thousands of North Korean refugees in a narrow strip of North Korea much less than 100 or so km deep, especially in the northern mountainous area, where roads and building spaces for refugee camps are limited.

[63] This is not to argue that the Chinese central government has authorized help for the North Korean WMD programs. But elements of the Chinese military may have done so, forcing the central government to take action to destroy the evidence of that assistance.

[64] For example, China could insist on U.S. withdrawal from the peninsula in exchange for Chinese withdrawal. Chinese possession of Pyongyang would put serious pressure on the ROK to accept such terms.

[65] According to one report, "[a]s of 2008, North Korea had W6,983.6 trillion (US$1=W1,126) worth of mineral resources" ("Economic Gap . . . ," 2011). Thus, North Korean minerals may be worth some $6.2 trillion.

[66] Lim, 2004. The author's references to a distortion of history refer to the Chinese Northeast Project discussed later.

China's infrastructure investments are already laying the groundwork for a Tibet-like buffer state in much of North Korea, to be ruled indirectly through Beijing's Korean cronies once the KFR [Kim family regime] unravels. This buffer state will be less oppressive than the morbid, crushing tyranny it will replace.[67]

Control of Pyongyang would also allow China to debrief North Korean leaders and examine North Korean documents, providing important sources of information. For example, from such sources, China could identify North Korean agents operating in China, agents whom China may want to suppress to avoid insurgency or other instabilities.

Some of these Chinese objectives were discussed in a U.S. interaction with members of the Chinese PLA:

> According to PLA researchers, contingency plans are in place for the PLA to perform three possible missions in the DPRK. These include: 1) humanitarian missions such as assisting refugees or providing help after a natural disaster; 2) peacekeeping or "order keeping" missions such as serving as civil police; and 3) "environmental control" measures to clean up nuclear contamination resulting from a strike on North Korean nuclear facilities near the Sino-DPRK border and to secure nuclear weapons and fissile materials.[68]

Potential Consequences of Chinese Intervention

Chinese intervention in a North Korean government collapse could have various consequences.

Forcing ROK and U.S. Intervention

If China decides to intervene in North Korea, the ROK population would likely be extremely upset. While the ROK might be reluctant to intervene in the North on its own, it would probably not view Chinese control of North Korea as an acceptable outcome of a North Korean government collapse. Thus, Korean nationalism could force the ROK

---

[67] Kaplan, 2006.

[68] Glaser, Snyder, and Park, 2008, p. 19.

government to intervene in the North when it would otherwise prefer not to. Moreover, while a ROK-initiated intervention in North Korea might have limited territorial objectives, seeking to deal with North Korean refugees, a Chinese intervention into North Korea would likely press the ROK to secure as much North Korean territory as possible.

The United States would likely feel less compelled by Chinese intervention into North Korea. But if the ROK is determined to intervene, the United States would almost certainly support its ally. In addition, the United States would recognize the potential for North Korean WMD use in such a situation and would likely decide that it needed to help secure North Korean WMD as rapidly as possible.

Derailing Unification?

Chinese intervention would give China control of at least some North Korean territory, if not most of it. Because relatively little of the North Korean military is deployed along the Chinese border, the Chinese should be able to advance rapidly into North Korea. Indeed, Chinese forces should be able to advance into North Korea much more rapidly than ROK and U.S. forces can advance from the DMZ, unless the ROK and the United States can co-opt North Korean groups along or above the ROK border. Potentially, China could race the ROK and the United States for Pyongyang, and depending on China's ability to co-opt North Korean forces (e.g., at the Pyongyang airport), could well secure Pyongyang and advance south of Pyongyang before making contact with ROK and U.S. forces.

China could decide to create a North Korean puppet state in whatever part of North Korea it is able to capture. If China decided to do so and thereby thwart Korean unification, it likely would try to seize Pyongyang before the ROK and the United States can. Then, once it had seized territory, it could include that territory in the new North Korea, subject to some form of Chinese oversight. One of the biggest problems China would face in such a move is that the most productive agricultural areas in North Korea are south of Pyongyang and are likely secured first by ROK and U.S. forces. Thus, a new, Chinese-dominated North Korea constrained to territory seized by China would have even less agricultural independence than today and would require major Chinese agricultural subsidies for continued survival. China may be prepared to trade such agricultural goods for North Korea's assessed mineral wealth.

Of course, China could intervene in North Korea but plan to withdraw once ROK and U.S. forces are able to stabilize the North. In doing so, China would know that, even in the best of circumstances, it would almost certainly take many months for ROK forces to reach the Chinese border area after intervening, and China would not be able to accept anarchy in that area in the meantime. Moreover, there is a risk that intervening ROK forces would never stabilize the North, especially as ROK ground forces decline in size (from 22 active duty divisions today to perhaps 12 in 2022[69]). Thus, China might plan a decision point after several months to see if ROK and U.S. forces have adequately stabilized the areas that they control. If the ROK and the United States have established stability in their part of North Korea, China could then decide to withdraw and allow the ROK forces to expand their area of control. But if the ROK and the United States have not established stability, China could remain and eventually create a puppet state. If China pursues this approach, it will be imperative for the ROK to have a strategy (including co-opting many North Korean forces and elites) and force size adequate for stabilization or lose the opportunity for complete unification and risk the spread of instability into the ROK.

If China seriously intervenes, the ROK and the United States could acquire some North Korean territory but probably not the majority of it. The ROK would achieve a degree of unification but probably not as much as desired. As will be shown in Chapter Five, only about 4 million North Korean civilians—about one-sixth of the North Korean population—live in the area south of Pyongyang. The ROK would likely be sorely disappointed if it is able to absorb only this much of North Korea.

---

[69] See the discussions of the ROK DRP in Chapter Six and of ROK force requirements in Chapter Ten.

Antagonism Between China and the ROK

The ROK will tend to view a North Korean government collapse as one of its best opportunities to achieve Korean unification. If China intervened and sought to thwart unification, the ROK population would probably be furious with China. The precursors of such feelings developed in the aftermath of North Korea's 2010 provocations, when North Korea sank the ROK warship *Cheonan* and shelled Yeonpyeong Island, and yet China refused to censor North Korean actions. By intervening in North Korea, China would be occupying territory the ROK claims and could deny full Korean unification at least in the short term. If China were to install a North Korean puppet government, the ROK population would view Chinese action as meddling in internal Korean affairs.[70]

For its part, China was concerned a decade ago about potential Korean claims to Manchuria, especially if Korea were to somehow reunify.[71] It therefore set up the "Northeast Project," which was assigned to examine the historical dynasties in Manchuria and northern Korea and identify whether they were Korean or Chinese. The outcome was critical because if the dynasty were Chinese, China would normally claim a historical right to control the territory ruled by that dynasty. Such a conclusion would allow China to defensively claim that Manchuria was indeed Chinese despite the large ethnic Korean population there. As one might expect, the Northeast Project determined that all the historical dynasties in the area examined were Chinese, including the Koguryo and others that were very clearly Korean.[72]

---

[70] China makes a strong point about other countries not meddling in its internal affairs. Chinese hypocrisy on this issue would certainly stir anger in the ROK.

[71] Chinese concerns in this regard are real: "Moreover, there is a movement in both Koreas for 'Korean irredentism to recover Manchuria' that calls for invalidation of the 1909 Gando Convention between Imperial Japan and the Qing dynasty" (Yoon Hwy-tak, "China's Northeast Project: Defensive or Offensive Strategy?" *East Asian Review*, Vol. 16, No. 4, Winter 2004, p. 100).

[72] According to *Chosun Ilbo*,

China's "Northeast Project" is a national academic project whose aim is to confirm that northeastern China, including early Korean kingdoms that once were located there, has always been under the Middle Kingdom's control. . . . Over a five year period from

This conclusion not only allows Chinese nationalists to feel secure in controlling Manchuria but would also lead many Chinese to feel a right to control parts or all of Korea. This issue arose when a summary of a lecture by a professor of politics at Beijing University noted:

> The North Korean regime cannot survive more than 10 years. If a pro-Chinese military faction grasps power following a collapse of the regime, China intends to incorporate North Korea into its military federation and eventually make it a subordinate state. The Northeast Asia Project now in progress is aimed at accumulating a historical basis for it.[73]

According to Professor Song Ki-ho of Seoul National University, "China isn't making the claims just for historical reasons but for political reasons to claim dominion over North Korea in case of a changing political situation in the region."[74] Koreans offended by the claims of the Chinese Northeast Project have demonstrated against the Chinese efforts to distort Korean history.[75]

2002 to 2007, the project cost an astounding 20 billion yuan, though its conclusions have been hotly contested. . . . On June 24, 2003, a journal for the Communist Party of China, *Guangming Ribao*, reported, "Koguryo was an ancient nation established by a Chinese minority tribe." In July of the following year, the Chinese Foreign Ministry made the same statement on its official website as the government embarked on a bid to register Koguryo remains as a UNESCO [United Nations Educational, Scientific and Cultural Organization] World Heritage Site. In the face of strong protests from the Korean government and civic groups, Beijing decided to back off from its irredentist claims. In August of 2004, Chinese Vice Foreign Minister Wu Dawei visited Korea and made a five-point verbal agreement including a pledge that the Chinese government and state-run media would not seek any distortions of history. Shortly after, the Chinese Foreign Ministry deleted the articles on its website. In 2005, after a Chosun Ilbo report on the issue, the Chinese government removed a signboard at a Koguryo site in Jilin Province that claimed the Koguryo people, "did not share the same blood as the Korean people."

"What China's Northeast Project Is All About," *Chosun Ilbo*, May 30, 2008. 20 billion Chinese yuan is equivalent to about $3 billion.

[73] As quoted in Kwon Dae-yul, "China's Alleged Plot to Annex North Korea," *Chosun Ilbo*, October 19, 2004.

[74] As quoted in "What China's Northeast . . . ," 2008.

[75] See, for example, "Govt to Establish Research Center on Goguryeo Studies," *Chosun Ilbo*, January 15, 2004.

After a North Korean government collapse, many in the ROK would likely claim that China was illegally intervening on North Korean territory. These claims could be met by Chinese counterclaims, with lots of emotion on both sides. Some ROK and Chinese military leaders could pursue aggressive military actions to secure territory that they felt was rightfully theirs. The Chinese tenacity over their perceived rights in the South China Sea, the Spratley Islands, the Senkakus, and various fishing areas surrounding Korea suggest the serious emotions and willingness to use force that could develop.

Conflict Between China and the ROK-U.S. Alliance

As chaos develops in North Korea, the ROK, the United States, and China would all likely send special operations forces (SOF) into the North for special reconnaissance, focused in particular on North Korean WMD facilities. Somewhere, the Chinese SOF would make contact with ROK and U.S. SOF, and unintended or accidental conflict could develop. This is especially likely around such facilities as the Yongbyon nuclear facility, where both sides would likely focus major reconnaissance efforts. The opposing nationalism and views of territorial ownership described above would only make conflict more likely and potentially more intense.

If Chinese ground forces advance into North Korea, some ROK and U.S. SOF could find themselves behind the Chinese lines, seriously complicating their situation. While special operations aircraft may be able to extract such forces, the aircraft may also be vulnerable to Chinese high-end surface-to-air missiles (SAMs) and fighter aircraft, creating other potential cases of unintended conflict.

The most serious risk of Chinese-U.S. conflict could actually be with aircraft. If the Chinese were to put their advanced SAMs (variants of the former Soviet SA-10) near the North Korean border, they could engage any ROK and U.S. air forces operating around Yongbyon and further north. The Chinese could declare this area a ROK and U.S. no-fly zone or could engage some ROK and U.S. aircraft working in that area (perhaps accidentally). Even if they do not declare the entire area a no-fly zone, they probably would insist that ROK and U.S. forces stay 50 to 100 km south of the Chinese border, a severe reduction in the ROK and U.S. ability to collect intelligence and use air forces to deal with North Korean threats. In particular, most of the North Korean NoDong and Musudan missile bases would be inside the Chinese SAM range,[76] potentially complicating counterforce or other actions against the North Korean missiles. This would be a particular concern if North Korean forces began using their ballistic missiles against the ROK or Japan. Imagine the ROK and/or Japanese response if it appeared that the Chinese were protecting North Korean ballistic missiles that are delivering WMD against locations in the ROK or Japan.

The second most serious risk of accidental conflict would be with Chinese and ROK-U.S. forces as they rush toward each other. Intent on trying to secure as much territory as possible, Chinese and ROK-U.S. forces would eventually make contact and suffer accidents as the forces from the two sides come within range of each other. In some areas, forces could be bypassed by forward elements of the other side and find themselves in the other side's rear area. If conflict were to begin between the ROK-U.S. forces and the Chinese forces, that conflict could escalate significantly in ways that neither side would want.

The consequences of Chinese conflict with the ROK and the United States would be extremely serious. Unless the potential escalatory spiral could be stopped, the two sides could escalate to nuclear in Chinese-run refugee camps, these North Koreans would likely not have a very good life. China would be challenged to assemble the building materials, bedding, and related supplies for refugee camps; the food and medicine; and the services, such as medical care, that the refugees would require. China may accept some international assistance in these areas, but the magnitude of the requirements would still be larger than the available supplies. Without these items, Chinese refugee camps could become a second humanitarian disaster in North Korea.

---

[76] China has imported versions of the Russian S-300 PMU SAMs, which have a range of 150 to 200 km. See Joseph S. Bermudez Jr., "Behind the Lines—North Korea's Ballistic Missile Units," *Jane's Intelligence Review*, June 14, 2011; S-300/Favorit (SA-10 'Grumble'/ SA-20 'Gargoyle')," *Jane's Strategic Weapon Systems*, December 23, 2011; and "HQ-9/-15 and HHQ-9 (RF-9/-15, FD-2000 and FT-2000)," *Jane's Strategic Weapon Systems*, December 22, 2011.

The North Koreans are unlikely to welcome Chinese intervention. In contrast to Chinese actions in 1950, the Chinese intervention postulated here would be intended to exercise control over North Korea. China might empower one of the factions to become a puppet government, but China would probably disarm other North Korean forces in the areas it controls. As a result, various factions in the North could oppose the Chinese intervention. One or more North Korean factions controlling ballistic missiles could use those missiles against China, potentially even including the employment of nuclear or other WMD warheads, consistent with the Kim Jong-Il declaration quoted earlier, that he would "destroy the earth" if North Korea were to lose a conflict (and a Chinese occupation would certainly constitute a loss). Depending on the nature of the North Korean attacks and the damage done, China could execute a severe retaliation, possibly including the use of its own nuclear weapons.[77] Thus, serious damage could be done in North Korea.

As Chinese forces established themselves in North Korea, they would likely offend many North Koreans. This would be especially true with North Korean nationalists. The Chinese might also stop the active border trade of many North Koreans, afraid that even traders might decide to stay in China and/or smuggle people into China. Thus, some North Koreans may decide to oppose the imposition of Chinese control, potentially establishing a North Korean resistance movement that could develop to include a combination of insurgency and criminal activities against the Chinese forces. The Chinese would likely react very aggressively against such opposition, potentially imposing large numbers of North Korean casualties.

Displaced North Korean people would likely turn south in reaction to Chinese forces moving into North Korea. Many would probably conclude that the ROK would treat them better. This would force the ROK to deal with an increased burden of refugees.

---

[77] If North Korea really did fire a nuclear weapon at China, China would be furious and would have a strong desire to retaliate, in part to demonstrate China's status as a great power. China would also want to respond strongly to deter other states from future use of nuclear weapons against China.

Potential Consequences of China Not Intervening

There is very little consideration of the consequences of China not intervening in North Korea after a collapse of the North Korean government. Yet there are several areas where such consequences exist and are trade-offs with the consequences described above.

The biggest problem that can develop if China does not intervene is with the ROK and the United States possibly being unable to handle the various military tasks in North Korea promptly and adequately. Even today, with a ROK Army of some 22 active duty divisions and a U.S. commitment to provide several more divisions, a ROK-U.S. intervention in North Korea is a demanding task, and it could take months for ROK and U.S. forces to reach all of North Korea, and even this level of forces may be insufficient to fulfill all the necessary missions. A recent study argued that even in the *most benign* of circumstances that could be associated with Korean unification, some 260,000 to 400,000 ground forces would be required to stabilize North Korea.[78]

The scenarios envisioned here could be far more demanding in terms of the troops required. For example, that study estimated that 3,000 to 10,000 ground force personnel would be required for finding, securing, and eliminating North Korean WMD when facing essentially negligible resistance.[79] It is more likely that ROK and U.S. forces would face opposition at many of the 200 or so WMD sites, requiring a commitment of roughly a maneuver battalion task force to secure each site, locate the WMD, and secure it until it can either be consolidated with other WMD stocks or eliminated on site (which is hard to do safely). The battalion would need to be augmented by various specialty forces, including reconnaissance and surveillance personnel, WMD specialists, intelligence specialists, and explosive ordinance disposal personnel. The total strength of the battalion task force could be around 1,000 personnel,[80] or a total requirement of 200,000 personnel

---

[78] Bruce W. Bennett and Jennifer Lind, "The Collapse of North Korea: Military Missions and Requirements," *International Security*, Vol. 36, No. 2, Fall 2011, p. 86.

[79] Bennett and Lind, 2011.

[80] A typical WMD elimination (WMD-E) task force could consist of three to four companies of infantry and armored forces (about 600 personnel) to seize and secure a WMD

to cover, near simultaneously, all 200 sites. With combat, leadership, and support forces at echelons above battalion, this 200,000 battalion-level estimate would grow to roughly 600,000 to 800,000 personnel, just to eliminate WMD. If the commander decided to accept the risk of visiting some sites, leaving behind a smaller (say 200 personnel) force to secure each site and move the battalion task force to a second site, the battalion-level personnel number could decrease to about 120,000, or about 360,000 to 480,000 total personnel. But in doing so, some 100 WMD sites would remain vulnerable to North Korean forces or criminals for a time, allowing them to seize and perhaps use or proliferate some WMD. This assumes that the location of all WMD sites would be known, which is unlikely.

But ROK demographics will make these levels of WMD-E commitments unlikely: The ROK Army has declined from 560,000 active duty personnel in 2000 to 500,000 or so today and is scheduled to fall to 385,000 or so in 2022—too little to provide even the needed manpower for WMD-E. With the added ground force requirements for demilitarizing the North Korean military and security forces and stabilizing North Korea, ROK forces will become insufficient even if the United States contributes several divisions of U.S. Army forces to the unification effort. See the discussion of this subject in Chapters Six and Ten.

Even with the current ROK Army size, several of the unification-related missions will be difficult to achieve, in part because of how long it will take the ROK and U.S. forces to reach key locations. These include distribution of humanitarian aid, eliminating North Korean WMD, and stabilizing North Korea. Chinese forces would provide substantial assistance in performing these missions, especially since many of the locations that must be reached are closer to the Chinese border. For example, the Yongbyon nuclear facility in North Korea is roughly 320 km by road from the DMZ but only 130 km by road from China, making it possible for Chinese forces to reach the facility far

---

site, plus a forward support company, reconnaissance elements, and WMD specialty forces to search the site and handle any WMD found, collect records, and debrief scientists and others.

sooner than ROK and U.S. forces traveling by road could. And while the ROK and the United States could execute an air assault against Yongbyon to arrive more quickly, they have insufficient heavy-lift helicopters to deliver even a battalion of infantry at a time, likely well short of the force needed to secure Yongbyon and potentially so short that it could be destroyed. If the advance on Yongbyon is executed by road, it could take weeks to get there in an environment of uncertain permissiveness, assuming no major bridges are significantly disabled at that. In the period of even a couple of weeks, any weapons and fissile materials at Yongbyon could be moved, along with scientists, records, and so forth. If Chinese forces could reach Yongbyon much more quickly, the potential for both nuclear weapon use and nuclear weapon proliferation could be significantly lower.

In other areas, Chinese forces could get humanitarian supplies to North Koreans along the border far more quickly than the ROK and the United States could. This would significantly reduce the number of refugees seeking to enter China. It could demilitarize North Korean forces along the Chinese border before many of them would defect to insurgency or criminal activity. It could reach some of the North Korean political prisons more quickly than ROK and U.S. forces, hopefully minimizing the efforts of North Korean prison staff to kill prisoners. And it could bring sufficient forces to bear in North Korea to promptly stabilize significant portions of North Korea. But if China does not intervene, these tasks could go unfulfilled for months in the northern parts of North Korea, causing serious consequences.

CHAPTER FOUR

Addressing North Korean Thinking About Unification

North Korean propaganda has depicted the ROK and the United States as the enemies of the North Korean people and has sought to make most North Koreans hate and fear the United States, in particular. If North Koreans harbor these feelings, the consequences of sudden unification could be exacerbated. Moreover, the ROK and the United States will have far less ability to mitigate these consequences unless they can gain the cooperation of North Koreans, especially the elites. Overcoming North Korean hatred and fear of the United States and the ROK is a starting point across almost all the potential consequences.

This chapter describes the challenges of these fears and the potential means of overcoming them. It proposes an approach to changing North Korean thinking about unification and about the United States and the ROK. It begins by describing the North Korean regime's efforts to distort the character and intentions of the United States and the ROK. The regime does this to alienate its people from their natural ROK brethren but also to provide enemies that the regime can blame for its own failings and its dedication of assets to military capabilities. The chapter then turns to describing the tasks required to make North Koreans more accepting of ROK-led unification. These tasks include transmitting a true picture of ROK society into North Korea, demonstrating that the United States and the ROK are not enemies, preparing policies that will make unification advantageous for the North Koreans, and communicating these policies to the North Koreans. These actions are best taken years before a sudden North

Korean government collapse to establish the credibility of the policies among North Koreans. The United States and the ROK also need to prepare to follow these policies, putting legal provisions in place and assembling the capabilities required to provide humanitarian assistance and other potential commitments. If the ROK and the United States are unprepared to provide the North Koreans a favorable life after unification, many North Koreans will become disaffected and potentially rebel against the development of a stable and prosperous unified Korea.

The recommendations in this chapter are those of the author, intended to illustrate the kinds of actions that the United States and the ROK could take. While some of these recommendations have been discussed with North Korean defectors, all these recommendations still need to be vetted, augmented, and integrated by professionals who have worked with North Korean defectors and are trained in psychological operations applied to North Korea. Such vetting would, hopefully, cause adjustments in areas where reactions not expected by the author could dominate over the expected reactions. Thus, this chapter should be read as a work in progress.

The Challenges of North Korean Indoctrination and Fear

The primary objective of the North Korean regime is to secure its own survival. The regime has sought to achieve this objective by pursuing a multidimensional effort to paint the prospects of any alternative to the North Korean regime as being unacceptable to the North Korean people. A key part of this effort has been North Korean propaganda that purposefully distorts the nature and interests of the United States and the ROK. The regime has thus depicted the ROK as poorer than the North and has claimed that the United States and the ROK are the perennial enemies of North Korea, determined to hurt the North Korean people. The regime has also sought to make the ROK and the United States the scapegoats for the multitude of North Korean failings, placing the responsibility for many failings on the United States and the ROK, verifying that they are the enemies of the North Korean people.

As a result, the North Korean people have many reasons for worrying about the collapse of the North Korean government and a subsequent ROK-led unification. The elites in particular must worry about their own futures should ROK-led unification occur. They probably worry that many of them will be imprisoned or even executed for crimes they have committed and, at very best, would be removed from their advantageous positions and potentially wind up starving to death. They have no confidence that the ROK government would find value in their participation in the resulting, unified Korean government, fearing a future analogous to the U.S. de-Ba'athification of Iraq. Many North Koreans likely wonder about the nature of the ROK business and political systems, including both the wealth of the ROK and the broad opportunities to participate in that wealth.

Many North Koreans, especially many of the elites, may therefore decide to at least oppose a sudden Korean unification, if not fight against it. And the ROK cannot afford the cost of major warfare, serious insurgency, and/or extensive criminal behavior added to the otherwise steep economic costs of a permissive reunification.

North Korea Is Rich, South Korea Is Poor

The North Korean regime has thoroughly indoctrinated its people to control their thinking, telling them how wonderful the Kim family and their country are. Indeed, the national propaganda depicts North Korea as the center of the earth, around which world events revolve.[1] North Koreans are told that their country is "paradise on earth,"[2] in sharp contrast to other countries and especially to South Korea. This comparison to South Korea may have been true in the past. After the Korean war, South Korea was one of the world's poorest countries, with only $64 per capita per year income.[3] Since then, the ROK has become a wealthy country, while the North Korean economy has languished.

Until about a decade ago, North Korea constantly depicted the ROK as an impoverished state, where people lived in far worse con-

---

[1] Andrei Lankov, "The World According to Pyongyang," *Asia Times,* July 13, 2007.

[2] Hyun Sik Kim, 2008.

[3] Mark Tran, "South Korea: A Model of Development?" *Guardian,* November 28, 2011.

dition than the people of North Korea: "[T]he survival of the North greatly depends on maintaining the myths about the South, such as it being a starving U.S. colony, a 'living hell, land of destitution and despair.'"[4] Some early defectors in 1987 said, "[w]hen we lived in the North, we were told that South Korea was a living hell."[5] A defector in 2006 said, "When I came to the South and saw how rich it was, I was very angry at the Pyongyang regime."[6]

The influx into the North of information about South Korea has weakened this propaganda line. While it is still repeated on occasion, now North Koreans are told that the South

> has lost its true national identity, so its inhabitants are full of admiration toward the spiritual purity of their Northern brethren. The southerners, the propaganda claims, also badly want to purify themselves under the wise guidance of the Dear Leader Kim Jong-il (allegedly a cult figure in both the South and the North).[7]

> Brian Myers, another remarkable specialist on North Korean culture and propaganda (not quite distinguishable areas, actually), recently wrote at length about a change of tune in Pyongyang propaganda: South Korea ceased to be depicted as the living hell, the land of depravation. The new image of the South is that of the country whose population secretly (or even not so secretly) longs to join its Northern brethren in their happiness under the wise care of the Beloved General.[8]

Apparently, DVDs and other information from the ROK have penetrated so much into North Korea that the argument of ROK impoverishment is not credible with many in the North and undermines overall

---

[4]   Lankov, 2008.

[5]   As quoted in Nicholas D. Kristof, "South Korea Welcomes Family Fleeing North," *New York Times*, February 9, 1987.

[6]   As quoted in Jennifer Chang, "Korean Propaganda Soars with Balloons," Al Jazeera, September 29, 2012.

[7]   Lankov, 2008.

[8]   Lankov, 2007.

North Korean propaganda. So an alternative approach is being taken to keep the multidimensional propaganda approach viable, claiming that the ROK is now poor in wise guidance and leadership.

The United States Is the Enemy

Several years ago, a tape emerged from North Korea that reportedly contained the comments of a high-level Central Committee member, Comrade Chang. He provided an excellent overview of North Korean propaganda about the enemies of North Korea and its people. Speaking of the hardships suffered by North Koreans,

> the audience was reminded that in the final count it is again the foreign forces who are to be blamed for these hardships. To quote Comrade Chang once again: "It is not because we do not know how to live better that we are not well off. Who is responsible for this? The US imperialists are responsible for this. That is why we call the US imperialists our mortal enemy with whom we cannot live under the same sky!"[9]

> According to the official North Korean world view, once again reiterated by Comrade Chang, the U.S. is responsible for everything that goes badly in Korea, and the constant military threat from the warmongering Washington is the major fact of North Korean life.[10]

While North Korean propaganda focuses on the United States as the enemy, it speaks of South Korean government officials as "lackeys" working with their "America masters."[11]

The North Korean propaganda begins at an early age:

---

[9] Lankov, 2007.

[10] Lankov, 2007.

[11] See, for example, "Rodong Sinmun S. Korean Conservative Forces' Conspiracy with Their American Masters Under Fire," Korean Central News Agency, October 30, 2012. The "NK News Database of North Korean Propaganda," undated, lists 211 references to the term *lackey* in North Korean articles from 1996 to 2012. It provides interesting bar graphs of the monthly frequency of word usage from searching the North Korean literature over time—for example, showing nearly 4,200 uses of the word *traitor* since 1996.

For North Koreans, the systematic indoctrination of anti-Americanism starts as early as kindergarten and is as much a part of the curriculum as learning to count. Toy pistols, rifles and tanks sit lined up in neat rows on shelves. The school principal pulls out a dummy of an American soldier with a beaked nose and straw-colored hair and explains that the students beat him with batons or pelt him with stones—a favorite schoolyard game, she says. . . . At the Kaeson Kindergarten in central Pyongyang, one of several schools visited by the AP [Associated Press], U.S. soldiers are depicted as cruel, ghoulish barbarians with big noses and fiendish eyes. Teeth bared, they brand prisoners with hot irons, set wild dogs on women and wrench out a girl's teeth with pliers. One drawing shows an American soldier crushing a girl with his boot, blood pouring from her mouth, her eyes wild with fear and pain. . . . "First, we start by teaching that the American imperialists started the war," said soft-spoken schoolteacher Jon Chun Yong, citing the North Korean version of how the war began. "From that time on, the tragedy emerged by which our nation was divided in two," said Jon, who has taught at the kindergarten for 15 years. "Since then, our people had to endure the pain of living divided for a long half-century."[12]

Another dimension of this propaganda is the unending nature of the United States being an enemy:

Compromise with enemies is impossible since they, especially the Americans, will never change their nature, will never stop dreaming about destroying the small and proud republic led by the Beloved General. However, the country has finally developed military means that make all enemies' schemes powerless. This project required great sacrifice, but the people who died during famine were in essence soldiers: their deaths saved many more lives.[13]

---

[12] "In North Korea, Learning to Hate U.S. Starts with Children," *USA Today*, June 23, 2012.

[13] This quote is reportedly from a lecture given by "a high-level Central Committee official" apparently to "a group of prominent academics and engineers." Earlier in the presentation, the speaker also said: "Until 2006, North Koreans were supposed to believe that the only

In summary, North Korean propaganda's depiction of the United States and the ROK as enemies complicates the process of dealing with a North Korean government collapse. Any North Korean believing the regime's propaganda will oppose ROK-led unification. Even North Korean children are taught to attack Americans. And even North Koreans who do not militarily oppose unification can disrupt the unification process in many other ways. Unless the United States and the ROK launch an effort to counter this propaganda, they could face significant difficulty in unifying Korea.

The Challenge of North Koreans' Fears for Their Future

I postulate that there are three major areas in which North Koreans, especially the elites, will be worried about their quality of life after unification: (1) the loss of societal, political, and/or military positions that have defined their privileges and influence; (2) the potential for criminal prosecution and imprisonment, execution, and/or disgrace; and (3) the loss of jobs, homes, property, and money wanted to fill their economic and physical needs and desires.

Positions and Privileges

With regard to the first, concerns about positions and privileges will vary by status in North Korea, as reflected in the sociopolitical classification of people (their *songbun*).[14] In this system, each person in North Korea is classified as core class, wavering class, or hostile class; almost all privileges in North Korea are associated with the person's *songbun*. The elites at the top of the core *songbun*, especially, have reason to worry, given the precedents of German unification:

> German unification completely deprived all East German Communist party and military leaders of their privileges and made them jobless. Kim Jong-il had the plight of former East German

---

reasons for the recent famine were huge floods that 'might happen only once a century'. Now it is admitted that the government needed money for missile and nuclear development, and hence had no other choice but to sacrifice some people to save the nation" (Lankov, 2007).

[14] See Robert Collins, *Marked for Life: Songbun; North Korea's Social Classification System*, The Committee for Human Rights in North Korea, 2012.

leaders photographed and shown to North Korean cadres. And many members of the elite, though they detested Kim Jong-il, thought they had no alternative but to follow him for fear of losing their privileges if the regime collapsed. That is why the regime did not collapse despite the 1990s famine that starved millions to death.[15]

Some of the North Korean elites likely worry about their futures after unification based on key ROK precedents. For example, the North Korean elites, especially the senior elites, will likely anticipate that their future under unification will be no better than the fate of the ROK's past presidents after they left office. These presidents have been taken to court, sentenced to death, and sent to jail, and past-President Roh Moo-hyun felt pushed into committing suicide. Why would the senior leaders in North Korea expect any better treatment? And if they do not, they may well decide to fight against unification under ROK control.

For the North Korean elite, their positions and authority have defined their lives and will be difficult to give up. For example, even if they are not imprisoned, North Korean military officers may be drawn to insurgency and/or criminal activity, in which they could once again command (even if they have authority only over smaller groups). Allowing them to do so would significantly complicate stabilization of North Korea, potentially making conditions much worse than the United States experienced in Iraq around 2006.

Criminal Prosecution and Imprisonment

North Korea is sometimes described as having a culture of criminality. As noted earlier,

> [a]ccording to defectors, it is practically impossible in modern day North Korea for ordinary citizens to survive and participate in the economy without taking part in illegal activities, such as smuggling or secret trade. For this reason, people find it necessary

---

[15] Kang Chol-hwan, 2009.

to cultivate close relationships with cadres in the legal system, who become the recipients of bribes in return.[16]

Thus, many officials could be subject to legal action after unification, as could the merchants and others who have offered bribes. Of more serious criminal concern would be the senior elites, who often exploit their positions to obtain wealth and do so employing questionable (illegal) means. Their positions have often allowed them to insulate themselves from criminal sanctions in North Korea, but the loss of their positions would leave them vulnerable to legal action. Some core *songbun* personnel have been the staff of the prison camps or other regime efforts to subjugate the population and should certainly be dealt with via criminal prosecution.

One paper by a law professor from Seoul National University proposes categories of illegal activities that should be dealt with in the aftermath of unification:

> Lee classified the North's illegal systems into four types: illegal acts to maintain the system such as torture, murder and detention by force; terrorism such as the 1987 bombing of a Korean Airlines flight; attempts to communize South Korea as exemplified by the Korean War on June 25, 1950; and illegal asset accumulation by high-ranking officials.[17]

If such a system were instituted, many North Koreans would be subject to prosecution. But the very fact that such actions are being discussed in the ROK may negatively affect the perceptions of North Korean personnel relative to their possible future after unification.

Achieving Economic and Physical Needs and Desires

Finally, North Koreans will likely ask: Will we be at least as well off after unification as we were under the North Korean regime? For the core *songbun* and the military, many have had some form of govern-

---

[16] Mok Yong Jae, 2012a.

[17] "System to Punish NK Leaders Needed After Reunification," *Dong-A Ilbo*, October 4, 2010.

ment job that they likely expect to lose, leaving them unemployed. Even if they do find a job, many of the elites will certainly not be able to command the kind of work conditions or salary that they have had in North Korea, having lost their position in society. The elites and many merchants will also worry about losing their wealth either due to inflation or ROK confiscation, and inflation may more broadly worry the population that basic necessities will become unacceptably expensive.

And those who better understand conditions in the ROK will realize that they are poorly trained for jobs in such a competitive environment; many will know that defectors have generally not done well economically in the ROK. Finally, those who are imprisoned or otherwise run afoul of the legal system may provide little or no economic security for themselves and their families.

Combined Quality of Life Perceptions for After Unification

Figure 4.1 roughly suggests the expectations that North Korean adults likely have today for their quality of life after unification. Thus, many (especially from the core class) will expect to be much worse off after

Figure 4.1
North Korean Quality of Life Expectations After Unification

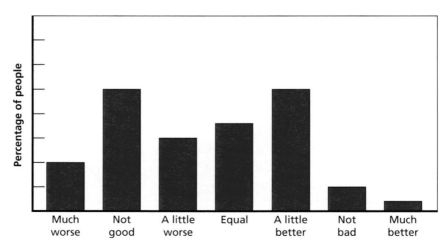

SOURCE: Notional data estimates by the author.
RAND RR331-4.1

unification because of lost jobs and positions and prosecution for illegal behavior, likely leading to imprisonment if not execution. Many others will expect to be worse off because their economic, physical, and sociopolitical situations will decline substantially and because they could be subject to ROK discrimination. The North Korean propaganda described earlier has focused these people on such downsides of unification. Still, some elites may hope that they could do well in a unified Korea (e.g., working as merchants and having reliable services, such as power 24 hours per day), including individuals from the top of the core class who have more contact with outside media than anyone else in North Korea.[18] Many in the hostile and wavering classes may also hope life will be at least a little better after unification. But if most of the core class perceives that unification would make them clearly worse off, it will be difficult to gain their cooperation with unification. And since they have the power to set policies and lead people, they could make unification very difficult to accomplish.

The wavering and hostile classes probably have not thought much about their lives after unification; any optimism they hold may be unrealistic because of their poor education and lack of experience with ROK culture. This highlights the fact that, while perceptions before unification are important, the performance of unification in its early days will further adjust attitudes and potentially cause people to take action against ROK control if they do not expect to be treated well.

ROK Reluctance to Counter These Perceptions

The ROK government has been reluctant to send information into the North to counter these perceptions, in part because there is no consensus in the ROK that such messages should be sent into North Korea. Many ROK progressives are concerned that sending these mes-

---

[18] According to Hwang Chang Hyun,

> It is well known that the higher up in the North Korean class hierarchy a family is, the more access its members have to South Korean movies and dramas (the media grouped together internationally as "Hallyu" or "Korean Wave"). This was a view confirmed yesterday by Park Jung Ran of the Center for Cultural Unification Studies at the release of the center's latest report, "Hallyu; The Wind of Unification."

Hwang Chang Hyun, "Winds of Unification Still Blowing . . . ," *Daily NK*, June 28, 2012.

sages could destabilize the North. Others in the ROK are unwilling to undertake the costs that unification could well entail. It is also difficult to create positive expectations because the ROK has yet to openly establish key conditions that would reassure North Koreans of their postunification lives. North Korean defectors who have come to South Korea have generally not found the much better lives they expected. Thus, the ROK government must step back and ask: What messages can and should be sent into the North with relative consensus from the South, and how should the ROK build on these messages over time?

Overcoming North Korean Indoctrination and Fear

Overcoming this fear is a key step in achieving North Korean cooperation in the unification process. Winning the "hearts and minds" of the North Koreans requires early, systematic engagement to help them learn the truth about the ROK and its many opportunities. Preparation in this area means taking actions to convince the North Koreans that reunification will be in their best interest: They will live better, more abundant lives and will not be subject to the arbitrary and capricious actions of the North Korean government and its various components. In terms of Figure 4.1, the desire is to shift many in the North Korean population to the right, helping them perceive that they will be better off after unification. But it will take time to convince the North Korean people that the regime's propaganda is false and that the ROK and the United States can be trusted in the opportunities being offered. This may be especially challenging with many of the elites.

Initial Messages: "The ROK Is a Great Country"

The first theme that the North Koreans need to understand is that life is far better in the ROK than in North Korea. This theme will run counter to the historical North Korean propaganda of the ROK being impoverished but must also identify the ROK as a country with identity and drive, happy to live without the influence of the North Korean Kim regime (countering the more recent North Korean propaganda). While some North Koreans have already gotten the prosperity message, many have not. The ROK status of economic plenty establishes a basis for North Korean interest in unification, with North Koreans anxious to gain the benefits that the ROK has to offer.

In practice, this message should be relatively simple to send because there should be broad ROK consensus on the underlying message: The ROK is a great country; it is a great place to live. Such a message could be part of a ROK national campaign, consistent with ROK nationalism and furthering national pride. But this message also needs to be sent into the North to adjust the expectations of the North Koreans. It could involve creating commercials and other advertisements demonstrating a bounteous life (which is certainly the case relative to the circumstances in North Korea).

ROK radio and television broadcasts could carry similar "public service" messages, including on the analog channels still being broadcast for consumption in North Korea.[19] The ROK government could arrange for similar commercials to be broadcast in China, across from the North Korean border—broadcasts that would reach into North Korea. It could also put several minutes of corresponding commercials on all DVDs manufactured in the ROK, at least some of which would get into North Korea. These messages would more coherently help the people of North Korea understand the South. They could do so by showing such things as

- **Food availability.** 60-second commercials could show pictures from several food or supermarkets in the ROK, with shopping carts holding diverse food products. Individuals could be interviewed, including those in modest jobs, to talk about the food they are able to purchase and to show the meals they are able to prepare. Surveys could be taken in the ROK and discussed in such commercials showing, for example, the fraction of meals in which ROK common people enjoy rice and meat (far less common in the North).
- **ROK farming.** Short commercials could show the equipment used on ROK farms, plus the fertilizers and insecticides employed,

---

[19] Cho Jong Ik, Government Agrees to Maintain Analogue TV," *DailyNK*, December 25, 2012.

and describe the resulting crop yields. The farms' sales of their products could also be demonstrated, showing that the ROK government and/or ROK Army does not simply come in and take much of the product away.

- **Modern cities, offices, and apartments.** The skylines of many ROK cities could be shown to illustrate the circumstances of those living in ROK cities. The plentiful availability of electricity and, along with it, elevators, appliances, and lights could be demonstrated. Even the traffic jams in Seoul and other ROK cities would speak to the strength of the ROK economy and the shared riches among the vast majority of the ROK population. Essentially, even a modestly paid worker in the ROK will tend to have a better lifestyle than many of even the North Korean core *songbun*.

- **High-quality construction.** The quality of ROK construction practices should also be demonstrated. This would include the nature of the construction equipment used in the ROK for buildings, roads, and other infrastructure. The ROK has many times the mileage of paved roads that the North has (which could be illustrated by showing paved roads in many rural areas) and has many buildings with "luxuries" that are seldom seen in the North.

- **Colleges and universities.** The ROK could film ROK universities, showing the large number of them and the percentage of young people given the opportunity for a college education. It could show classrooms unencumbered by Kim family doctrine and show facilities, such as libraries with their vast printed and electronic resources.

- **Advanced nuclear physics research.** The ROK should provide general information on the nature and quality of its nuclear physics research (and other areas of major scientific advancement). This should include pictures of physics laboratories and the equipment both at ROK universities and in ROK companies. Any North Korean scientists should yearn for an opportunity to work in such environments.

- **Many excellent nuclear plants.** The ROK should show pictures of its 23 nuclear power plants and contrast them with the very small North Korean Yongbyon nuclear reactor. The ROK reactors also produce nearly one-half of the electricity the ROK consumes, while the Yongbyon reactor was reportedly never attached to the electrical grid.[20] In a video, radiation detectors could demonstrate that the ROK plants are clean and well maintained, a serious contrast to the Yongbyon facility, which is apparently very much contaminated with radiation.[21]

- **Broad computer and Internet availability.** The ROK should show families and schools with large numbers of advanced computers. It should discuss the percentage of families with Internet connectivity and regular use, including connections to a wide variety of international sites. The ROK should present the common use of computers by nearly all high school and college students, with many employing laptop computers. It should demonstrate the kinds of information readily available on the Internet (but not to most North Koreans).

- **Advanced medicine.** The ROK should show ROK hospitals as well lit, agreeable facilities with ample supplies of antibiotics and other drugs and advanced diagnostic and operating facilities. It should show the pharmaceutical companies in the ROK and their production of medicines, as well as the availability of such medicines to almost everyone in the ROK.

- **Strong manufacturing.** The ROK should show how ROK industrial facilities are no longer manpower intensive but use substantial automation. A good example would be an automobile production line. The output of such facilities should be demonstrated to show the effectiveness of automation, and the programming of the equipment could also be illustrated.

- **Modern airlines, airports, and transportation.** ROK international transportation infrastructure should be illustrated, including the advanced aircraft ROK airlines use, the airport facilities that are available, and the degree to which common people can use these facilities to travel broadly within the ROK or interna-

---

[20] Nicholas Eberstadt, "A Skeptical View," *Wall Street Journal*, September 21, 2005, p. 26.

[21] See, for example, "N.Korea's Nuclear Facilities 'a Disaster in the Making,'" *Chosun Ilbo*, April 19, 2011.

tionally. Families of common workers could be interviewed to talk about their ability to go to exciting places and about their freedom of travel. The KTX trains traveling at 300 km/hour and other rail advances could also be shown, along with the schedules and reliability of both regular and KTX train service.[22]

All these are examples of areas in which South Korea truly is a great state and in which conditions in North Korea are backward and even primitive by comparison. While ROK soap operas showing such images are already extremely popular in North Korea,[23] giving some of the feel of ROK society to the people of the North, many in the North may feel that the soap operas reflect the lifestyles of only the ROK elites. North Koreans need to learn about the abundance of ROK society illustrated above, especially that these advances are not just reserved for the ROK elites but rather are shared by the ROK common people. A twist on messages about ROK plenty would be to follow families of factory workers or farmers and show their lives across these topical areas.

But the ROK would need to be careful with these messages. It does not want to create an impression in the North that unification will instantly bring about North Korean wealth—that will not be possible. Thus, the messages need to emphasize the *many years* that most ROK citizens have worked to achieve their quality of life. Otherwise, North Koreans could become disaffected after unification, an outcome to be carefully avoided.

This kind of information campaign should continue through Korean unification and perhaps beyond. It is an initial effort in the sense that it lays the basis for people in North Korea to begin thinking that things could be better with a different government. Some people in North Korea have already likely reached this conclusion (hence the many defectors to the ROK, despite the challenges of defection), but many likely have not. The potential for North Koreans to gain a better

---

[22] Korea Train eXpress (KTX) is Korea's bullet train.

[23] Shin Hae-in, "Changes Brewing in 'Not so Isolated' North," *Korea Herald*, December 15, 2010.

life through unification becomes the basis for many of the subsequent messages that the ROK wants to send to North Koreans.

Next Steps: The North Korean People Can Attain ROK Plenty

Once North Koreans come to believe that a better lifestyle is available in the ROK, they will also need to feel that they can, over time, become part of that lifestyle through unification. This second step is a more difficult message because the ROK does not appear to have prepared adequately to make this case. Moreover, some in the North, especially some of the elites, likely cannot become part of the ROK lifestyle because of their unwillingness to adapt or because of crimes they have committed that the ROK will be reluctant to forgive. Nevertheless, the ROK government needs to make most North Koreans feel that unification will give them, personally, a better life. These messages would include the following:

- **Merchants are welcome in the ROK.** Many people in the ROK are merchants and are not persecuted for such activities. This is in sharp contrast to North Korea, where most merchants are viewed with concern at best and where merchants must often turn to bribing public officials to avoid incarceration. Many people in North Korea became rich via market activity, only to see that activity attacked by the North Korean currency revaluation of December 2009 and other actions.[24] Such attacks would not happen in the ROK. Pictures of major ROK shopping areas, such as Myeong-dong, would demonstrate the acceptance of market activity in the ROK. Actual stories of merchants may be even more compelling in drawing contrasts with the life of North Korean merchants.

---

[24] In December 2009, North Korea revalued its currency, exchanging 100 old won for 1 new won. It also severely limited the amount of currency that could be exchanged, apparently trying to wipe out the capital stock of North Korean merchants. The North Korean regime wanted to do so because many merchants had accumulated significant amounts of cash that in part allowed them to bribe officials so that they could avoid the dictates of the political leaders. See, for example, Blaine Harden, "In N. Korea, Resistance Is the New Currency," *Washington Post*, December 27, 2009.

- **North Koreans will live well after unification.** North Koreans, especially the North Korean elite, need to feel that the high quality of living in the ROK will extend into the North. This is the area in which the quality-of-life message discussed above should be introduced. An improved quality of living will need to be a part of the plans for unification, with capabilities to achieve that objective demonstrated before a North Korean collapse and with actual improvements achieved at least in part early in a unification. For example, from a short-term perspective, the ROK and United States need to be prepared to deliver humanitarian aid promptly to the North (see Chapter Five), demonstrating an ability to improve the quality of life. From an information perspective, the ROK needs to be able to say that it has addressed these issues, has meaningful plans and resources to deal with them, and can move promptly to implement its plans if a collapse occurs and the conditions for unification develop. But saying so will likely generate opposition from ROK progressive groups; thus, this effort needs to be done as discussed in Chapter Ten.
- **North Koreans can live well in a ROK-governed society.** It would be ideal to show the lives of many North Korean defectors and argue that they have done very well in the ROK. While some such individuals will be found, many North Korean defectors have not done so well in the ROK, in part because of the limited education they received in the North, in part because of ROK discrimination (the language, accents, and cultural differences of North Koreans make them identifiable as having come from North Korea), and in part because the skills learned in North Korea often do not correspond with job skills required in the ROK.[25] To send this message, the ROK government needs to do more to train defectors for jobs and to overcome discrimination. But it should also encourage North Koreans to stay in North Korea after unification; the ROK government needs to prepare to apply resources to improving life in North Korea, as will be

---

[25] See, for example, "NK Defectors Fail to Assimilate Into S. Korean Society," *Donga Ilbo*, October 26, 2009.

discussed in Chapters Five and Six. In practice, massive North Korean migration into the ROK is likely to create even more discrimination as some South Koreans lose jobs or perceive that they have lost jobs to North Koreans and as such migration otherwise tests ROK willingness to absorb North Koreans.

- **Even the North Korean military can live well in a unified Korea.** The North Korean military can pose the biggest threat to Korean unification, potentially engaging ROK forces outright or transitioning to insurgent or criminal activities. The ROK thus needs to be able to largely demobilize the North Korean military into civilian life but to do so in a way that provides jobs for the demobilized military personnel and allows the North Korean officers, especially, to retain their dignity and some elements of their privileged status. The ROK needs to develop such programs as described in Chapter Six and inform the North Korean military of ROK intentions. But ROK progressives will be even more likely to oppose this message because it destabilizes the North. The message thus needs to be made under appropriate circumstances.

While the ROK government will want to send these messages into North Korea, it is difficult to do so before a consensus is built in the ROK that would support these actions. Therefore, the ROK first needs to send messages to overcome North Korean propaganda and prepare people in both the ROK and North Korea for the messages.

Building Positive North Korean Postunification Quality-of-Life Expectations

As described in Chapter Three, if most North Koreans feel that unification will not be in their interests, the ROK may have to impose unification, rather than just usher it in. Imposing unification will be far more costly, in terms of both lives lost and money spent, and could even fail. Therefore, developing positive expectations among the North Koreans is the foundation on which a successful unification must be built. This subsection outlines the key elements needed to change North Korean perceptions and the preparations required to achieve these elements.

Ironically, many people in the ROK or the United States will have difficulty understanding the reluctance of the North Koreans to overthrow the oppression of the current North Korean government. Historically, many South Koreans have shed considerable amounts of blood and tears to secure democracy and a free economy in South Korea, as did Americans of previous generations. But North Koreans have not experienced the freedom and economic opportunities that would exist in a unified Korea. It will therefore be critical to personalize North Korean perceptions of the future and specifically address key concerns of the North Koreans.

The German Example

At the time of German reunification, most East Germans appeared to feel that reunification would personally be good for them. They viewed West Germany as more economically advanced and rich and thus anticipated that unification would give them an economically better life. Many also preferred to work with their brother Germans than to continue to be subjugated to the Soviet Union.

But there were other important attractions as well. Some time after German reunification, a ROK colleague was sent to East Germany to talk with the former leaders of the East German secret police, the Stasi. His assignment was to determine why the Stasi leadership had failed to put down the demonstrations in East Germany in the fall of 1989 that eventually precipitated German Unification. The Stasi leaders were fairly unified in identifying two reasons. First, for many years, the West German government had promised a general amnesty for East German leaders—the promise had been given for so long that the Stasi leaders felt confident that West Germany would abide by it. Second, the West German government had announced pension plans for East German government personnel, and the plans were more lucrative than what the Stasi leaders anticipated from the East German government. Since the senior Stasi leaders were all approaching retirement, the offers of amnesty and generous pensions convinced them that they would be better off after unification than under the East German government.[26] So they were only lukewarm in their efforts to put down the demonstrations.

But many of the less senior East German elites did not fare as well, as discussed relative to Kim Jong-Il's filming reported above. They were too young for retirement and yet could not find good employment after German unification. The ROK and the United States need to decide how to develop appropriate post-Korean unification employment for the North Korean elites.

Selective Amnesty Against Criminal Accusations

As argued above, many North Koreans are involved in activities that would be considered criminal based on either North Korean or ROK law. The offering or acceptance of bribes is particularly commonplace. The personnel involved in such crimes, especially the elites, will likely fear criminal prosecution and imprisonment, causing them to have potentially the worst possible perceptions of personal postunification conditions. This is of particular concern with the North Korean military; senior commanders alienated from unification may draw many of their subordinates and peers with them into military units that fight against unification, either directly or as insurgents or criminals.

The ROK therefore needs to develop some form of selective amnesty. In contrast to the German general amnesty discussed above, it is difficult to imagine that the Korean or international communities will simply ignore the egregious human rights abuses that have been practiced in North Korea, and they should not. So the delicate trade-off will be in identifying what the ROK is willing to forgive through selective amnesty and whether the imposition of justice in other areas is worth the price the ROK will likely pay in terms of combat, casualties, insurgency, and criminal activities.

Nevertheless, the ROK cannot afford to apply criminal justice to any significant fraction of the North Koreans. The ROK legal system would have difficulty dealing with tens of thousands of criminal prosecutions against North Koreans, and the ROK prison system has an official capacity of only 44,430 people, relative to which it was already

---

[26] Interview with senior ROK official in September 2009.

filled with 46,503 prisoners as of mid-2011.[27] While the ROK could use the North Korean prisons to hold North Koreans accused or convicted of crimes committed before unification, the stigma, especially of the North Korean gulags, will likely make their use unacceptable in international terms. Even if the ROK were extremely aggressive, it likely could not handle criminal actions that would lead to the imprisonment of as many as 40,000 North Koreans,[28] or about 1 percent of North Korean adults from the core *songbun*.[29] To avoid alienating many of the other 99 percent in the core *songbun* plus some people from the other *songbun*, the ROK government needs to decide which roughly 1 percent of the core *songbun* it feels has committed the most serious crimes, plan to prosecute them, and offer amnesty to the rest of the North Korean population.

In making this decision, the ROK likely wants to focus on human rights crimes (especially torture and murder, generally practiced by less-powerful individuals). In this regard, the State Security Department, which performs many secret police functions, reportedly numbers some 50,000 personnel,[30] many of whom have been involved in serious human rights abuses. Others among the various security and police organizations may also warrant criminal action for their human rights crimes, likely filling the number of prosecutions possible. Therefore, there should be less focus on economic crimes, especially since many of most powerful North Koreans who could fight unification

---

[27] International Centre for Prison Studies, "World Prison Brief," website, undated.

[28] The lack of prison space would be a critical constraint on those prosecuted. Imprisoning even 40,000 North Korean criminals would require the use of some North Korean prison facilities. While the gulags would be inappropriate, some of the "labor-training camps" and perhaps some of the "correctional" centers that exist in each North Korean province could be used; see Ken E. Gause, "Coercion, Control, Surveillance, and Punishment: An Examination of the North Korean Police State," Washington, D.C.: Committee for Human Rights in North Korea, 2012, pp. 80–81. But the political ramifications of using these could still be problematic for the new unified Korean government.

[29] Per the 2008 census, there were about 16.5 million North Koreans of age 20 and above. The core *songbun* is about one-fourth of the North Korean population, about 4 million adults. See Collins, 2012, p. 25.

[30] See Gause, 2012, p. 17.

would be guilty of such. But the choice is up to the ROK because it will pay a people and economic cost for North Koreans who decide to oppose unification in insurgency and/or criminal behavior but will also pay a moral cost for being too lenient with criminal offenders.[31]

Once the ROK government has made an amnesty decision, it will be important to communicate this plan to the North Korean people. As in the German case, the North Koreans will likely need to be reassured on amnesty repeatedly over a period of years. But it will also be difficult to secure ROK public opinion to support an amnesty program. The ROK government therefore also needs to explain the reasons for amnesty, the German precedent, and the prices that will likely be paid for not being generous in this area.

Providing Hope of Economic and Physical Security

The ROK also needs to decide the basic economic and physical quality of life to offer to the North Koreans. North Koreans need to expect that they will at least have food and other essential goods (such as electrical power) and also that they will have physical security. Problems in these basic areas have historically led people in other countries to displace from their homes and eventually become refugees.

From a strategic perspective, the ROK will want most North Koreans to remain where they have been living in the North or to return there if they have displaced. In these areas, many North Koreans would have places to live, jobs, and supporting infrastructure. Once people leave their homes and jobs, their humanitarian needs grow significantly, and their ability to become self-sufficient over time decreases greatly. Moreover, if many North Koreans seek to enter the ROK or China to obtain food and good jobs, they could overwhelm the humanitarian capabilities of both countries, flood their job markets with vast numbers of low-skilled laborers; raise opposition in China and the ROK against these immigrants, who would steal jobs and

---

[31] The author is not aware of any work going on in the ROK on defining unification-based amnesty. But that work may be going on within the Ministry of Unification, without public disclosure.

other resources; and politically destabilize at least the border areas.[32] This subject is addressed in more detail in Chapter Five.

Within this framework, the ROK needs to adjust the North Koreans' expectations to obtain their cooperation or at least their support of unification and to do so in several critical areas:

- If, after a collapse, North Korea suffers from a food shortage as expected, the immediate concern of many North Koreans will be short term: How are they going to eat today and tomorrow and the rest of this week? A ROK ability to deal promptly with such a humanitarian crisis would provide a sharp short-term contrast between unification and a continuing collapse in North Korea. The discussion in Chapter Five of providing humanitarian aid describes how the ROK could perform such a function and also the messages that should be sent into North Korea well in advance of a government collapse to convince the North Korean people that the ROK is prepared to meet their humanitarian needs should the North Korean government fail.
- The ROK government needs to decide on an approach to handling North Korean property. There are two major issues:
  - Many North Koreans who fled to the South during the Korean War will claim property in the North, property that, in many cases, others have used for decades. Turning this property over to South Koreans would definitely alienate the North Koreans and lead to an incredible legal quandary. Such property rights cases in East Germany overwhelmed the German courts after German unification, and many have reportedly yet to be resolved. Property tied up in such cases may become unusable by either party and not be maintained.
  - Property ownership could become a major advantage of unification for many North Koreans, giving them rights and resources that they lack today because the North Korean

---

[32] Indeed, because China does not want these refugees crossing into China, China may be forced to intervene deeply in North Korea to create refugee camps and barriers to stem the flow of refugees. See Chapter Nine.

state owns most property. Ownership could also provide an incentive for North Koreans to stay home: The ROK could announce a program for North Koreans to become the owners of their residences and of related land areas. Such a program could require the North Koreans to continuously inhabit these locations for three to five years after unification to receive ownership. It would then also need to limit the ability of North Koreans to sell this property for perhaps ten years or more. In East Germany, many people sold their recently acquired property within the first year, giving them a short-term economic windfall but a long-term loss of property ownership—not an advantageous outcome.[33] See Chapter Eight.

- The ROK also needs to decide what financial resources North Koreans will be allowed to retain. For the elites, such assets as cars, cash, trading goods, and food will be important. The ROK may decide to take some of these assets away because of the (potentially exploitive) manner in which they were acquired. But taking too much away could lead to conflict and rebellion. The ROK will also need to consider the implications of the exchange rate it sets for North Korean currency, as well as any limits imposed on currency exchange.
- Most North Korean adults will need jobs after the short-term humanitarian aid has stabilized economic conditions in the North. According to the 2008 North Korean census, some 12 million North Korean adults have jobs, not counting the military.[34] Many of these jobs should be able to continue after unification. The ROK should be prepared to provide short-term capital for North Korean firms so that they can weather the transition to unification and continue operating. The ROK should also provide business assistance to help North Korean firms transition to

---

[33] Allowing the North Koreans to promptly sell the property they have been inhabiting would mean a loss of ownership and thus interest in maintaining the property. The sales would also cause a sudden availability of money among many in North Korea, creating excessive demand and with it a surge in prices—inflation—because there will not be a sufficient opportunity to augment the supply of available goods very quickly.

[34] Central Bureau of Statistics, 2009, p. 176.

a free market, including help with both the paperwork required and product improvement (low-quality North Korean products are unlikely to sell very well once higher-quality ROK and other products become available).

- The ROK will especially need to address employment for those North Koreans who may not expect to have jobs in the aftermath of a North Korean government failure. This will be particularly true of several categories of people: (1) North Korean political prisoners,[35] (2) most of the North Korean military, and (3) many North Korean government employees.[36]

- Most North Korean elites, especially government personnel, will expect unification to end their positions of power and strong influence. Yet in many cases, these people will be difficult to replace in the short term, suggesting that at least some of them will need to be retained, either in their existing positions or as advisors to their replacements. The ROK needs to evaluate these positions and decide whether retention will be preferred and, if so, the type of retention that should be pursued, as well as plans for retirement or alternative positions after the need for their assistance has significantly declined. These plans need to be explained to the North Korean elites. Moreover, these people need to be reassured that they will not be purged and that most will be offered amnesty, as discussed above.

- Some older and/or senior North Koreans should likely be retired immediately, and others will be retired over time. These people should be offered a competitive pension, one that will allow a reasonable lifestyle. They should feel that, with their pension, unification will either be good for them or at least not be a bad outcome. To generate a favorable response, the nature of the planned pension should be publicly announced. The cost of such pensions

---

[35] There are many criminal prisoners in North Korea. Unification should not immediately change their circumstances but presumably should lead to an eventual review of their sentences.

[36] Chapter Seven deals with the approach for helping the prisoners; Chapter Six discusses the North Korean military.

would be far less than the damage these people could cause if they decided to rebel against the unified Korea. But giving these people pensions could also cause a political problem in the ROK. Therefore, the implications of North Korean expectations for the future needs to first be discussed broadly in the ROK media.

- Most North Koreans outside of the core *songbun* have had limited education opportunities, with few going to college. Even the core *songbun* members who have gone to college have often received politically focused and generally outdated training. Thus, higher education will need to be a key focal point of the ROK after unification. The ROK will need to update and expand university and related programs and to offer many scholarships. Plans for such efforts should be very attractive to many North Koreans, especially those in the wavering or hostile classes.

- To what extent will North Koreans be stigmatized because of what they did in support of the North Korean regime? Even if North Koreans are provided amnesty and an adequate financial future, if they expect to be stigmatized for their roles and/or actions under the North Korean regime, they will likely anticipate a lesser quality of life.

The ROK needs to communicate its plans in these areas to North Koreans. But it first needs to make these plans and commit to providing the resources for them. The ROK does not want to tell people in the North that they will be taken care of in some way, then have the ROK press show that the ROK government has no plans or capabilities to meet these commitments. Such behavior would undermine the credibility of the ROK government, and the ROK government needs credibility with the North Korean people to succeed in unification.

In the planning process, the ROK government may conclude that it cannot do everything on this list—the cost would be just too high, or the ROK population may be unwilling to underwrite the security of the North Korean elites. At the very least, ROK authorities need to estimate which parts of North Korean society are likely to accept unification and which are likely to fight against unification, given different amnesty, quality-of-life, and privilege arrangements, and should seek a combination that would truly allow a successful unification. As argued above, a successful unification will require convincing a significant part of the North Korean population that unification is in their interest and, better still, convincing these North Koreans to cooperate in the unification process. The ROK can pay for unification by making life better for many North Koreans, or it can pay for unification through conflict and dealing with insurgency and criminal activity. I believe that, while the former costs will be high and very visible politically, they be will far lower than the latter costs, which would likely grow significantly over time.

The ultimate challenge will be to convince the ROK population of the wisdom of this approach. The programs underlying the assurances to North Koreans outlined above will be expensive and imply a tax burden on ROK citizens that they will be reluctant to bear. The ROK government needs to justify these expenditures by describing a unified Korea as an investment in the future of the Korean people, something that will most benefit the children of those paying the costs in the short term. Given recent debates in the ROK on even creating a fund for unification to which people could voluntarily contribute, these programs will be hard to sell.[37] The former ROK Minister of Unification rightly described the needed approach:

> People have gotten used to the division. And up until now we have always only emphasized the costs of reunification, but never the costs of division. Those aren't just the costs related to refugees or humanitarian aid programs for Pyongyang, for example to help fight famines. There are also security policy and social policy costs. But we would only have to pay the money for reunification once, and the benefits would be for ever.[38]

---

[37] According to one report, "[a]nticipating popular resistance to the establishment of a punishing 'reunification tax', a number of expert voices are now being raised in support of finding a way to build up a reunification 'war chest' through greater voluntary participation" (Kim Yong Hun, "Alternative Ways to Unification Funding," *DailyNK*, August 18, 2011).

[38] Manfred Ertel, "South Korea's Unification Plan: 'No One Wants to Just Swallow up the North,'" interview with Yu Woo-ik, *Spiegel Online International*, March 10, 2012.

Organizing and Timing These Messages

How should the ROK government send messages into North Korea to convince those in the North that unification will give them a better life? One approach would be to selectively demonstrate ROK abundance. For example, the North could be invited to send some sick children and their mothers to ROK hospitals for pro bono care. Or several North Koreans could be invited to attend a major ROK university. Or a couple of North Korean building engineers could be invited to come to the ROK and observe the construction of ROK buildings, including the use of a variety of advanced equipment.[39] These North Koreans would return to the North with amazing stories, and even if the stories were shared only with North Korean security personnel, the message of ROK citizens living a life of plenty and the potential for North Koreans sharing it would be very powerful.

In addition, the importance of North Korean provocations must be recognized. In the immediate aftermath of North Korean provocations, the ROK government can take actions that would otherwise be very difficult in normal circumstances. As an illustration, President Roh Moo-Hyun ordered that the military conscription period be shortened from 24 months (for the ROK Army) to 18 months by 2014.[40] While it was within the power of President Lee Myung-Bak to change this order after he assumed the presidency in 2008, it was considered politically impossible for him to deal with this issue: Both young voters and their families would likely have seriously opposed any change to President Roh's order. But in December 2010, shortly after the North Korean shelling of Yeonpyeong Island, President Lee ordered that the conscription be kept at the then-current level of roughly 21.5 months. Interest-

---

[39] For obvious reasons, the North Korean authorities would be reluctant to let such interactions occur and may prevent them. But even offering these interactions should have a psychological payoff.

[40] The conscription period is the length of time that conscripts serve in the military. Thus, a 24-month conscription period means that conscripts would serve for two years. Note that President Roh decreased the conscription period for the ROK Army from 26 to 24 months, then set it to shorten a little each month through 2014, when it would have declined to 18 months.

ingly, little political response occurred: Koreans were so angry at the North Korean provocation that they did not act against this change.

Indeed, the entire story illustrates an important point: The ROK has historically focused on countering and deterring North Korean provocations using military means, forgetting that the major reasons for its provocations are political: Demonstrating the empowerment of the regime, supporting the North Korean military, and seeking to strengthen North Korean military support for the regime. ROK military responses to North Korean provocations may damage the North Korean military, but that damage is likely to further strengthen North Korean military support for the regime. Instead, the ROK government needs to consider more political responses to North Korean provocations, responses that directly impose costs on the regime and thus hopefully deter it from further provocations. The ROK government needs to posture such a response against North Korean claims that its regime is stable and empowered, that the ROK and the United States are the enemies that cause all of the problems in North Korea. Doing so will also enlighten the North Korean people.

Revisiting the Yeonpyeong Island Shelling

Consider, for example, the North Korean shelling of Yeonpyeong Island in 2010. President Lee could have announced that evening that the North Korean regime carried out this provocation not because it was strong but because it was weak and unstable. Indeed, the North Korean regime was sufficiently weak that it was prepared to risk a general war with the ROK and the United States by committing an act of war against the ROK. The North Korean regime being so unstable gave President Lee no choice but to prepare for the possibility of "sudden change" in North Korea—a North Korean collapse. While a collapse was not necessarily imminent, the North Korean regime was demonstrating concerns for its own stability by carrying out such a provocation. The ROK could impose a real cost on the North Korean regime by making these statements contrary to the North Korean regime's claims of stability and strength: At least some of the elites and others in the North would believe President Lee's statement, and others would begin wondering and be more susceptible to future comments of this kind. The ROK government is most anxious to deter North Korea, and deterrence is based on the opponent's cost-benefit trade-offs. The ROK seldom imposes serious costs on the North Korean regime itself, but such an effort would impose costs and likely reinforce future deterrence.[41]

President Lee could have continued that the ROK therefore needed to prepare better for a collapse, so that it would be ready if and when such an event occurred. He could have ordered the ROK Marines to assume a major new assignment: Preparing to deliver humanitarian aid along the North Korean coastlines. As noted above, almost any collapse would lead to a severe food shortage as part of a humanitarian disaster; President Lee could have offered that the ROK needs to bear some responsibility for being ready to mitigate the resulting crisis. The role of ROK Marines would be critical because (1) about 9 million of the North Korean civilian population live in the coastal counties of North Korea; (2) the aid would need to be delivered across the beach (and not just in ports) in some areas; and (3) unless the ROK military delivered the aid, North Korean criminal organizations would likely take much of the food and other aid. ROK willingness to prepare for delivering such aid should clearly show that the ROK is not the enemy of the North Korean people, something President Lee should have specifically said.

President Lee could have then directed the ROK Marines to train for this kind of humanitarian mission by loading rice onto amphibious ships at Pusan or Pohang, moving a few miles up the ROK coastline, then unloading this food across the beach. The ROK government controls over a million tons of rice reserve and thus could afford thousands of tons for such exercises.[42] This training could have been filmed, including testimonials from young ROK Marine officers talking about how anxious they are to help their starving North Korean brethren.

---

[41] Making a strong political response against North Korea does carry the risk that North Korea could escalate. The ROK must also prepare to deter North Korean military attacks that the North could consider as part of an escalation. Few in the world would view a North Korean military escalation as warranted if the ROK limited its actions to political responses.

[42] "Rice Reserve Exceeds 1.5 million Tons," *Korea Times*, March 1, 2011.

President Lee could have threatened the North Korean regime that, if it committed another provocation, the films of this training would have been openly broadcast into North Korea. Then President Lee could have used a subsequent provocation as justification to begin these broadcasts, arguing that the North Korean regime had been warned; North Korean bad behavior had forced the ROK government to deliver on its warning to punish the North Korean regime (as opposed to North Korean soldiers) for its provocation and to strengthen deterrence of future provocations.

An even more severe political response would have been for President Lee to invite U.S. Marines to participate in the training with the ROK Marines. He could also have requested that a contingent of U.S. Marines be permanently stationed in the Pohang area to work on this mission with the ROK 1st Marine Division located there, with the U.S. Marine amphibious shipping based nearby. Assuming that the U.S. government accepted this request, President Lee could have then announced that the bad behavior (provocation) of the North Korean regime was responsible for U.S. Marines being based in the ROK. The North Korean military would be furious about such a development because of its strong dislike of U.S. Marines, a result of experiences during the Korean War.

Finally, President Lee could have, at some point, offered to have the ROK and U.S. Marines deliver aid to some North Korean coastal county particularly hard hit by North Korean famine, before a North Korean government collapse. If the North Korean regime had refused, many of the North Korean people would have still learned that the ROK and the United States tried but that the regime had prevented this assistance. If, instead, the regime had accepted the aid, the ROK and U.S. Marines would have begun to establish important relationships with the local North Korean leaders and demonstrated the ability to deliver help.

Deterring a North Korean Nuclear Weapon Test

Similarly, the ROK government needs to pose a meaningful deterrent against a future North Korean nuclear weapon test. The ROK president could tell the North Korean regime that, if it carried out a nuclear weapon test, South Korea would saturate Yongbyon and other North Korean nuclear facilities with leaflets that showed ROK university nuclear facilities and ROK nuclear power plants, offered jobs in these facilities to any North Korean nuclear scientists who defected, and offered to pay such scientists a reward of, say, 5 billion won for senior scientists or 2 billion won for midlevel scientists who defected to Seoul. The North Korean regime would, of course, shift security to prevent such defections, but the regime would still have to worry that it could fail and be shown ineffective before the North Korean military and other elites if even one scientist defected. Even if no scientists were able to defect, such messages would alert them to the value the ROK places on them and the fact that they would likely obtain employment postunification, which is exactly the kind of message this chapter seeks to deliver.

Do Not Go Too Far: North Korea Is Not Yet Ready for Open Rebellion
The ROK government needs to exercise care and discretion in preparing people on North Korea to support ROK-led unification. North Korea is not yet ripe for an "Arab Spring"–like set of developments, and may never be.[43] The North Korean government is still coherent, and the security services still impose serious penalties on those acting against the government. Thus, it is premature to send messages to North Korea encouraging the open rebellion of the North Korean people: Such messages will only get potential rebels killed or imprisoned. Moreover, as suggested above, many in the ROK would oppose sending such messages.

The Failures of the North Korean Government
It is difficult for the North Korean government to cover up all its failures or to blame the ROK and the United States for them all. Nevertheless, it tries to do so, and some significant percentage of the North Korean population apparently believes the North's deceptions that

---

[43] But even a peaceful unification would require some preparation of the North Koreans for a ROK-led economic environment given the dominance of ROK economics over those of the North.

alienate the North Korean people from the ROK. Therefore, the ROK at some point also needs to inform the North Korean people of the regime's failings. These would include such North Korean actions as the 2009 currency revaluation and the money spent on the North Korean ballistic missile program, as opposed to on food for the North Korean people. North Koreans should also be told about the regime's actions against merchants, actions that restrict the availability of goods to many in North Korea. The ROK could also argue that the North Korean government could feed everyone in North Korea very well on the perhaps $4 billion or so that the Kim family has apparently accumulated in private slush funds.[44]

Other Key Messages

ROK culture needs to be explained to North Koreans, especially the elites. Key issues would be the rule of law (as opposed to the growing culture of criminality with bribery and black market activity in the North), plans for providing humanitarian aid, and the nature of freedom associated with ROK society. The ROK also needs to demonstrate ROK and U.S. military superiority, showing, for example, how a sensor-fuzed weapon could simultaneously engage and destroy several tanks (the video image being key).

Meanwhile, to better understand the secretive North Korean society, the ROK and the United States should seek defectors from the core elite, including the military. The approach would be similar to that for the nuclear scientists described above. Again, even if these efforts fail to yield defectors, they will highlight the value that the ROK places on this portion of the North Korean elite.

Preventing North Korean Disaffection

Even if successful in gaining acceptance of ROK-led unification from many of the North Korean people, the ROK and the United States could lose that support early in an intervention, as suggested in Figure 4.2.

---

[44] "How N.Korea's Ruling Family Swells Its Private Coffers," *Chosun Ilbo*, April 28, 2010.

Key factors that could cause North Korean disaffection include a failure to deal promptly with the humanitarian disaster that would likely accompany North Korean government failure (including food shortages, disease, and the loss of other government services), security failures (associated with criminal activity, insurgency, or warfare), the lack of jobs and thus money to pay for necessities, Chinese intervention, the influx of individuals who will try to exploit the conditions in the North (carpetbaggers[45]), and property rights issues, as discussed earlier. After ROK and U.S. intervention, North Korean criminal groups and insurgents can be expected to maximize their attacks, in part seeking support from other North Koreans and seeking to convince some North Koreans to join their ranks.

The United States has had serious difficulty with its plan to demilitarize Taliban insurgents in Afghanistan. The lure of the program has been a commitment to amnesty, initial monthly stipends, jobs, and land in exchange for disarmament the departure from the insurgency.

Figure 4.2
Challenges in Sustaining North Korean Support

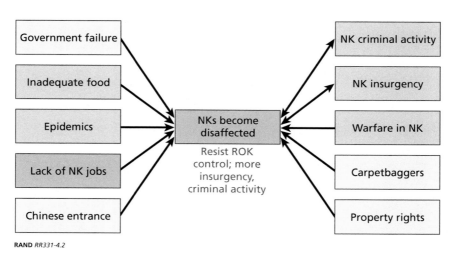

RAND RR331-4.2

---

[45] Carpetbaggers would include people and corporations trying to buy assets in North Korea cheaply, expecting to make big financial returns over time. But North Koreans will view these people or companies as exploitive, leading many to a negative reaction.

The problem has largely been that the village development plans that were intended to provide the jobs for the insurgents have not been started in many areas, leaving the insurgents generally without jobs. In addition, the insurgents who have been disarmed have been targeted by their former Taliban comrades, causing some losses to those no longer having weapons.[46] This illustrates that there is a security component required to sustain support.

There is no guarantee that disaffection can be prevented—unification will be a difficult task, with many potential circumstances that could alienate the North Koreans. The best prospects for avoid disaffection would be associated with (1) prompt ROK and U.S. intervention in the aftermath of a North Korean government collapse,[47] (2) preparation of the North Koreans to believe that unification can be good for them, and (3) ROK and U.S. preparation to rapidly address the challenges outlined in Figure 4.2. Subsequent chapters will have more to say about these preparations.

---

[46] This paragraph is based on Azam Ahmed, "Afghan Amnesty Program Falls Short, Leaving Ex-Insurgents Regretful and Angry," *New York Times*, January 9, 2013.

[47] The ROK in particular will probably want to wait to see how a North Korean government collapse develops. But waiting will likely allow the situation in the North to deteriorate, in part by giving time to the groups opposed to ROK-led unification to increase their strength.

CHAPTER FIVE

Challenges of and Responses to Humanitarian Disaster

This chapter characterizes the challenges that could lead to a humanitarian disaster and how to mitigate them. North Korea suffers from a humanitarian disaster even today: As discussed above, in many parts of the country it has insufficient food to feed its people, inadequate medicine, and unacceptable water. A collapse would only exacerbate these conditions, based on a series of challenges. While North Korea's inability to produce the food it needs would provide the basic challenge, a North Korean government collapse would terminate the existing food distribution system and lead many people holding food to hoard it, reducing the food supply well below subsistence levels. The food supply could be reduced further by criminals and other disruptions and by various problems in introducing international aid. These conditions will only worsen if there is a significant delay before the ROK decides to intervene and before it can bring food and other humanitarian supplies into most of North Korea.

Efforts to mitigate these challenges will need to flow a substantial amount of aid into North Korea and to distribute that aid to the vast majority of the population in their home locations. It would also need to provide support for the North Korean currency, overcome disruptions to aid distribution, and rebuild farm efficiency in the North.

Challenges That Would Contribute to a Humanitarian Disaster

Figure 5.1 illustrates the challenges that would contribute to the consequences of a humanitarian disaster and the subsequent consequences of massive North Korean refugee flows. The challenges that contribute to humanitarian disaster are associated with several overall problems:

- **Inadequate national supply.** North Korea has inadequate supplies of food, medicines, and other humanitarian needs in part because it is unable to produce enough of these items and in part

Figure 5.1
Humanitarian Challenges After a North Korean Collapse

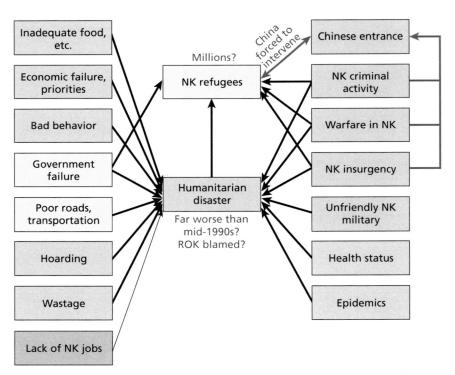

NOTE: Thick lines indicate a strong influence; thin line indicates a moderate influence.
RAND RR331-5.1

because its failing economy does not provide the resources to purchase adequate supplies from other countries. In part, the North Korean government has also given economic priority to its military, spending economic resources on the military rather than on feeding and caring for its people. Moreover, North Korean bad behavior (e.g., provocations, proliferation, and human rights violations) has made North Korea a pariah in the international community, making many potential donors unwilling to provide aid.

- **Inadequate local supplies.** The North Korean government has taken control of much of the food and other humanitarian supplies and distributes these supplies with preference to the elites and the military. A government failure would end government control of these confiscation activities, likely leaving many of the elites (especially mid- and lower-level personnel in Pyongyang) with little in the way of supplies and allowing the military to take what it wants (see supply disruptions, below). In addition, transportation within North Korea is limited. Since most production of food is south of Pyongyang but most of the population is north of Pyongyang, the result is regional disparities in access to humanitarian supplies. This was particularly true during the famine of the mid- to late-1990s, which affected people most in the northeast portion of North Korea. But a collapse may well stop much of the transportation system (such as the railroads) that the government, which would no longer exist, normally controls.

- **Lack of individual financial resources.** Even when food is available in an area, many North Koreans lack the financial resources needed to acquire food. As noted above, standard North Korean salaries are inadequate to feed a family. After a government collapse, many government employees and others likely will no longer have a job or will not be paid regularly, exasperating their efforts to obtain food.

- **Supply disruptions.** As argued in Chapter One, the hoarding of food and other goods seems likely in the aftermath of a government collapse. Thus, the already limited supply of food in North Korea will be further reduced. Moreover, hoarding and the many failures of distribution will likely increase food wastage, further reducing supply. The North Korean military will likely seize many available food supplies for its own use, unfettered by the elites who normally control military misbehavior. The North Korean military and criminal organizations (which will likely be affiliated with each other) will be particular deterrents to humanitarian assistance from international humanitarian organizations because these organizations will know that deliveries to the North will almost certainly not go to the population unless under military escort from ROK or other forces. Further, any warfare or insurgency in the North could divert food or prevent its distribution where it is most needed.

- **Complicating situations.** Food and medicine supplies in North Korea are already chronically inadequate, undermining the health of the population and making them more susceptible to illness or death. In addition, many basic diseases are well established in North Korea because of a lack of appropriate vaccines and other medicines. North Korean use of biological weapons (either purposefully or accidentally) could also lead to a public health disaster in North Korea, where the poor health of most people makes them vulnerable to disease and where there would be inadequate medicine to treat any significant number of people exposed to disease. Thus, the health chaos in the aftermath of a government collapse could well lead to epidemics in the North.

Massive refugee flows are a natural result of a humanitarian disaster. But they usually occur in combination with either a relaxing of internal security that allows people to move or a serious degradation in internal security that forces people to move, fearing for their safety and even their lives. Humanitarian disaster challenges are thus also challenges for refugee flow, but refugee flow is more likely when accompanied by warfare, insurgency, or criminal activity and related abusive behavior. As noted earlier, recent estimates suggest that 3 million or more North Korean refugees could flow just to the ROK after a North

Korean government collapse.[1] Similar or perhaps even larger numbers of people would likely flee toward China, which wants no refugees from North Korea to cross its border. Such a refugee flow would be a major inducement for a Chinese intervention in North Korea. Russia could also face some refugees across its small border with North Korea, and some North Koreans could attempt to reach the ROK, China, Russia, or even Japan by boat.

The hoarding of food and other humanitarian supplies could become one of the greatest challenges. Figure 5.2 compares the hoarding and its affects after the December 2009 currency revaluation to what could happen after a government collapse. In 2009, the North Korean won had depreciated to the point that it needed a 100:1 revaluation (trading 100 old won for 1 new won). But to wipe out much of the financial capital stock merchants and traders possessed, the exchange was initially limited to roughly $100 worth of won at the black market exchange rate. Moreover, the use or even holding of foreign currency

Figure 5.2
Challenges That Could Lead to Humanitarian Disaster

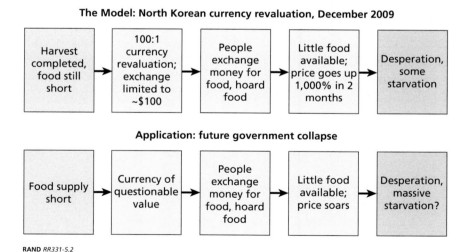

RAND RR331-5.2

---

[1]   "Sudden Unification . . . ," 2012; Na Jeong-ju, 2007.

was banned, preventing foreign currency from being an alternative means of holding capital and wealth. Therefore, at least some North Koreans exchanged money for food, planning to hoard that food and use it to hold wealth. Apparently, this hoarding dramatically reduced the food supply; the normal laws of supply and demand caused the price of food to increase 1,000 percent in two months.[2] The result was that many people could not afford food, making them desperate and causing some starvation.

The bottom of Figure 5.2 provides a comparison to the aftermath of a North Korean collapse. Depending on the time of year, the food supply could be much lower than it was in early December 2009 (especially from March to May or so). Moreover, after a government collapse, the North Korean currency will be of questionable value, to say the least, leaving many people without a currency with which to buy food and other goods. North Koreans would thus be likely to exchange North Korean won for both foreign currency and for such goods as food, which they would hoard because the goods would be one way of their holding wealth. In addition, many North Koreans in possession of food will likely be reluctant to sell it, hedging against the uncertainties of the future supply for their own consumption and anticipating that the price of food will go up significantly based on historical precedent for periods of low supply. The result would likely be very little supply and a lot of demand, causing inflation and leaving many people without food, and leading to potentially more deaths and suffering than previous famines. Moreover, the ROK government could be blamed (within the ROK, within North Korea, and internationally) for the severity of the disaster if the ROK is slow to intervene (as might be expected) or is unprepared to provide the needed aid promptly.

---

[2]   In fairness, the currency revaluation also distributed a small amount of money to each North Korean, many of whom chose to use that money to buy food. Thus, the supply went down and the demand went up, causing serious inflation.

Mitigating the Humanitarian Disaster Challenges

This subsection addresses actions that the ROK government could take to mitigate North Korean humanitarian disasters and subsequent refugee flows following a North Korean government collapse. It begins by discussing some of the policies required to deal with the challenges that contribute to these consequences. It then describes some strategies that could be used in pursuit of these polices. Finally, it discusses the other preparations that would be required to deal with these humanitarian disasters and refugee flows.

Policies for Mitigating Humanitarian Disaster

In the aftermath of a North Korean government collapse, the humanitarian disaster in North Korea would almost certainly involve both inadequate supplies (including food) and threats to individual security. The ROK would want to mitigate both aspects of the humanitarian disaster. If it does not, unification could well fail, the result of both a lack of security and disastrous conditions in the North that could lead to an overwhelming refugee flow and many of the other disastrous consequences described in Chapter Three for both the ROK and China. The ROK will simultaneously strive to overcome the causes of the humanitarian disaster so that the ROK does not have to provide substantial humanitarian aid to North Korea for a matter of decades.[3]

In the short term, the ROK needs to seek the welfare of the North Korean people through humanitarian aid. The ROK should be prepared to provide a substantial percentage of food and other needs across all of North Korea in an effort to prevent starvation, disease, and other serious difficulties there. By delivering most of the basic humanitarian needs in the short term, the ROK should also be able to break the pattern of hoarding these items and should be able to lower the prices of these supplies to make them relatively affordable. It must simultaneously seek to rebuild government functions in North Korea,

---

[3] The ROK does not want to transform the North into a welfare state in which the population expects major ROK subsidies in perpetuity. Not only would such an approach be bad policy, but it would also likely be financially infeasible and would be an unfair burden on the ROK population.

create economic stability in the North by providing jobs for the North Korean people, repair their infrastructure (including transportation and power, as described in Chapter Six), and make their farming and other efforts more productive. These activities will seek the medium- to long-term welfare of the North Korean people through jobs and increased self-reliance.

To establish security and stability in North Korea, the ROK will need to insert military forces in the North. These ROK forces will seek to neutralize the North Korean military and security force threats outlined in Chapters Six and Seven, while providing security for the distribution of humanitarian aid—making sure the aid actually gets to civilians. While some would likely prefer not to involve the ROK and allied military forces, instead employing international humanitarian organizations to deliver the aid, the humanitarian organizations alone would likely only be able to perform limited parts of the humanitarian effort for several reasons:

1. In the immediate aftermath of a North Korean government collapse, international humanitarian organizations would likely have neither the quantity of aid needed nor the means available to distribute aid to most of the North Korean people.[4] Especially in areas away from major ports and airfields, many North Koreans could be put in jeopardy of starvation or at least would displace from their homes seeking food without the resources of the ROK and other governments and their military delivery means.

2. This would be particularly true in the short term, when international humanitarian organizations would be unlikely to have the food and transportation means in place in the ROK or China to support delivery to North Korean families.

3. After a North Korean government collapse, the jeopardy to personal security in North Korea (to both North Korean civilians

---

[4] With some preparation time, they could get ready, but a lot of food is perishable over time. It is thus difficult to be fully prepared for a North Korean collapse and sustain that preparation over possibly many years.

and humanitarian organization personnel) is likely to be significant. Without ROK and allied military intervention, most aid delivered to North Korea by international humanitarian organizations would likely be commandeered by the North Korean military and security services, seeking to provide for their own sustenance and also to make up for salary payments that may not occur after collapse. While one might hope that the North Korean military would then pass the aid on to civilians, it is more likely that the North Korean military would operate as a black market, seeking payment for whatever aid they did pass on. This approach would not solve the humanitarian disaster in the North.

One could argue that the international organizations should at least be allowed to try to deliver aid and see how well they can do before involving ROK-allied military force. But, in practice, if the ROK waits many weeks or several months before intervening with military forces, the humanitarian disaster could get out of control, both from a stabilization perspective and in terms of starvation, refugee flows, and other concerns. Prompt military intervention is required for the ROK to avoid losing the initiative.[5]

Note, however, that the objection here is to a purely civilian effort to provide humanitarian aid. International humanitarian organizations should be encouraged to work with the military and provide as much aid as they can while receiving ROK and allied military security. The ROK and allied militaries should then focus their aid in areas that the international humanitarian organizations cannot reach.

Strategies for Providing for North Korean Welfare Through Humanitarian Aid

In providing humanitarian aid, a ROK and U.S. intervention should strive to keep people in their homes, jobs, and normal day-to-day envi-

---

[5] The use of military force to perform humanitarian operations has a mixed history. Such an effort would require considerable preparation and very specific planning, a part of which already appears to be going on in the ROK Ministry of Unification.

ronment. Once people leave their homes and jobs, their humanitarian needs grow significantly (for shelter, clothing, cooking implements, water, etc.), and their ability to become self-sufficient over time is greatly impeded. Moreover, if many North Koreans become refugees, entering the ROK or China to obtain food and good jobs, they could overwhelm the ability of both countries to absorb immigrants, flood their job markets with vast numbers of low-skilled laborers, raise opposition in China and the ROK against these immigrants who would be perceived as "stealing" jobs and other resources from the local population, and politically destabilize at least the border areas. Indeed, because China does not want any of these refugees crossing into China, China may be forced to intervene deeply into North Korea (at least 100 km or so to create refugee camps and barriers to stem the flow of refugees). The ROK and the United States will want to strive to avoid the development of situations that would press China into such an intervention or to minimize the Chinese perception of the need to hold substantial parts of the North Korean territory if it does decide to intervene.

Figure 5.3 provides a frame of reference for doing so. This figure shows aggregated locations for the civilian population based on the 2008 North Korean census. Some 3.3 million North Koreans live in the coastal counties of the northeast, while 6 million live in the interior counties north of Pyongyang.[6] Considering the territory slices moving north from the DMZ, relatively few North Korean civilians live south of Pyongyang (not quite 4 million: 1.1 plus 2.3 plus 0.5 million), a good number live in the Pyongyang slice (about 8 million: 1.4 plus 5.8 plus 0.7 million), and nearly half of the population lives in the slice north of Pyongyang (about 11 million: 1.8 plus 6.0 plus 3.3 million). The last group would likely be most affected by a famine because the most productive farming area of North Korea is south of Pyongyang. Alternatively, about 4.3 million North Koreans live in the coastal counties

---

[6]   Comparing the 2008 census to the 1993 North Korean census (the only other one available) suggests that there is considerable falsification in the 2008 census—the civilian population numbers are too high (for example, the North Korean authorities apparently wanted the 2008 census to suggest that few North Koreans had died during the famine in the mid-1990s, which was certainly not the case). Still, the overall magnitude of falsification is probably not much greater than 15 percent.

Figure 5.3
Providing Humanitarian Aid: Geographic Requirements

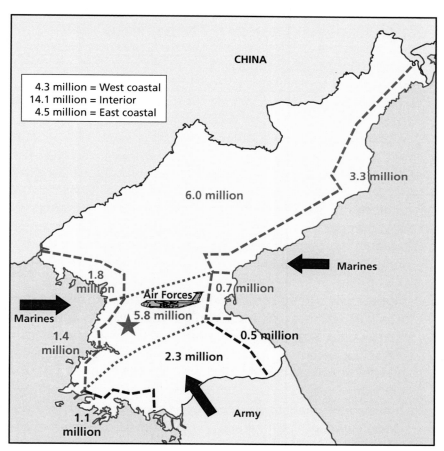

CHINA

4.3 million = West coastal
14.1 million = Interior
4.5 million = East coastal

3.3 million

6.0 million

1.8 million

Marines

Air Forces   0.7 million

Marines

5.8 million

1.4 million

0.5 million

2.3 million

1.1 million

Army

RAND RR331-5.3

on the west coast, and about 4.5 million live in the coastal counties on the east coast, or almost 9 million civilians in the coastal counties.

To keep North Koreans at home, the ROK and the United States should therefore seek to deliver humanitarian aid to their home areas throughout North Korea—effectively using aid as the leading element of any ROK and U.S. intervention. Key principles of a strategy for taking humanitarian aid into North Korea are:

- Until the North Korean military is demobilized and North Korean criminal organizations are largely neutralized, humanitarian aid going into North Korea will require a ROK and U.S. military escort to prevent its loss or diversion. Still, some of the aid will need to be given to North Korean military forces to secure their cooperation; this subject is discussed under demobilization of the North Korean military in Chapter Six.
- The North Korean road network is extremely limited, and most of it is unpaved.[7] Neither the roads themselves nor the bridges supporting the roads are likely to sustain major vehicle traffic without significant construction efforts that will reduce the flow for some time (and this assumes no adversary attempts to damage the bridges or tunnels or even the roads). This flow limitation is especially true across the DMZ. ROK aid escorted across the DMZ by the ROK Army could thus be marginal in meeting the needs of the 2.3 million civilians in the interior counties south of Pyongyang and would certainly be challenged to also cover the 1.6 million civilians in coastal areas south of Pyongyang.
- Figure 5.3 thus proposes that much of the humanitarian aid would be delivered to North Korea through ports along the North Korean coast and, where the ports are too far away or inadequate, across the beach (especially on the west coast). This aid would potentially need to cover the 7.2 million civilians in coastal counties from Pyongyang and further north, although aid delivered from the sea might also need to cover the coastal areas south of Pyongyang, raising the total requirement to 8.8 million civilians. ROK and U.S. Marines could provide a significant part of the military escort, with some ROK and U.S. Army assistance. But the combined military force, military logistics, and humanitarian aid traffic may exceed the capacity of the transportation assets (e.g., trucks) available to the assigned military forces and the capacity of the road network out of the ports and off the beach-

---

[7] North Korea has some 26,000 km of roads, but only 724 km (3 percent) are paved. In contrast, South Korea has four times as much total roads (103,000 km), 80 percent of which are paved. See CIA, 2012.

es.[8] This traffic would also be vulnerable to interdiction by rogue military forces and by criminal organizations.

- While the population of the interior of North Korea could simply be induced to displace to the coastlines to receive humanitarian aid, any displacement of people increases the burden required to meet civilian needs, as discussed above. It would therefore be better to deliver humanitarian aid to the interior locations where North Koreans live. While roads could be opened and improved to do so, such efforts will take more time than is likely available before many civilians would displace from their homes. Thus, in the interior, from Pyongyang and further north, humanitarian aid would likely need to be delivered by cargo aircraft. But there are inadequate airfields for delivering and distributing the aid, and some of the aid will thus need to be delivered via airdrops.

- When airdrops are used, the aid needs to be packaged in small packages (e.g., 0.5-kg packages) rather than on pallets that can hurt people when dropped to the ground and can be easily taken by criminal groups. Small packages pulled from a transport aircraft by a drag chute would be distributed over a wide area, making it more likely that civilians in need receive much of the shipment. Of course, Chinese concerns would also apply to airdrops of food; China may insist on ROK and U.S. aircraft not approaching closer than 50 or 100 km from its territory or its forces.

- Before aircraft can deliver such aid, the North Korean air defense system needs to be blunted in each area. Since the ROK military will not want to attack the air defenses and thereby appear to have made North Koreans its enemy, the ROK military will need to

---

[8] Because of the limited transportation assets, the United States should consider transferring many of the mine-resistant, ambush-protected trucks it extracts from Iraq and Afghanistan to South Korea so that they would be available to deliver aid, thereby reducing the number of trucks taken away from the ROK economy. Most military planning focuses on the logistical requirements of U.S. and/or ROK military forces; in this situation, many more trucks would be needed to carry humanitarian aid. Mine-resistant, ambush-protected trucks are not primarily for hauling but could deliver some of the needed cargo. They would also be relatively secure against improvised explosive devices and other threats North Korean military, insurgent, or criminal forces might pose.

carry out an aggressive information campaign that offers a cease-fire with food delivery in areas where air defenses are not fired at ROK and U.S. aircraft. The ROK and the United States would need to send negotiating teams to the commanders of these North Korean military forces to convince them not to attack ROK and U.S. forces (see the discussion of stopping conflict in Chapter Six). North Korean air defenses that violate such a cease-fire (e.g., any radars that are turned on) would then be subject to suppression.

A major challenge with this aid will be with how far north China will allow it to be delivered. China has always been sensitive about ROK and U.S. naval operations, especially in the West/Yellow Sea. For China, the advantage of allowing humanitarian aid delivery by air is that it would prevent many North Koreans from displacing toward China. And aid delivered along North Korea's coastlines would attract displaced North Koreans to the coastlines, rather than giving them little choice but to move to the Chinese border in search of food. China would certainly prefer to have the ROK and the United States meet the humanitarian needs of these North Koreans but will be suspicious of U.S. and ROK security intentions. More will be said about this in Chapter Nine, on Chinese intervention.

Average food consumption across North Korea is about 15,000 tons per day (almost 5.5 million tons per year). Depending on the food available in the North and how it is hoarded, the ROK and the United States may initially need to deliver close to this much each day—let us assume 80 percent, or 12,000 tons per day—to break the hoarding of food. Based on the population locations, the ROK Army forces would need to deliver about 1,200 tons per day across the DMZ; the marine and navy forces (with any army forces that would be assisting them) would need to deliver and distribute up to 4,800 tons per day along the coasts; and airlift would need to deliver 6,000 tons per day to the interior. In terms of airlift, this would require about 108 C-17 sorties per day, or some 400 C-130 sorties per day, a daunting requirement. As noted earlier, airlift would not even be possible until the North Korean air defenses could be blunted. But it would be a mistake to fail to deliver humanitarian aid to the interior of North Korea for a period of months: Much of the population could decide to displace before aid arrives. Thus, the air defense situation must be managed within weeks.

Prompt delivery of adequate humanitarian aid throughout North Korea should greatly reduce the refugee flow to China and the ROK. Efforts to provide jobs in North Korea and to stabilize the security situation (the latter discussed in Chapter Six) could further reduce the flow. In addition, ROK efforts to guarantee North Koreans a good quality of life will also be helpful because those who expect criminal prosecution, poor jobs, or stigmatization may well seek to escape to China, hoping to have a better life there. A North Korean government collapse will certainly cause some North Koreans to become refugees regardless of the best efforts of the ROK government, but the various actions described in Chapter Four and in this chapter should significantly help reduce refugees.

Finally, the ROK needs to begin delivery of humanitarian aid to the North promptly after a North Korean collapse. But for many reasons, the ROK may be reluctant to intervene promptly. Indeed, whether a collapse has actually occurred may not be clear for some time, especially given the North Korean propensity to deny information on the North. For some time, one or more factions may also claim to be the legitimate government of North Korea, with some uncertainty about whether or not they really are. Also, ROK perceptions of the cost of intervening in the North would be so high that there would be a tendency to "wait and watch." Nevertheless, the condition of North Korea is likely to deteriorate seriously over time after a government collapse, whether or not that deterioration is observed. The longer it takes the ROK to intervene, the more serious conditions could become in the North, and the North Korean population will likely blame the ROK for those conditions, risking North Korean disaffection with unification. The ROK may therefore want to consider providing humanitarian aid in coastal areas and along the DMZ soon after the appearance of any major disruption of the North Korean government and then subsequently decide on a full intervention focused on unification.

Strategies for Providing for North Korean Welfare Through Economic Stability

While providing humanitarian aid, the ROK also needs to work on bringing economic stability to the North to resolve mid- to long-term humanitarian issues. The ROK would need to rebuild government functions in North Korea, improve North Korean infrastructure (using the former North Korean military units, as described in Chapter Six), while creating a more secure environment. The ROK would also need to develop jobs so that the economy can begin carrying more of the economic load, shifting away from a focus on aid.

A key issue noted previously is the status of North Korean currency. The ROK government should decide on an exchange rate from the North Korean won to the South Korean won and should support that rate to stabilize the North Korean won and limit the perceived need in North Korea to use food and other goods as an alternative for holding wealth. A prompt transition to the use of the South Korean won, at the set exchange rate, would also combat inflation in North Korea and help secure the wealth of North Koreans (as discussed in Chapter Four).

The ROK already has plans for rebuilding government functions in North Korea. The ROK has selected individuals to become the governors and other officials in North Korea, and has tasked these people to prepare plans well in advance of unification.[9] Once the ROK begins its intervention in North Korea, it should work as much as possible with existing North Korean officials to keep them employed, although monitoring for any misbehavior or sabotage. Because North Korea has had a state-directed economy, governmental organizations will be needed at first to coordinate and sustain economic activity until ownership of North Korean economic enterprises can be established to allow private-sector operations. In addition, the governmental organizations in the North will need to provide priorities for infrastructure repair and rebuilding, especially as part of the public-service activities described in Chapter Six, to develop jobs for the population, to oversee

---

[9]   Interview with the Chairman of the Korean Ministry of Unification's Commission of the Five Provinces (of North Korea), July 2010.

improvements in agricultural production, to supervise the distribution of humanitarian aid, to rebuild the police and other forces that may be corrupted, and to deal with criminal and even insurgent activities.

The formation of jobs is particularly critical. Even if most North Koreans stay at home and retain existing jobs, several groups will need new jobs, including many in the North Korean military, North Korean political prisoners, and North Korean government employees who are no longer needed for various reasons. The ROK will need plans for developing industry and other economic activities in North Korea within the bounds of property ownership, as discussed in Chapter Eight.

Other Preparations Required

To fulfill the strategies described above, the ROK government will need to make a number of preparations.

Setting North Korean Beliefs and Expectations

A part of the reason for pursuing humanitarian assistance to the North is to provide the North Korean people hope that unification will give them a better life and, by so doing, secure the cooperation of many North Koreans in unification. But to be effective, the ROK must let the North Koreans know about its plans for humanitarian assistance long before the North Korean government collapses and convince them that these plans are real and resourced. Strategic communications about ROK humanitarian assistance plans must thus be made regularly and for some time. The ROK would strengthen its credibility by training ROK Marines and others in the delivery of humanitarian aid, filming the training, then broadcasting these films into North Korea. It would also help to announce the quantity of supplies being prepared, the likely locations where deliveries would begin, and how deliveries would be performed (including military escort for security purposes).[10]

Once a North Korean government collapse happens, the ROK needs to be truly prepared for humanitarian assistance and to execute

---

[10] Many North Koreans are aware that aid that reaches North Korea is often commandeered by the military or the black market, so the plans for securing aid delivery will be important in convincing the North Koreans to take these plans seriously.

this effort effectively. ROK credibility among North Koreans will hinge on the initial operations of the humanitarian assistance effort. A ROK failure in any geographic area will convince many North Koreans (especially those who have been told they will receive aid in the second or third phase of aid efforts) that they cannot trust ROK commitments, causing the North Koreans not to support unification.

The ROK could be more effective in its strategic communications on humanitarian assistance if it could arrange to deliver some humanitarian aid well before a North Korean government collapse. The ROK might select one or two coastal counties in North Korea that are being particularly hard hit by famine and offer to the North Korean government to have ROK Marines deliver humanitarian assistance to people in these counties. If the North Korean government refuses to accept the assistance, the ROK government could then blame the North Korean government for the loss of this humanitarian aid. If the North Korean government accepts the assistance, the ROK can begin building some expertise in actual aid delivery and, in the process, establish contacts with some key North Koreans. Either outcome would be a partial win and thus worth the effort.

International Coordination

Well before a North Korean government collapse, the ROK must coordinate its plans for humanitarian assistance with at least the United States and China and with international humanitarian organizations. The ROK will need U.S. and other help in delivering humanitarian assistance, especially over the longer term. The United States could offer U.S. Marines and their amphibious ships for the aid delivery, bringing more capacity for aid delivery by amphibious ships than the ROK itself has, and likely offering some humanitarian aid of its own. The ROK should share with the United States its own studies of requirements for unification and seek U.S. assistance, especially in areas the ROK cannot adequately handle itself.

China has traditionally objected to U.S. or ROK naval ship operations in the Yellow/West Sea, especially north of the ROK coastal islands. China might be even more concerned about U.S. or ROK naval ships going into such areas after a North Korean government collapse.

Therefore, the ROK needs to coordinate this issue with China. Because China normally refuses to talk about North Korean collapse, fearing to alienate the North, the ROK may need to pursue several kinds of interactions with the Chinese on this subject—more likely with academics than with government people, at least as a start. For example,

- ROK academics should be commissioned to write papers on options for ROK responses to natural disasters in North Korea. These papers might consider a massive earthquake, as happened in China in 2008, or a famine caused by unfavorable weather conditions (either a lack of water or flooding). These papers should be published in academic journals, including journals of international standing. Many in China and likely even some in North Korea would eventually read these articles and probably spread the concepts to their peers and to government.
- The ROK should offer to discuss with North Korea how the ROK could organize disaster relief for North Korea if a severe famine of some kind were to affect the North (using a Track 2 kind of discussion). Such discussions would necessarily have to address access to coastal areas along both the west and east coasts, where China might be sensitive. North Korea might reject holding such discussions, at which point the ROK participants could explain the situation to potential Chinese participants and encourage their participation. The best outcome would be if the Chinese were willing to participate, but even if they are not, the ROK participants could proceed and then publish the results of their work in academic journals accessible to both North Korea and China, perhaps as follow-ons to the papers mentioned immediately above. Having been notified of the effort, at least some of the Chinese would read the articles and pass along the concepts.
- The ROK could hold some nongovernmental tabletop exercises that explicitly examined collapse, seeking to explore key policies and operations. Chinese observers could be invited to these exercises, not to probe them for information but to allow them to witness the challenges presented. Afterward, they would hopefully carry the lessons learned back to various Chinese audiences.

- ROK academics and perhaps some government personnel who specialize in collapse and unification could regularly write articles in the ROK media (and especially op-eds) that explain ROK thinking about dealing with a North Korean collapse. These articles would convey to China ROK expectations for how to handle a collapse situation that leads to unification. Chinese experts in this area can be expected to eventually write their own articles to support or contradict ROK concepts, beginning an informal international dialogue on how to deal with these issues.
- Eventually, official government (Track 1) exchanges on these subjects should become possible between the ROK and China, perhaps involving other regional players, such as the United States, Japan, and Russia. These should be pursued initially to outline alternative strategies for unification but should eventually seek to build consensus on appropriate policies and strategies.

Supply, Equipment, and Financial Preparation

The humanitarian aid required in North Korea will include food, medical assistance, sanitation, and purification of water sources. Total North Korean food requirements are estimated as just over 5 million tons of cereals per year. The ROK might need to provide 80 percent as much (4 million tons[11]) the first year to overcome hoarding and hopefully less in subsequent years as hoarding eases and self-sufficiency increases. While much of this can probably be provided from other countries over time, perhaps three to four months of supplies need to be held in the ROK for immediate delivery, or 1 million or so tons of cereals. In recent years, that quantity of rice, alone, has been available in the ROK.[12] Other supplies, for example, for medical assistance, are likely not available in the ROK in such large quantities, and the medical professionals required to use these supplies would almost certainly

---

[11] This assumes that China does not intervene. If China intervenes, as discussed later, the aid the ROK provides could be proportionately less, depending on how much of North Korea China decides to occupy.

[12] It has been noted that "Korea's rice reserve exceeded 1.5 million tons in the 2010 food grain year, the highest reached since 1994, the government said Tuesday." "Rice Reserve Exceeds . . . ," 2011.

not be available in sufficient numbers from the ROK alone. The ROK therefore needs to outline the total humanitarian supplies it believes it would need in the short term in North Korea after a government collapse and should arrange with allies and other partners to provide parts of such aid in a time-critical manner. The ROK will also need to arrange for all kinds of aid to be provided in the subsequent period, to be delivered to North Korea starting at about three to four months. In part, it can purchase this aid, but it will also require donations from allies and friends.

Providing humanitarian aid in the required quantities will not be cheap, but neither will it be overwhelmingly expensive. The ROK needs to pursue more rigorous examination of the various costs and to identify alternative assumptions associated with the costs. The ROK then needs to prepare at least a voluntary contribution fund, as ROK Unification Minister Yu Woo-Ik has recommended,[13] or a unification tax, as ROK President Lee Myung-bak earlier suggested,[14] to provide the funding for humanitarian assistance and other aspects of unification. For just the food, the price of rice allows us to approximate the funds needed. If the ROK would need to provide 4 million tons of food aid per year and if this were primarily rice (which is available at roughly $600 per ton[15]), the total cost would be about $2.4 billion for food aid in the first year and hopefully less in subsequent years. Some amount would also be required for medical assistance, for sanitation, for purifying water sources, and for delivering supplies. The total might amount to $10 billion to $20 billion per year.

Building ROK Political Consensus

There is no consensus in the ROK about how the humanitarian challenges in the North should be handled after a North Korean government collapse or even whether the ROK should play a major role in

---

[13] See, for example, Ertel, 2012.

[14] See, for example, "No 'Unification Tax' Right Now, Lee Promises," *Chosun Ilbo*, August 18, 2010.

[15] See "Rice Monthly Price—US Dollars per Metric Ton," Index Mundi website, August 9, 2012.

providing such aid. The ROK government needs to build such a consensus over time. During the administration of President Lee Myung-Bak, the ROK conditioned any substantial renewal of aid to North Korea on improved North Korean behavior, which conditions have not been met, given North Korean provocations in recent years and its unwillingness to negotiate denuclearization. But if the ROK government wants to prepare for unification, it needs to take a more positive role in justifying humanitarian aid to North Korea and providing more of that aid in the short term, much as President Park Geun-Hye has proposed. This is not to say that the North Korean government deserves ROK assistance but rather that building a consensus in support of unification will depend on establishing behaviors now that help meet the humanitarian needs in North Korea.

The role of humanitarian organizations will depend on the specifics of North Korean collapse, but such groups, regional and international, may be able to play important roles and help increase capacity. The ROK should consider how these organizations might be able to participate and engage them in advance planning to the extent feasible.

CHAPTER SIX

Challenges of and Responses to Conflict and Military Forces in North Korea

This chapter addresses conflict that could be associated with the collapse of the North Korean government and the means for dealing with North Korean military forces. One conflict possibility would involve the North Korean government ordering a diversionary invasion of the ROK, trying to avoid a collapse, but that invasion would likely fail and cause a collapse. In another, North Korean provocations could lead to an escalatory spiral that does considerable damage in both North and South Korea before the North Korean government fails. Alternatively, a civil war could break out between the factions in the North, each trying to seize the resources of others because no faction would have adequate food and other resources. Eventually, as the ROK and U.S. intervene, the North Korean military could oppose the intervention, much as it would oppose a counteroffensive into the North after a North Korean invasion of the ROK. Finally, a North Korean insurgency could develop in the aftermath of ROK and U.S. intervention in the North. The large North Korean military and its heavy indoctrination would be major challenges across these kinds of conflict.

Mitigating conflict and its related challenges will require serious short-term efforts to stop the conflict plus medium-term efforts to remove the military threats in North Korea and adjust the attitudes of the former military personnel. This chapter examines challenges for each of these areas. It examines efforts to reach out to the senior North Korean military leaders to convince them to terminate their attacks and to accept cease-fires. Modifying their allegiance from the

North Korean regime to the unified Korean government would facilitate these efforts. As promptly as possible, the ROK government would also need to begin demobilizing and demilitarizing the North Korean military forces and eliminating North Korean WMD, especially given the potential of WMD to escalate any conflict.

The Challenges from Conflict in North Korea

As described in Chapter Three, conflicts of various kinds resulting from a North Korean government collapse could cause damage, especially in North Korea, that would resemble the damage done in classical assessments of an invasion of the ROK. This damage could include casualties, infrastructure damage, and WMD contamination. Conflict could also cause damage in the ROK, including perhaps tens of thousands of military casualties; the damage could be sufficient to undermine the ROK's military and financial ability to achieve unification. This would be particularly true if worldwide markets fear the WMD contamination of Korean goods and Korean personnel who perform services.

Figure 6.1 identifies some of the challenges that could complicate these consequences. First and foremost, North Korea has a very large active duty military (perhaps as many as 1.2 million men[1]) and a very large number of weapons. It is a military that is poised for mobilization as soon as a major crisis develops (with reportedly 7.7 million reserve personnel[2]). A government collapse would lead to at least some mobilization, yielding perhaps several million North Korean personnel in arms. The North Korean military also possesses WMD, which could give it the ability to damage its opponents substantially. Today, many in the North Korean military—perhaps most—would be unfriendly toward unification, fearing ROK and U.S. control of North Korea, in large part as the result of North Korean indoctrination. The regime has used this indoctrination to influence both North Korean career military personnel and conscripts to have significant loyalty toward

---

[1]   ROK MND, Defense White Paper, 2010, p. 340.

[2]   ROK MND, 2010, p. 340.

Figure 6.1
The Challenges from Conflict in North Korea

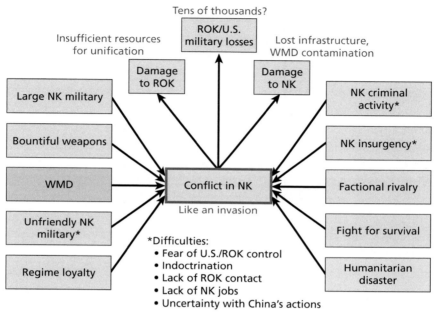

the North Korean regime and to fear a serious decline in their quality of life in a ROK-led unification. As a result, after a collapse and subsequent unification, many North Korean military personnel could be led into criminal activity and/or insurgency against the unified Korean government. In addition, the North Korean military could become involved in civil war because of factional rivalry. If it does, such contests would be a fight for survival that would compel the factions to very escalatory action if they feared they might lose. All this would be fueled by the humanitarian disaster that would accompany a North Korean government collapse.

After a North Korean government collapse, the North Korean military would almost certainly break into factions focused on regaining control of North Korea and their own survival. Some soldiers (perhaps many) would desert to escape military life and return to their families. Over time, a civil war or regular opposition to intervening

ROK and U.S. (and Chinese) forces could give way to insurgency and criminal behavior, as suggested in Figure 6.2. The large size of the North Korean military and the vast stocks of weapons would allow at least some people and weapons to be turned to these purposes. Should hunger and instability grow, many of the military, and especially the special forces, would be likely to join criminal groups. The failure of North Korean control mechanisms, including the security services, would contribute to this migration.

Instability in North Korea would grow as insurgency and criminal activity grow. And in turn, insurgency and criminal activity would grow as instability grew. In the end, stability in the former North Korea is critical to a successful unification; thus, the ROK would need to deal with these threats and suppress them as best possible.

Finally, weapons will also be a complication after a North Korean government failure, especially WMD. Figure 6.3 shows some of the challenges of trying to achieve ROK and U.S. control of these weapons. North Korea has a bountiful supply of weapons of many types, including potentially enough weapons to arm a significant fraction of its active duty and reserve forces. As noted in Chapter One, it also appears

Figure 6.2
The Challenges of North Korean Instability

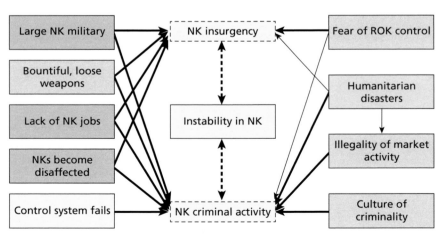

NOTE: Thick lines indicate a strong influence; thin lines indicate a moderate influence.
RAND RR331-6.2

Figure 6.3
The Challenges from Uncontrolled WMD and Other Weapons

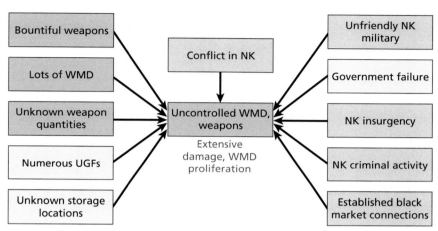

RAND *RR331-6.3*

to have a significant quantity of WMD, amounting to perhaps 2,500 to 5,000 tons of chemical weapons,[3] and the nuclear materials for at least five to ten nuclear weapons, although some evidence suggests that imports and uranium enrichment could make the numbers as high as 20 or so.[4] The ROK MND has stated that the "North is also suspected of being able to independently cultivate and produce such biological weapons as anthrax, smallpox, and cholera."[5] But the exact quantities of any of the North Korean weapons are unknown, which would complicate any effort to collect and eliminate them. North Korea also has a large number of underground facilities (UGFs), reportedly more than 10,000,[6] in which many of these weapons are stored. Among these

---

[3]   ROK MND, 2010, p. 35.

[4]   Bennett, 2009.

[5]   ROK MND, 2010.

[6]   The *Boston Globe* has reported that "[a] South Korean intelligence source estimates that there are several hundred large underground factories in North Korea and more than 10,000 smaller facilities. Joseph Bermudez, the author of three books on the North Korean military, puts the total number between 11,000 to 14,000" (Barbara Demick, "Vision on Tunnels Drives N. Korean Defense," *Boston Globe*, November 28, 2003).

UGFs and other potential storage locations, it appears that the ROK and United States do not know where many of the weapons are stored, making it difficult to prioritize sites to be visited for weapon collection and elimination or even to know where to check for weapons. ROK and U.S. forces are likely insufficient to guard the large number of weapon storage and related facilities simultaneously, so a consolidation effort would be required.

Other challenges are associated with who controls the weapons, especially the WMD. After a North Korean government collapse, the military or other elites that control weapons will likely try to disperse many weapons and related production capabilities to retain control of them and to reduce the chances of the weapons being destroyed by ROK and U.S. attack.[7] Thus, even if the ROK and the United States thought they knew where the WMD was located before the North Korean government collapses, they may still need to search most UGFs and pursue WMD in other locations after the collapse. The North Korean military would use its various weapons, likely including WMD, if it were ordered to invade the ROK (especially if the regime is trying to prevent a collapse via a diversionary war). Alternatively, after a collapse, these weapons could well be used in a North Korean civil war or in support of an insurgency or criminal activity. Any groups gaining control of these weapons might well sell them to third parties to gain cash for food and survival. If WMD is sold, there is a serious potential that it will eventually make its way to rogue states or terrorist groups through established international black market connections. Terrorist groups would have strong interest in using WMD against the United States, and deterring them from doing so would be very difficult.

---

[7] The production capabilities would include the scientists, engineers, and technicians who know how to produce WMD; the raw materials used in production; and the equipment used in production.

The ROK Demographic Challenge

In dealing with North Korean conflict and other North Korean military threats after a collapse, the ROK will depend heavily on its ground forces (ROK Army and Marines). Ground forces will have the main role in demilitarizing and demobilizing the North Korean military and in finding and eliminating North Korean weapons, especially its WMD. While the ROK military has historically been relatively large (690,000) and has heavily emphasized ground forces (over 85 percent of the total ROK military in 2000), the ROK military will have declined in active duty personnel by some 25 percent by 2022, and the percentage of its ground forces will have been reduced to under 80 percent. These changes will significantly challenge ROK responses to a North Korean government collapse and subsequent Korean unification.

For many years, the ROK was able to retain an active duty military force of about 690,000 personnel. Of these personnel, some 560,000 were ROK Army personnel, and about 25,000 were ROK Marines, for a total ground force capability of almost 585,000. But in the early to mid-1980s, the ROK experienced a significant reduction in its births, which just after the year 2000 was reflected in the 20-year-old age cohort that is subject to the draft in the ROK. As shown in Figure 6.4, from 1977 through about 2003, 400,000 or so young men turned draft age almost every year, enough to sustain the 690,000 or so personnel active duty personnel. Over 75 percent of the total personnel were conscripts, obtained by drafting almost all young men who did not volunteer for military service. By 2020, the number of 20-year-old young men will be just under 320,000, and by 2025, the number will be only about 225,000. This reduction in available manpower means that the ROK military manpower will grow smaller in coming years. In addition, former ROK President Roh Moo-Hyun set in motion reductions to the draft service period from 26 months for the Army to 18 months (by 2014) that would further reduce the number of active duty military personnel, although in December 2010, ROK President Lee Myung-Bak froze the conscription period at the 21.5 months that the reduction had reached. But President Park Geun-Hye promised to

Figure 6.4
The ROK Military's Demographic Problem

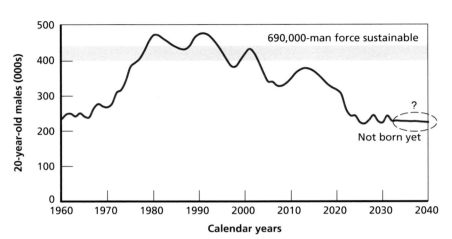

SOURCE: Korean Statistical Information Service, "Projected Population by Age,"
January 2013.
RAND RR331-6.4

reduce the conscription period to 18 months during her 2012 election
campaign; experts expect her to do this over time.

The relatively straight lines in Figure 6.5 show the size of the
ROK military and of the ROK Army as projected by the ROK DRP
1230,[8] the current ROK military modernization plan. The ROK military is projected to fall to about 520,000 active duty personnel in
2022,[9] of which somewhat over 385,000 would be ROK Army personnel—the ROK Army absorbing effectively all the personnel reduction.
This almost one-third reduction in the ROK Army involves cutting
the number of active duty combat divisions from 22 to 12 or so, but
retaining two ROK Marine divisions, for 14 or so total ROK active
duty ground force divisions. The ROK Army would also have some 16
reserve divisions in 2022, although many ROK military leaders dis-
count the value of the ROK reserve divisions because reserve personnel

---

[8] The plan name reflects the fact that it was designed to run from 2012 until 2030.

[9] Interview within ROK MND, June 2012; see also Kim Eun-jung, "S. Korea Pushes to
Cut Troop Levels to 522,000 by 2022," Yonhap News Agency, August 23, 2012.

Figure 6.5
Projected Active Duty ROK Military, Army Force Size

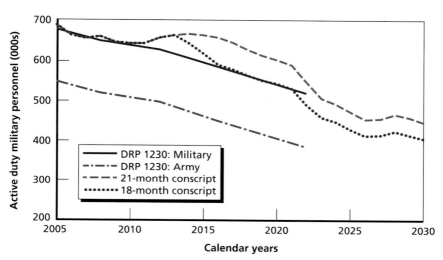

RAND *RR331-6.5*

train only three days per year. In contrast, the North Korean Army has some 30 active duty combat divisions and 60 reserve combat divisions (and North Korean reserve divisions get far more training each year).[10]

The dashed line at the top of Figure 6.5 is based on a simple spreadsheet model of ROK military manpower levels the author developed. For this line, the model assumes the reduction in the conscription period President Roh Moo-Hyun started in 2008,[11] then President Lee Myung-Bak's freeze at 21.5 months in late 2010. This line suggests that, through 2023 or so, the ROK military could actually be somewhat bigger than currently planned, but thereafter, the ROK active duty military will decline to even smaller sizes.[12] The dotted line shows the military manpower that would be available if President Park imple-

---

[10] ROK MND, 2010, p. 340.

[11] President Roh Moo-Hyun directed that the ROK Army conscription period be gradually dropped from 24 months in 2008 to 18 months in 2014, falling a couple of days each month.

[12] The ROK also uses conscripts in its national police force and in other roles; thus, any excess in available military manpower will likely be used to support these organizations.

ments her promise to reduce the conscription period to 18 months over the next three years. Note that this line fairly closely matches DRP 1230, leaving few conscripts for other roles.[13] Beyond 2022, these lines suggest that ROK military manpower will fall below the 2022 levels by perhaps another 100,000 personnel if the 18-month conscription period is chosen. If the ROK Army is forced to absorb all these reductions, it would be smaller than 300,000 personnel by 2026.

These numbers are important because they show a decline over time in the ability of the ROK ground forces to deal with the North Korean military and the other challenges in this chapter. Even today, the ROK military would need substantial cooperation from the North Korean factions after a North Korean government collapse to de-escalate conflict, demobilize the North Korean military, eliminate WMD and other weapons, and stabilize North Korea quickly enough to avoid disaffection. The North Korean military is not prepared today to provide such cooperation. Even with the modest ground force that the United States will be able to provide to support the ROK, the ROK military will not have sufficient force to compel all North Korean factions to abandon conflict and military threats while the ROK military also protects the ROK.

By 2020 or so, ROK ground forces will be far smaller. To adequately handle a North Korean government collapse, the ROK will need to take some combination of five actions:

1. Get a greater U.S. force commitment. The ROK anticipates a major U.S. force commitment to any contingency with North Korea: "US augmentation forces, including the Army, Navy, Air Force and Marine Corps, are comprised of approximately 690,000 troops, 160 naval vessels and 2,000 aircraft. These forces will be deployed in the event of a contingency to defend the ROK."[14] But such a commitment would amount to roughly one-half of all U.S. active duty forces, more than the United

---

[13] Of course, a model like this includes many assumptions that could vary depending on actual ROK policy and practice. Thus, these are very approximate estimates.

[14] ROK MND, Defense White Paper, 2006, p. 56. A similar statement is included in the 2010 white paper.

States could likely deploy in coming years. The United States has come to view most conflicts as being longer-term (multiyear) commitments, requiring a rotation base of deployable forces. The preferred rotation base is currently two forces in reset and preparation for each force deployed, limiting the United States to employing about one-third of its deployable ground forces, or about three active duty U.S. Army ground force divisions and one U.S. Marine Corps division. Thus, the United States is unlikely to deploy even 690,000 personnel to a Korean contingency, let alone more beyond this number to make up for the ROK ground force reductions.

2. Maximize the size of the ROK active duty forces. The ROK could increase the size of its own active duty forces by sustaining or increasing its conscription period and by generating a larger fraction of military volunteers. These options are considered in more detail in Chapter Ten.

3. Rely more heavily on ROK Army and Marine reserves. The ROK has some 3.2 million military reserve forces. Most of these are organized as ROK Army individual replacements; the ROK does have 22 reserve maneuver divisions, but this number is also declining.[15] This reserve force structure is apropos to a defense of the ROK rather than military operations into North Korea. The ROK needs to organize more reserve units and provide some of its reserve personnel more than three days of training per year. Options for organizing a more effective ROK reserve force are discussed in Chapter Ten.

4. Co-opt more of the North Korean forces. If the ROK can co-opt more of the North Korean forces, it will require fewer ROK forces to stabilize North Korea and perform other necessary missions, such as de-escalation, demobilization, and WMD-E. The ROK is very unlikely to secure a significant level of cooperation without substantial preparation in the next few years.

5. Seek Chinese military support. As argued in Chapter Three, China is likely to intervene in North Korea after a North

---

[15] ROK MND, 2010, p. 340.

Korean government collapse. China could perform missions in parts of North Korea that reduced ROK ground forces would be no longer able to control. The options for working with Chinese forces are discussed in Chapter Nine.

These options present the ROK with some difficult choices, none of which are likely to be popular within the ROK. Nevertheless, the failure to take an appropriate combination of these actions may make it impossible to unify Korea beyond some point in the next three to five years due to ROK Army reductions, and will certainly increase the cost of unification significantly. See Chapter Ten.

Mitigating the Conflict Challenges

This section addresses actions that the ROK government could take to mitigate conflict that occurs in Korea after a North Korean government collapse. Efforts to mitigate conflict and its related challenges will require serious short-term efforts to stop the conflict and medium-term efforts to remove the military threats in North Korea and adjust the attitudes of the former military personnel to avoid a major insurgency and/or criminal activity. This section focuses on the short-term efforts that seek to avoid or end conflict. It begins by discussing some of the policies and strategies required to deal with conflict. It then discusses the other preparations that would be required to deal with conflict. Subsequent sections discuss actions required to demilitarize the North Korean military forces and to collect and eliminate North Korean weapons.

Concepts and Policies for Mitigating Korean Conflict

Korea cannot be unified if conflict prevails and imposes continuing damage and insecurity in Korea. If conflict has begun before or soon after a North Korean government collapse, the ROK and the United States must try to stop that conflict promptly, avoiding acts that could escalate the conflict. They must also seek to prevent conflict from developing, including insurgency and criminal behavior.

The key ROK and U.S. effort must be to achieve a cease-fire promptly or at least a significant reduction in hostilities. As long as most parties in such a conflict are fighting for their survival, some will come to feel that they are losing. Such worries would change their deterrence calculus and could justify their taking extreme actions to avoid losing, including serious escalation. This would be true of factions fighting a civil war, for the North Korean military embroiled in an invasion of the ROK, or for North Korean forces that might be defending against a Chinese intervention. Only if the conflict is stopped with a cease-fire or significant de-escalation are the parties likely to feel a degree of security.

But as long as the parties stay armed, especially armed with major weapons, such as WMD, the potential for serious escalation remains. Thus, a cease-fire or serious de-escalation must be followed by efforts to demilitarize the forces in North Korea. In addition, the parties must be deterred from using the cease-fire as an opportunity to rearm or create new alliances, which they then employ in returning to conflict. Efforts to disarm and demilitarize North Korean forces will be addressed later, under "Demilitarizing the North Korean Military Forces."

Strategies for Mitigating Conflict in North Korea

The ROK and the United States will need to use some combination of approaches to stop or de-escalate conflict. The approaches chosen will depend in part on the conflict situation being addressed.

Some Approaches to Stopping Conflict

The following are the available approaches:

- Provide inducements in exchange for a cease-fire in place. This approach would use food, money, amnesty pledges, and other inducements to get one or more parties to agree to a cease-fire. The parties should also be promised ROK and U.S. military protection against their opponents. The magnitude of the inducements will likely be a function of the military power of the group: Groups that think they can win will be difficult to buy off, whereas groups that fear losing should normally welcome a cease-fire. While these inducements will likely be expensive, preventing the damage that conflict would otherwise cause and avoiding even more costly escalation would almost certainly justify the investment. Problems could develop with the cease-fire if one or more parties try to use it to rearm or seek new allies or otherwise strengthen themselves militarily; thus, such activities must also be prevented or moderated to sustain the cease-fire.

- Draw a separation line that parties are not allowed to cross. The ROK and the United States could draw a separation line between factions in North Korea to separate them, likely as part of a cease-fire. Drawing a separation line with China could prevent accidental conflict between ROK-U.S. and Chinese forces. It is easiest to impose such a line before conflict starts or after a cease-fire has been achieved. While it is difficult to enforce such a line, and mistakes will happen, a line is still one of the few ways to avoid large amounts of accidental conflict.

- Coerce parties to secure a cease-fire or deterrence while protecting forces and other assets. This approach would apply military pressure against the various parties to achieve a cease-fire and deter their escalation of the conflict. The basic principle of deterrence is to threaten costs and/or the denial of benefits to the other parties, and the most powerful threats would be attacks against the leaderships themselves. Still, such threats will appear hollow if ROK and U.S. forces are not prepared to protect themselves against retaliation from the parties, especially retaliation with nuclear weapons or other WMD. But this protection likely needs to focus on defensive measures, as opposed to attacks on the parties' military forces, because such threats of attack could be destabilizing, likely prompting preemption by one or more parties.[16]

- Destroy or secure particularly threatening weapons. A more aggressive approach would be to destroy or secure the weapons of

---

[16] Whenever an effort is made to destroy a party's major weapon systems, that party is put into what is referred to as a "use them or lose them" quandary. That is, if it appears that the United States will destroy the party's weapons, it may well be prompted to launch the weapons before they can be destroyed. If the weapons involve WMD, as is likely in North Korea, the damage such parties do could escalate the situation rather than de-escalate it, especially if urban areas are targeted.

one or more parties, especially the more dangerous weapons, such as WMD. Once these weapons have been destroyed or secured, the ROK and the United States will have greatly reduced the conflict that is possible and will have increased incentives for the parties to accept a cease-fire. But since the parties are likely to view these weapons as key to their survival, the parties are likely to oppose attempts to destroy or secure the weapons, leading to conflict with the ROK and the United States and perhaps even escalation. Thus, until conflict is de-escalated, this is a risky approach that will likely increase the intensity of conflict before being able to reduce it.

- Destroy or eliminate military capabilities of the party(s). This final approach involves the ROK and the United States directly fighting one or more parties—an escalation of conflict striving to eventually de-escalate by defeating the parties involved. The cost to the ROK and the United States of this approach is likely to be high, and the threat of serious escalation would also be high. Thus, this approach is something to be avoided, if possible. Still, if one or more parties are antagonistic and causing major damage to other parties or the ROK and the United States, there may be no choice but to pursue this approach.

Note that, if China also intervenes in North Korea, as seems likely, it will also have these approaches available in dealing with any conflict in North Korea, including conflict its intervention precipitates with the North Korean parties along the Chinese border. Thus, the ROK and U.S. approach on conflict needs to be coordinated with the Chinese forces. For example, if the Chinese intervene in support of some North Korean faction, seeking to defeat other factions, the ROK and the United States must convince China also to de-escalate, or the opposing factions are likely to escalate against the faction that China is supporting and potentially even against Chinese forces, likely leading to a major conflict.

To achieve a cease-fire, achieve deterrence, or establish a separation line, the ROK and the United States will need negotiating teams to work directly with the North Korean parties and potentially with

Chinese forces at several command levels. These teams would be sent for face-to-face negotiating with the various North Korean leaderships. They would support ROK and U.S. commanders who would need both the resources and authorities to provide the incentives required to secure cease-fires and related agreements. Given Korean culture, these negotiating teams would likely need to be headed by senior ROK and U.S. officers (lieutenant or major generals, likely from the reserves or retired officers[17]) to achieve the respect of the North Korean commanders. These teams would seek to determine the situation in North Korea, who is in charge, and how to de-escalate the conflict. Because of the uncertainties in these factors, some of these teams may go into unexpectedly hostile situations and be lost; but even such an outcome would give the ROK and the United States vital information. But if the ROK and the United States properly prepare to use these teams, the payoff of their successful negotiations could be substantial in stopping conflict and the damage it would cause.

Formulating Strategies Based on the Conflict Type

The selection of these approaches will depend in part on the nature of the conflict in North Korea. In most cases, some combination of these approaches will be needed in dealing with the various parties in North Korea:

- A North Korean invasion of the ROK. In trying to avoid a government collapse, the North Korean regime could order an invasion of the ROK as a diversionary war, hoping to keep the military unified in support of the regime. But if rebellion against the regime was already developing, the invasion could precipitate government failure, especially if the invasion suffers serious reverses. The forward North Korean forces would then feel particularly vulnerable and potentially prone to escalation if the government has failed, leaving them on their own, threatened with destruc-

---

[17] In some circumstances in which these teams would be used, a senior ROK officer would be most useful in reassuring the North Korean commanders; in other situations, a senior U.S. officer would be most useful. Because the circumstances cannot be predicted, sending both officers appears to be the best approach.

tion. Offers of protection of their forces coupled with provision of food and other essentials could be sufficient to motivate these forces to accept a cease-fire. ROK and U.S. negotiating teams could make these offers, thereby reducing the fears of these North Korean forces and hopefully facilitating a cease-fire in place, or better still a cease-fire that includes North Korean withdrawal across the DMZ (a particularly viable separation line). If the North Korean forces are unwilling to accept a cease-fire or some de-escalation, coercive action or direct military attacks could be used to give them reasons for terminating the conflict.

- North Korean provocations. In the aftermath of North Korea's 2010 provocations (sinking of the warship *Cheonan* and shelling of Yeonpyeong Island), the ROK has issued many threats about executing serious retaliation in response to future provocations. The ROK and the United States would certainly want to stop North Korean provocations from one or more factions, should such provocations develop in the aftermath of a government collapse. While negotiating a cease-fire may be possible in such circumstances, the ROK and the United States would more likely need to take a coercive approach to make the costs of such provocations greater than any benefits that would accrue to the perpetrator. This likely means threatening the leadership of the parties carrying out provocations and sustaining the intelligence needed on the leadership location so that meaningful retaliations would be possible against the offending parties. Such retaliations would be escalatory and may thus also require some attention to disarming the parties of at least their WMD.

- A North Korean civil war. North Korean factions fighting in a civil war would be particularly prone to escalation because some would likely fear that they are in a losing position (especially given the concentration of much of the North Korean conventional force south of Pyongyang). The weaker factions would likely be receptive to offers of a cease-fire coupled with protection of their personnel and provision of food. But stronger factions would likely be more difficult to convince, potentially requiring coercive threats backed by punishment for their continued aggression.

Indeed, even if such stronger factions accepted a cease-fire, they might decide to cheat and continue selected attacks on the weaker factions, expecting that there will be little punishment. While the most effective punishment would be attacks on the leadership of such a faction, that leadership would likely use the negotiating teams working with them as hostages, trying to avoid attacks. The ROK and the United States would therefore need to be prepared to attack either lower-level leaders responsible for any given attack or key faction force capabilities to convince the faction that continued conflict is not in its best interest. But doing so would be risky and would require ROK and U.S. forces postured to deter escalation. The ROK and the United States would also want to impose separation lines between the factions so that responsibility for any infractions would be clearer.

- Insurgency and criminal behavior. The options of a cease-fire and deterrence may not be very effective against a North Korean insurgency or criminal behavior. To deal with these threats, the ROK and the United States likely need to be prepared to destroy or eliminate the military capabilities of these parties, much as the United States has practiced in Iraq and Afghanistan. At the same time, the ROK and the United States will want to provide individual insurgents or criminals with incentives to abandon such activities, including financial incentives and some form of amnesty. The ROK and the United States also need to develop favorable relations with the majority of the North Korean population to undermine the base of support for either insurgency or criminal behavior, but this will take time.
- Chinese intervention. Chapter Nine addresses this issue.

In each of these cases, a failure to achieve meaningful de-escalation or a cease-fire would likely force the ROK and the United States to escalate to destroying or securing at least the WMD the parties involved hold, if not pursuing military defeat of the parties. Such decisions would make a mutually agreed on outcome difficult to achieve and would leave serious bases for disaffection among the targeted groups.

Other Preparations Required

Several other kinds of preparations are needed to achieve cease-fires or substantial de-escalation.

Setting North Korean Beliefs and Expectations

North Korean groups accepting a cease-fire or substantial de-escalation when their survival is at stake will require substantial trust in the ROK and the United States. In practice, it would be more likely to achieve that trust if China is a participant in the effort, as discussed in the next paragraph. In addition, the ROK and the United States need to demonstrate their reliability in other ways, such as by delivering humanitarian aid to North Korea as promised, rewarding scientists or other defectors as promised, and taking meaningful retaliation against North Korean provocations or criminal activities. That is, the ROK and the United States will not only need to build trust in benefits offered but also trust in ROK and U.S. actions to punish violators because various groups in North Korea will be seeking ROK and U.S. guarantees of protection as conditions for accepting a cease-fire. If the ROK and the United States have not appeared to take action against provocations, as would tend to be the case today, the North Korean groups may be unwilling to accept a ROK-U.S. guarantee of their safety.

International Coordination

As suggested immediately above, North Korean groups are more likely to trust Chinese cease-fire assurances than ROK and U.S. assurances, especially given North Korean propaganda on ROK and U.S. commitment failures. The ROK and the United States should therefore work closely with China (and also Russia) in trying to achieve a cease-fire. Of course, such multilateral negotiations take time, time that some North Korean groups will likely feel they do not have. Thus, it would be ideal for the ROK, the United States, and China to have agreed to means of achieving a cease-fire well before a collapse occurs. While China has been reluctant to have such discussions, the ROK and the United States can at least organize discussions on this subject and invite Chinese observers or provide results to the Chinese after the completion of the discussions. At some point, Japan and Russia should also be involved because they will each have a stake in any regional conflict.

If China has also entered the conflict, special efforts must be applied to avoid an immense escalation of violence. Chapter Nine addresses that issue.

Supplies, Equipment, and Financial Preparation

The ROK and the United States will need to have food, medicines, money, and other incentives to offer the various North Korean groups to encourage them to accept a cease-fire. The groups will most likely want both immediate compensation and also regular resupply thereafter to sustain their needs. The ROK and the United States need to decide which organization(s) will be responsible for negotiating these agreements, what authorities they will be given, and how the incentives are to be delivered. In the aftermath of a North Korean government collapse, the leaders of different factions in North Korea may have only tenuous control of their areas; thus, any delivery of incentives will likely require ROK and U.S. military escort to reach the parties making the agreement.

Building ROK Political Consensus

Many South Koreans will likely oppose ROK intervention in a conflict in North Korea, fearing the conflict would spread into the ROK. In practice, a failure to achieve an early cease-fire in the North is the most likely route to attacks on the ROK, allowing the conflict in the North to spiral out of control. This problem needs to be explained to the ROK people to help justify an early focus on a cease-fire, even if one or more factions escalate to using WMD.

There will also likely be serious ROK opposition to providing incentives to the North Koreans to cease conflict. Many in the ROK already fear the potential cost of Korean unification, and offers of incentives to stop conflict would appear to be the first of a series of very expensive steps. The ROK government thus needs to discuss with the public the risks of not containing conflict in North Korea and how the costs of providing incentives would likely be far less than the costs of damage suffered in the ROK otherwise.

Demilitarizing the North Korean Military Forces

Mitigating the conflict will provide a short-term resolution of the North Korean military threats. A longer-term resolution will require disarming most North Korean military personnel, demobilizing them, and reintegrating them into civil society. This disarmament, demobilization, and reintegration (DDR) process is the subject of an extensive literature, having been performed over time in numerous locations around the world. Some North Korean military personnel may also be integrated into a combined Korean military force. Civil reintegration and military integration are the two approaches usually described in the DDR literature. This section recommends focusing on a third option: public service organized at least initially within the combined military. This section describes proposed approaches to each.

Ideal Disarmament, Demobilization, and Reintegration Thinking

The UN describes the DDR process as follows:

- Disarmament. Disarmament is the collection, documentation, control and disposal of small arms, ammunition, explosives and light and heavy weapons of combatants and often also of the civilian population. Disarmament also includes the development of responsible arms management programmes.
- Demobilization. Demobilization is the formal and controlled discharge of active combatants from armed forces or other armed groups. The first stage of demobilization may extend from the processing of individual combatants in temporary centres to the massing of troops in camps designated for this purpose (cantonment sites, encampments, assembly areas or barracks). The second stage of demobilization encompasses the support package provided to the demobilized, which is called reinsertion.
- Reinsertion. Reinsertion is the assistance offered to ex-combatants during demobilization but prior to the longer-term process of reintegration. Reinsertion is a form of transitional assistance to help cover the basic needs of ex-combatants and their families and can include tran-

sitional safety allowances, food, clothes, shelter, medical services, short-term education, training, employment and tools. While reintegration is a long-term, continuous social and economic process of development, reinsertion is a short-term material and/or financial assistance to meet immediate needs, and can last up to one year.

- Reintegration. Reintegration is the process by which ex-combatants acquire civilian status and gain sustainable employment and income. Reintegration is essentially a social and economic process with an open time-frame, primarily taking place in communities at the local level. It is part of the general development of a country and a national responsibility, and often necessitates long-term external assistance.[18]

According to this framework, both active duty and reserve military personnel are first disarmed to resolve much of the threat they pose. They are then demobilized—discharged from active duty military service. Then, to assist them in transitioning to civilian life, they may be offered short-term and long-term assistance.

If, instead, the military personnel are to be integrated into a combined military force, they may bypass the entire DDR process. In practice, however, there is seldom much interest in creating a combined military force with substantial numbers of formerly opposition military personnel. Thus, three years after German unification, only 2 percent of the East German military personnel in the late-1980s were still part of the combined German military. These personnel are usually retained because of their experience with opposition military equipment that is to be retained or to serve other transition functions.

Note that this approach is largely in contrast to what happened in Iraq in 2003. The United States had developed some plans for DDR of the security forces that involved the reintegration of many of them into the new Iraqi Army. Propaganda efforts thus called on Iraqi units to surrender in formation. However, in the face of the "melting away"

---

[18] UN, "Integrated Disarmament, Demobilization and Reintegration Standards," New York, 2006, p. 2.

of Saddam's armed forces (which had generally gone home, some with their weapons), the United States decided instead to abolish the Iraqi Army. Because this was done with no promise of job training or payment (a stipend and pension system was set up within a few weeks but only after protests and complaints, and many saw it as insufficient), many former officers and personnel were left frustrated. Some did end up joining the new Iraqi Army, but unknown numbers likely did support and/or join insurgent forces.[19]

Problems Applying the Traditional Approaches to North Korea

The DDR process for North Korea will be complicated in many ways. The biggest problem will be with handling the size of the North Korean forces: The North Korean active duty military today is several times the size of the Iraqi active duty military in 2003 (perhaps 1.2 million[20] versus Iraq's 389,000[21]). In addition, North Korea has some ten times as many reserve forces as Iraq had in 2003. The ROK Army and Marines will have difficulty getting to all North Korean units promptly, then managing the disarmament and demobilization process, and finally simply guarding the surrendered weapons. While many North Korean reservists will be able to return to existing jobs once demobilized,[22] the active duty personnel will find it more challenging to integrate into civilian society. Not unlike the situation in Iraq in 2003, North Korea can be expected to have few civilian jobs to spare for demobilized active duty personnel and will not have the infrastructure required for serious reinsertion and reintegration efforts, given the large numbers of North Korean military personnel.

At the same time, alternative employment for North Korean military personnel will likely develop rapidly in criminal organizations and insurgency. North Korean criminal organizations already exist, associated with the widespread North Korean black market. Many in

---

[19] In practice, DDR is often conducted in ways far less than the ideal described earlier.

[20] IISS, *The Military Balance 2012*, London, 2012, p. 256.

[21] IISS, 2002, p. 105.

[22] The challenge here will be with North Korean government personnel, as it is unclear that their jobs will be retained.

the North Korean military appear to already be associated with black market activities. And some North Korean military units already appear to be preparing to transition to insurgency against ROK and U.S. forces.[23] The roughly 200,000 North Korean special forces are of particular concern with both criminal and insurgent activities.

Figure 6.6 illustrates these challenges. As ROK and U.S. forces enter North Korea, they will likely encounter a mixed reception from the North Korean forces. In some areas, the North Korean commanders may not oppose the ROK and U.S. forces, especially if they come offering incentives for cooperation. For example, some factions may fear being defeated by other faction(s) and may prefer to ally themselves with the ROK and the United States. The x-axis in this figure measures the percentage of areas where the ROK and the United States would face serious opposition. Some North Korean soldiers may also decide not to fight. Perhaps they would desert their units, or perhaps they

Figure 6.6
The Challenge of North Korean Demobilization

---

[23] Jung Sung-ki, "US to Chart Steps Against N. Korea's Insurgency Tactics," *Korea Times*, June 29, 2008.

would simply decide not to fire at ROK and U.S. forces. The percentage of soldiers opposing the ROK and the United States is shown on the y-axis. The actual North Korean reaction is uncertain, but these two factors are likely correlated. Therefore, the actual probabilities are reflected by the ellipse in this chart, in which the more solid the color, the higher probability of occurrence. Wherever the ROK and the United States do encounter opposition, they will likely experience conflict and difficulty in demobilizing North Korean forces.

North Korean military opposition can be reduced in several ways. The ROK and the United States could convince the North Korean military commanders not to oppose unification, employing the negotiating teams discussed above to both achieve cease-fires and begin the disarmament and demilitarization processes. The ROK and the United States could also convince individual soldiers not to fight by providing them both short-term incentives (e.g., food and pay) and medium- to long-term incentives (e.g., jobs and homes).

The other problem will be with North Korean security forces, especially the personnel embedded in the military to impose regime control. For the North Korean military, the Military Security Command provides most of these forces, which number less than 10,000 personnel,[24] or about 1 percent of the North Korean military. These personnel could decide to fire when their commanders agree to be disarmed, hoping to prevent their unit from being easily co-opted.[25] In addition, some number of the North Korean Ministry of People's Security (the broader secret police) would also need to be disarmed and demobilized,[26] and this ministry has some 210,000 personnel plus 100,000 civilian staff.[27] See Chapter Seven.

---

[24] Gause, 2012, p. 36–37.

[25] I often refer to this threat as the "Red October effect"—from the book and movie *The Hunt for Red October*, in which a cook is actually a security person who tries to blow up a submarine whose officers are defecting.

[26] Much of this force provides security along the Chinese border. If Chinese military forces intervene as expected, the Chinese will need to deal with those personnel.

[27] Gause, 2012, p. 26–27.

Concepts and Policies for Demilitarizing the North Korean Military Forces

The large numbers of North Korean forces need to be disarmed promptly, under ROK military supervision. Their weapons then need to be collected, likely in large UGFs in each province, the weapons consolidated in relatively secure locations to minimize the ongoing security requirement. The North Korean reserve personnel then need to be returned to their jobs.

Disarmament takes weapons away from the military forces. Even for North Korean military personnel integrated into the combined Korea military, some degree of disarmament will occur (e.g., removing tanks and combat aircraft and naval combatants from the personnel). Most North Korean military personnel will have to surrender all their weapons, having no need of them in subsequent public service (probably 80 percent or so of the North Korean military). This process also involves debriefing military personnel to identify the location of North Korean weapon stocks away from the units, weapons that could be used if not eliminated.

ROK and U.S. forces would have three options for demobilizing active duty North Korean military personnel after they have disarmed:

1. Civil reintegration. They can be subject to civil reintegration, although likely without much in terms of assistance from the ROK because the North Korean military is so large. Therefore, this activity should be limited to selected individuals who can secure jobs in the civil economy, such as scientists and some engineers, and to senior personnel due for retirement. Those being retired should be provided an adequate pension.

2. Military integration. Almost all active duty North Korean soldiers should be integrated into a combined Korean military force. They should be kept in the military so that military discipline would still apply and debriefings could be carried out when convenient. These soldiers should then be divided into two groups: Those doing military service in the combined military and those doing public service (below). Those doing military service could amount to maybe 20 percent of the North Korean

military and would include personnel assigned to disarm North Korean military units, to guard North Korean weapons, to deal with insurgents and criminals, and other tasks.[28] Many of those doing military service would retain small arms for protection and would be monitored by teams of ROK soldiers. Others would maintain former North Korean military equipment and may not need to be armed. Within a year or so, the number of retained North Korean military personnel would likely drop from 20 to 10 percent, and within three or so years, the numbers would likely fall to 3 to 5 percent.

3. Public service. Most disarmed North Korean military units should immediately be put to work to perform infrastructure repair, new construction, or other activities. Because most North Korean roads are not yet paved, many of these units should be assigned to work on the North Korean road network so that ROK and U.S. ground forces can gain sustainable access to the North Korean interior for delivery of humanitarian aid, establishing a safe environment, and securing WMD and other weapons. These personnel should also be provided resources for building necessary housing where units have insufficient housing for the soldiers, spouses, and children. The personnel would be fed and paid, enough to allow their families to be with them (many of the military families in North Korea have been sent home to parents because even military units lack sufficient food). And the ranks of personnel would be respected.[29]

---

[28] It is unlikely that sufficient ROK maneuver forces will be available for all of the functions for which they would be needed. Therefore, the ROK should decide to leave some number of North Korean military units with small arms so that they could continue to perform a security role or perhaps assume a police role. For example, the North Korean guards around weapons facilities may be kept in place under the supervision of a smaller ROK contingent. Care should be taken in choosing these units, although in practice, North Korean special forces units may be the best for such assignments if their indoctrination with North Korean propaganda can be overcome.

[29] It will take years to convince many North Korean military personnel that such offers are serious; thus, the ROK ought to begin to make such offers long before a North Korean government collapse.

It would be best for the ROK and the United States to keep North Korean units together. This approach would involve disarming them but employing the unit together as a means of monitoring their military service or public service and thereby simplifying the process of providing incentives, such as housing (much of it in existing barracks) and food. Keeping the units together and monitoring the personnel under military discipline will allow the combined Korean government to pursue those leaving to join criminal or insurgent groups as deserters.

Many North Korean military personnel, especially the officers and noncommissioned officers (NCOs), likely expect to be treated as prisoners of war and subjected to war crimes trials. But the Korean constitution (making even North Koreans citizens of the Korean state) would limit incarceration to those specifically identified as having committed crimes (e.g., many of the prison camp guards). The capacity of the ROK justice system would limit those prosecuted, many of whom would likely have been known for their brutality and thus they would be expected by their peers to be prosecuted (see Chapter Four).[30] Most of the remainder of the military personnel should be treated well, being provided food and housing for themselves and their families as long as they are in military or public service. Many of the military personnel would be debriefed, but this should not be a hostile experience, except for those specifically identified as having committed crimes.

The ROK will need to set several policies for these efforts:

- The disarmament should occur promptly—within weeks where possible and within a few months elsewhere.
- Most North Korean reserve personnel would be expected to return to their civilian jobs. However, for reserve personnel unwilling or unable to do so, provision should be made to adding them to public service units at their ranks in the North Korean military.
- Most North Korean active duty personnel should be retained on active duty to provide some control of their actions but processed

---

[30] For example, many North Korean officers and NCOs have likely accepted bribery. But because there will likely be insufficient capacity to prosecute and incarcerate these individuals, amnesty should probably cover such crimes. See Chapter Four.

into public service activities, especially infrastructure repair and improvement. These assignments will keep the personnel gainfully employed and will also, hopefully, instill in them a sense that they are contributing to the greater good of the combined Korea. The assignments will also prepare many of them for jobs after public service is terminated; for example, it will likely take many years to finish paving North Korean roads.[31]

- Most North Korean military defectors already in the ROK will likely want to return to be with their parents or other family members. Efforts should be made to enlist these individuals in the public service activities done in their home areas.

- North Korean military personnel should be treated well, fed and paid regularly, and provided reasonable housing. It will be particularly important to set a positive precedent early in the process so that word of mouth and other communications will convince the North Korean military personnel not involved in the initial transitions that the ROK will treat them well.

- Provision should also be made for educating the North Korean military personnel on the ROK democratic society and culture, as well as on the nature of a free-market economy. All North Korean military personnel could be given a tablet computer containing a basic instruction course that they would need to pursue at a specified rate. Such a device could also provide job-related training. A modest number of teachers could be assigned to each unit to make sure the educational material is studied and that required tests are taken and passed; when the North Koreans fail to pass the tests, the teachers could provide extra instruction.

Strategies for Demilitarizing the North Korean Military Forces

The demilitarization process should involve a sequence of steps, first applied across the DMZ and in the coastal areas where aid and other

---

[31] The North Korean provincial and local governments may thus eventually extend roadwork jobs to such North Korean former military units. The ROK government should provide business advice to these units to help them organize into construction companies, likely unifying with other construction units to form a construction firm.

incentives can be initially delivered. The process needs to begin by contacting North Korean commanders and offering an exchange of incentives for demilitarization, simultaneously committing to good treatment of the North Korean military personnel. Negotiating teams would then be inserted to determine the details of demilitarization, followed by insertion of ROK and U.S. forces and aid to use in the local demilitarization process. These forces would likely do a partial disarmament (removing heavy weapons but not small arms) of these first North Korean forces that they first contact and transition them to becoming military service units assigned to disarm their North Korean counterparts, with ROK and U.S. military monitoring. Once sufficient North Korean forces have been assigned to this disarming role, most North Korean Army forces would be transitioned to public service after being disarmed.

However the North Korean government collapse develops, many of the North Korean forces will still likely be in or close to their peacetime locations. At the corps level, these are depicted in Figure 6.7. The ROK 2010 Defense White Paper talks about nine regular corps (I, II, III, IV, V, VII, VIII, IX, and X) plus the Pyongyang Defense Command (PDC) and two mechanized corps (425 and 108).[32] Historically, the mechanized and armored forces south of Pyongyang were also considered corps (806, 815, and 820), but they have since been designated divisions.

ROK responsibility for the North Korean forces would be given to whichever force can most easily reach the North Koreans. Thus, the ROK Army would be given initial responsibility for dealing with the three North Korean DMZ corps (I, II, and V) and the three heavy divisions (806, 815, and 820) behind them. The ROK and U.S. Marines would have responsibility for the west coast corps (IV, III, PDC, and 425) and the east coast corps (VII, IX, and 108). While this alignment would appear to put responsibility on the marines out of proportion with their force size, the North Korean corps that the marines would have to deal with are smaller than the corps the ROK Army would have to handle. In addition, the two northernmost coastal corps (VIII and

---

[32] ROK MND, 2008, p. 32

Figure 6.7
Dealing With the North Korean Corps

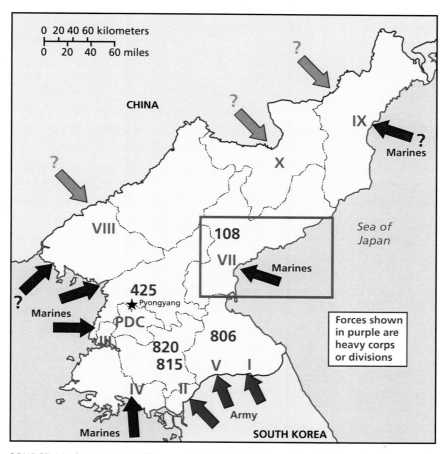

SOURCE: Marine Corps Intelligence Activity, *North Korea Country Handbook*,
MCIA-2630-NK-016-97, May 1997, p. 51.
RAND *RR331-6.7*

IX) are within the area that China would rapidly secure if it intervened
(it would also take control of the X Corps area); thus, the marines may
not need to deal with them. If the ROK Army has more forces available
than are needed to advance across the DMZ, these extra forces could
also be used along the coasts in addition to marines.

The Example of Hamhung

One of the first areas in which ROK and U.S. Marine forces would want to operate would be the Hamhung area on North Korea's east coast, reflected by the box in Figure 6.7. The Hamhung area would be under the protection of the North Korean VII Corps; the North Korean 108th mechanized corps is also located in the same area. To illustrate this process, demilitarization of the Hamhung area could proceed as follows:

1. Strategic communications to prepare. Over the coming years, the ROK and United States need to carry out a strategic communications with the North Korean military in the Hamhung area (and other parts of North Korea). This campaign would seek to divide the North Korean military from the regime, identifying the regime as the cause of ROK and U.S. problems and depicting the North Korean military as the victim of poor regime policies. This communications campaign would argue that the shortages the North Korean military has suffered in food and equipment and modernization are the regime's fault, with which the military must cope. Thus the ROK government could declare the following to North Koreans today:

    The ROK military is not the enemy of the North Korean military, but rather preparing to assist it with food and other aid if the regime did not stand in the way. Should the North Korean government ever collapse, the ROK military is prepared to provide assistance in a prompt manner.

    The ROK would then want to provide various means for the North Korean commanders in the Hamhung area to contact ROK forces and arrange assistance in event of an emergency. The ROK would also want to provide the North Korean commanders the names of the ROK personnel whom they could contact, updating the list when command changes occur. And some of the ROK and U.S. strategic communications should focus on the culture of the ROK military as a means of educating the North Koreans. These communications should include demonstrations of high-tech weapon systems (such as sensor-fuzed weapons) that could prove devastating to North Korean forces if a conflict were actually to occur.

2. Liaison with the local corps command. As instability builds to significant levels in North Korea, the ROK will want the negotiating team assigned to work with the North Korean VII Corps to begin reaching out and communicating with it. The negotiating team assigned to the North Korean 108th Corps should also establish contact. Once a government collapse does occur, these two negotiating teams should offer to deploy to the North Korean corps headquarters to arrange for North Korean cooperation in exchange for food and other incentives. These teams would also have a major role in intelligence collection, determining who is in command of each unit, the locations of the units, any defections of subordinate units, and so forth. They should also request permission to send negotiating teams to each of the divisions within the VII Corps and possibly teams to work with the maneuver brigades of the 108th Corps. As part of the process,

    a. Each of the North Korean corps commanders should be given a choice: They can work with the assigned negotiating teams, or the ROK and the United States will bypass the corps leadership to work with the divisions, attacking the corps leadership, if necessary, to avoid its interference.

    b. It will generally be difficult to predict how a North Korean corps leadership will behave. Some negotiating teams will be taken hostage, and some may be killed. These would be unfortunate losses. The ROK and the United States will need to take some risks to promptly demilitarize North Korean military forces.

    c. Where the corps commanders and their subordinates refuse to cooperate, the ROK and the United States may eventually have to attack the North Korean forces and compel their demilitarization. This option should be left as a last choice. Before accepting combat, various efforts should be made to eliminate the unresponsive corps commanders or to disrupt their command authority (e.g., by encouraging desertions to nearby areas, where the cooperative parts of units could be reconstructed).

3. Liaison with division commands: Negotiating teams led by peers of the North Korean division commanders would next be committed to work with these commanders on the demilitarization process.

4. Deliver and distribute aid to the military and civilians; provide security. The negotiating teams should arrange for larger ROK and U.S. maneuver forces to be introduced into the Hamhung port. They would bring with them the first increments of food, medicine, and other supplies. The negotiating teams should explain the incentives being offered and the procedures that would be applied to disarmament and demilitarization. They would encourage the corps and division commanders to maintain the discipline and cohesion of their forces, avoiding desertions, as both military service and public service would continue under military discipline. They would arrange for the insertion of the ROK and U.S. maneuver forces needed to perform the initial disarmament processes and to secure WMD. The teams would also arrange for military support of the forces being disarmed if they are attacked by other North Korean units.

5. Secure the port area. The inserted ROK and U.S. maneuver forces would initially secure the port area so that food and other aid could be delivered while avoiding interdiction by rogue military units or by criminals.

6. Disarm the local battalions. The inserted ROK and U.S. maneuver forces would first disarm battalion-sized units in the port area, then move beyond the port to other North Korean units. The initially disarmed North Korean units should be considered for assisting subsequent disarmament and/or guarding weapon stocks (in which case, they would retain small arms), doing so with significant ROK and U.S. monitoring teams. During this process, biometric records should be created for all North Korean personnel so that future investigations of crimes or insurgency have a good chance of identifying the perpetrator(s).

Over time, biometrics should also have a deterrent effect on criminal behavior as the North Koreans learn how biometrics facilitate identifying those responsible for criminal behavior.[33]

7.   Begin public service. All disarmed units would retain their housing and other resources. The units not committed to some form of military service would be given a public service work assignment. Much of the early work would likely involve road and other infrastructure repair and improvement, including work on housing repairs and additions for the North Korean personnel and their families.[34] For example, a North Korean battalion might be assigned responsibility for 3 to 5 km of the main road headed north from Hamhung so that humanitarian aid can be taken in that direction. The North Korean personnel would continue to operate as a battalion under the North Korean battalion commander and other officers and NCOs. A ROK monitoring unit should be assigned to the battalion to prevent abusive behavior or other misdeeds. The North Korean units performing such infrastructure maintenance or improvement should be provided some equipment and supplies to perform their work—initially, shovels and, eventually, bulldozers and machines to lay asphalt or concrete. The North Korean units should also be incentivized to help them learn about capitalism. For example, several North Korean battalions might compete for a financial prize based on the quality of the road section they are maintaining.

8.   Secure and guard collected weapons. Some element of the ROK and U.S. maneuver forces would be responsible for securing the collected weapons in a small number of storage facilities so that the weapons can be monitored at a reasonable cost in manpower. The local ROK-U.S. commander will likely want to use some of the retained North Korean security forces to guard these facili-

---

[33] It may take some time for such a deterrent effect to develop because North Koreans will not be familiar with how biometrics facilitate law enforcement.

[34] The ROK wants to make sure that North Korean military personnel see that unification has significantly improved their quality of life.

ties under ROK monitoring. And the ROK may also decide to load some of these weapons onto the ships that brought in food and other supplies, planning to extract the weapons from North Korea so that they can be dealt with in the ROK.

9. Search for WMD storage, weapon depots. As North Korean forces are being disarmed and demobilized, the ROK and U.S. forces will also want to pursue North Korean WMD and other weapon storage. This process is described in the following section on eliminating North Korean WMD.

10. Disable air defenses. As ROK and U.S. forces move into North Korea, they will need to be able to deliver supplies by aircraft, deliver quick reaction forces by helicopter, and provide air support (both intelligence and attacks) for the ground forces. The ability to do so will depend on disabling North Korean air defense systems. In a wartime environment, this would be done by attacking all North Korean SAM systems and destroying all combat air bases. In a collapse environment, this kind of offensive behavior would alienate many North Koreans because these attacks would kill or otherwise affect both North Korean military personnel and civilians. As long as the collapse environment is largely permissive, the ROK and the United States will want to notify the air defense operators that they will be safe from attack if their radars remain off but will be attacked if the radars are turned on, especially if they fire. Combat aircraft that take off will be shot down. Then, as ROK and U.S. ground forces advance, they should disable the air defense radars that they come into contact with so that they no longer need to rely on North Koreans being responsive to the coercive policy.[35]

11. Establish facilities for force projection. As this demilitarization process proceeds, North Korean military groups may arise that seek to stop the work of the ROK and U.S. forces by attack-

---

[35] In practice, the ROK and the United States may need to disable the North Korean SA-5 SAMs and, once deployed, the KN-06 SAMs because these will pose threats to aircraft over a large area, with potentially high lethality. ROK and U.S. special forces may need to be given this mission, although negotiating teams should first try to secure cooperation of the North Korean SAM commanders.

ing them. While it would be ideal to hold a sizeable maneuver reserve force in each operating area to deal with such challenges, the ROK and U.S. forces are, in practice, unlikely to have much more force available than is required to support the disarmament and demilitarization process. Therefore, as ROK and U.S. forces move out to perform these functions, they need to identify areas where they could pull back to defend themselves. Air and sea power should be available to support them, as well. While this situation would be unlikely to occur very often, it would probably occur at least once in the demilitarization process, especially given the degree of indoctrination of many of the North Korean forces. If the ROK and U.S. forces prove to be vulnerable to such attacks, other North Korean forces may be encouraged to try similar attacks. Such a development should be avoided.

In summary, disarming the North Korean military forces but sustaining military cohesion will be critical to accomplishing many objectives with the North Korean military personnel. A key objective will be to avert desertions to insurgent and criminal groups. At the same time, this approach will provide food and housing for the military personnel, rather than pushing them into potentially disastrous humanitarian conditions that might lead them to desperate actions undermining local security. Another objective will be to provide job-related training for the military personnel. This approach will also provide time to debrief military personnel while they are still subject to military discipline. In a related matter, this approach would allow time for ROK and U.S. authorities to apply biometrics to the North Korean military personnel.

As more North Korean forces are demobilized, some North Korean conscripts may well want to return home to their families. The ROK and the United States could arrange to transfer such personnel to public service units in the vicinity of their families. If the number of personnel seeking transfers is as large as could be expected, such transfers could lead to a substantial redistribution of the public service personnel. Most active duty North Korean military units are located near the DMZ, away from the families of personnel and the cities where civilian employment opportunities are more likely to develop over time. But any major transfers would likely overflow the military barracks in the cities and require many soldiers to live at home, away from regular surveillance, especially at night. Thus, these transfers may need to be delayed for months until more barracks spaces can be created in the cities and then tested as an experiment, looking for ways to make these transfers without suffering major defections to insurgency or criminal activity.

Jumping Ahead

Once the ROK and U.S. maneuver forces are introduced across the DMZ, in ports, and in some cases at airfields, they need to begin expanding their areas of control. But the direction and pace of the expansion will depend on the priorities of facilities, forces, and other areas surrounding them. In many cases, the ground forces will not want to wait for movement on the ground but rather will want to project ahead by airborne, air assault, or amphibious insertion to reach priority locations; alternatively, airpower could be used to attack some facilities or at least prevent access to and exit from them. Figure 6.8 suggests this approach, paying particular attention to promptly reaching the ballistic missile and related WMD facilities.

To facilitate these jumps ahead, negotiating teams should be sent into the corps and divisions in these areas to arrange for cooperation in exchange for food and other incentives. Some of these teams should include air defense disablement units that would be responsible for dealing with the North Korean air defenses in the areas of advance, thereby allowing insertion of food and other aid by air. The airborne, air assault, and amphibious forces would extend their control to key inland facilities while the forces across the DMZ and at coastal ports and airfields extend their control more linearly but in the direction the jumps have gone, making an eventual linkup possible to facilitate better logistical support.

Other Preparations Required

Demilitarization of the North Korean military forces will require a number of other preparations.

Figure 6.8
The Need to Jump Ahead of the Ground Advances

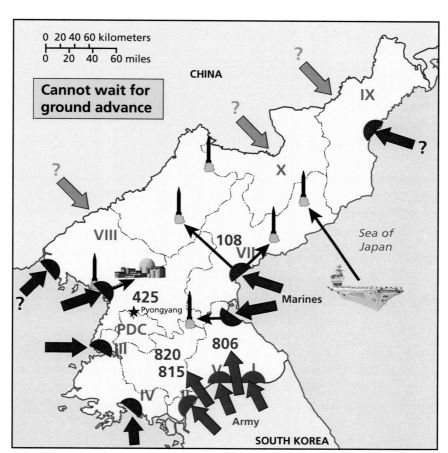

SOURCES: Marine Corps Intelligence Activity, 1997, p. 51; Im Jeong Jin, "Yangkang Province Gets New 10th Corps," *Daily NK*, December 16, 2010; and ROK MND, *Defense White Paper*, 2010, p. 29.
RAND RR331-6.8

Setting North Korean Beliefs and Expectations

All the concepts described in Chapter Four that would create an expectation of an improved quality of life after unification would support the demilitarization process by helping North Korean military personnel become more likely to believe such commitments from ROK and U.S.

military personnel. ROK and U.S. military personnel need to begin reaching out to the North Korean military and showing them acts of kindness and understanding while still being firm and professional, even today. This means increasing the contacts with the North Korean military, especially at senior levels, and showing extreme patience with the anticipated North Korean rudeness. In part, creating the proper environment will require demonstrating ROK and U.S. military superiority to the North Korean military leadership, helping them understand the potentially devastating capabilities of ROK and U.S. forces.[36]

To help set expectations, the United States might want to find films of German demilitarization after World War II. By contrasting the treatment of the Nazi political elites with how the German troops who surrendered were treated, the United States could begin creating an image of equitable U.S. treatment of military personnel demilitarized from even a hated regime.

Military Preparation and Training

As ROK and U.S. forces proceed in an intervention, they must treat the North Korean military well, establishing a precedent. This means avoiding conflict wherever possible (thus seeking a cease-fire before demilitarizing North Korean forces and not carrying out unnecessary attacks against air defenses, road traffic, and other possible targets). But ROK and U.S. forces would want to employ devastating responses to the guilty parties when conflict does develop. Avoiding conflict will require extreme discipline among the ROK and U.S. forces, especially since some security personnel among the North Korean forces will likely try to create conflict by firing on ROK and U.S. forces against the orders of their military superiors.

---

[36] The U.S. military television channel in South Korea regularly shows "commercials" with pictures and films of U.S. and ROK military exercises and activities. But the lethality and capabilities of U.S. and ROK forces are seldom demonstrated. While appropriate care needs to be taken not to divulge classified information, the United States and the ROK want the North Korean military personnel to gain visual understanding of the lethality of precision munitions or the multiple kills achievable with scatterable munitions or the intelligence an unmanned aerial vehicle can collect. These images would help the North Koreans perceive the devastation they could suffer in a conflict with the United States and the ROK.

International Coordination

ROK and U.S. forces will want to involve international partners in the demilitarization process. The presence of such forces will likely help assure the North Koreans of internationally approved treatment.

International support could be particularly important financially. The process of employing North Korean units in public service will be fairly expensive for the ROK. It will therefore want to seek international support for this effort, likely by having other countries or international humanitarian organizations take the responsibility for providing for the needs of North Korean units in specific areas. This could work particularly well on the east coast, where there are more ports for delivering cargo. But the ROK and the United States would need to monitor these arrangements and make sure that the full range of needs is met. For example, if several European countries decided to take responsibility for the North Korean public service units in the Wonsan area but were only able to provide food and money, the ROK and the United States might still need to provide medicine and doctors and may also need to provide interpreters to facilitate communications.

The ROK and the United States must work closely with China and Russia if they decide to intervene in North Korea. Under such circumstances, as ROK and U.S. forces move into North Korea, they will eventually run into Chinese and perhaps Russian forces also advancing into the North.[37] Avoiding accidental conflict with these forces will be a high priority for ROK and U.S. forces. While far from an ideal approach, the best chance of avoiding accidental conflict would be to establish a separation line across North Korea, north of which the ROK and U.S. forces would commit not to go, and south of which the Chinese and Russian forces (if any) would commit not to go. If Russia is involved, a separation line may also be required between Russian and Chinese forces, although defining such a line would be far more difficult because any major Russian advance into North Korea would divide Chinese forces from the ports of Rajin and Sonbong and

---

[37] Russian intervention is possible but not likely, and if Russia does intervene, it will likely play a minor role, in contrast to China. Thus, the remainder of this report focuses on Chinese intervention.

perhaps even Chongjin, where China is making major infrastructure improvements in exchange for long-term rights to use and even control parts of these ports. The approach with China is discussed in more detail in Chapter Nine.

China and Russia (if involved) would also want to pursue demilitarization in the North. It would be ideal if each country took a similar approach to demilitarization, especially since the ROK will be anxious for Korean unification and eventual Chinese and Russian withdrawal that would leave the ROK responsible for any commitments made to the North Korean forces that are demilitarized. But it seems unlikely that China (and perhaps Russia) would be prepared to treat the North Korean units as carefully as suggested above for ROK and U.S. forces. The ROK and the United States must therefore be prepared to encourage China to treat the North Korean units well but to explain to North Korean audiences how the Chinese approach differs from the ROK-U.S. approach when necessary. The ROK, in particular, may need to speak on behalf of individual North Korean officers—especially senior officers—to prevent China from imprisoning or executing them.

Supply, Equipment, and Financial Preparation

The essence of the approach outlined above is to provide the North Korean military forces with significant incentives—food, medicine, money, and so forth—in exchange for their cooperation and demilitarization. ROK-U.S. negotiating teams and senior commanders for the North Korean operation will also need to have the authority to employ these assets. In addition, to live up to these commitments in a timely manner, the ROK and the United States will need a significant supply of these items and associated transportation ready for delivery into the North soon after a North Korean government collapse; they can acquire follow-on supplies from international markets, but these will likely not be available in significant quantities for several months. Because criminal efforts to interdict U.S. supply lines into Afghanistan could resemble the threats that develop in North Korea, the ROK and the United States need to learn from the supply efforts in Afghanistan. For example, they will need excess supplies to make up for supplies that are stolen, plus trucks that are less susceptible to roadside ambush, such as U.S. mine-resistant, ambush-protected vehicles.

North Korean officers will also likely want commitments addressing amnesty and pensions similar those made to the East Germans before German unification. The North Koreans will be reluctant to accept demilitarization if they believe they will then be thrown into prison or otherwise subjected to harsh legal treatment. Still, many North Korean officers likely have a history of exploitive behavior, taking bribes for promotions and participating in or at least allowing the operation of the black market. The senior officers will also likely conclude that they will not be retained in the North Korean military for very long and will want to know about pension provisions. These are areas in which ROK policy, in particular, needs to be established and prepared for implementation. The ability of the negotiating teams to overcome the inbred North Korean propaganda of ROK and U.S. hate for them will turn significantly on the provisions in these areas and on the commitments to provide the North Korean officers a good quality of life in the future.

Building ROK Political Consensus

Today, many in the ROK will likely oppose having to pay for North Korean military cooperation. The ROK government needs to explain this situation to the ROK people over time, addressing the steps required to achieve unification at a minimal cost. The ROK government has worried that even a minimal cost will appear prohibitive and cause may ROK citizens to oppose unification. The ROK government needs to explain to the ROK citizens the consequences of alternative outcomes to a North Korean government collapse (e.g., Chinese control of North Korea, civil war and perhaps anarchy in North Korea, or a follow-up North Korean government that could be even more threatening than the Kim family regime), as well as the long-term advantages of a unified Korea. See Chapter Ten for more discussion of this subject.

Legal Challenges

Some North Korean military personnel will likely rebel against demilitarization regardless of how well the ROK and U.S. forces handle it. ROK and U.S. forces will therefore need a legal framework for dealing with rebels, despite their being citizens of the combined Korea (per the ROK constitution). The ROK needs to decide how harshly it should treat such rebels to discourage further rebellion while, at the same time, giving hope to individuals who may initially make bad decisions.

Military Preparation and Training

ROK and U.S. military forces need to be prepared to achieve North Korean demilitarization without becoming so harsh as to encourage rebellion. The North Korean regime has apparently told its military to expect ROK and U.S. harshness, conditioning them to react negatively to a ROK and U.S. unification effort. But at least some North Koreans likely already question the regime's propaganda. The ROK and the United States must train their forces to appear more mild and not overly aggressive yet thoroughly prepared to deal with any serious opposition. This training must avoid large numbers of standoff attacks, rather seeking to neutralize North Korean defenses through coercion and military action only if the North Koreans commit aggressive acts. This kind of behavior is challenging but not unlike U.S. actions in Iraq and Afghanistan over the last ten years.

Meanwhile, ROK and U.S. forces need to be prepared to go after and eliminate North Korean pockets of resistance of either insurgent or criminal character. The U.S. use of drone aircraft to monitor and carry out strikes would be a key approach to this responsibility, but the North Korean integrated air defense system must be disrupted and then disabled to allow such operations. ROK and U.S. forces must also create favorable relations with the North Korean civilians, in part by delivering humanitarian aid to them, to turn them away from the insurgents and criminals. ROK and U.S. civil affairs and information operations will be critical to this effort.

Eliminating North Korean WMD and Other Weapons

One of the priorities for U.S. forces going into North Korea after a government collapse would be elimination of North Korean WMD. In the U.S. defense strategic guidance from January 2012, one of the ten priority missions for the United States military in coming years is countering WMD.[38] The United States worries that North Korean military forces may use the large quantity of WMD they appear to have and/or proliferate it to third parties, who could use the WMD against the United States or its allies. Collecting the WMD in North Korea will generally be easier than trying to mitigate the consequences of WMD use or trying to find the WMD in criminal or terrorist networks in various parts of the world.

WMD-E is the process required to resolve the WMD threats. It involves destroying the WMD through standoff attacks or using ground forces to secure the WMD and assess it; the ROK and the United States would then need to eventually destroy it. WMD-E is complicated by the demands of the nuclear Nonproliferation Treaty, which specifies that only nuclear powers, such as the United States or China (but not the ROK), are allowed to deal with key nuclear materials. The ROK is not prohibited from dealing with chemical or biological weapons and would likely take a major role in eliminating them.

North Korea also appears to have vast stores of conventional weapons, in keeping with its plans to outfit some 9 million active duty, reserve, and paramilitary personnel. While these weapons are less fearsome than WMD, they also could cause significant losses in the ROK and to U.S. and ROK forces and therefore need to be eliminated. This section focuses on collection of WMD, but the same means for doing so would eventually need to be dedicated to collecting all North Korean weapons, generally in similar manners.

Concepts and Policies for Eliminating North Korean WMD and Other Weapons

Fortunately, the ROK has some idea where WMD is stored or has been produced. For example: "'There are about 100 sites related to the nuclear' program in North Korea, South Korean Defense Minister Kim Tae-Young told lawmakers during a parliamentary audit. 'We

---

[38] U.S. Department of Defense, "Sustaining U.S. Global Leadership: Priorities for 21st Century Defense," Washington, D.C., January 2012, p. 5.

have a complete list of them,' he said."[39] But others are not as certain that the facilities are all known: "A South Korean intelligence official said last month that North Korea has been secretly enriching uranium that could be used to build nuclear weapons at three or four undisclosed locations."[40] Still, even if all the WMD facilities were known, significant quantities of the WMD and of other weapons will likely have been dispersed by North Korean military leaders within days to weeks after a North Korean collapse to increase the chances of weapon survival, to prepare for weapon use, and/or to facilitate weapon proliferation. Thus, the ROK and the United States need to maintain continuous and intrusive surveillance of North Korea, especially around known WMD facilities, but also looking for previously unknown WMD facilities. This will be hard to do until the North Korean air defense system has been controlled or suppressed, so some losses of collection aircraft should be expected.

WMD-E should start with likely weapon storage areas, with ROK and U.S. forces trying to collect weapons and related materials. Attention then needs to shift to likely dispersal sites, many of which would be UGFs, part of the reportedly 10,000 or so North Korean UGFs.[41] The forces pursuing WMD-E should also visit key North Korean military headquarters (such as the headquarters of the Strategic Rocket Forces announced in 2012[42]), where information about the dispersal process likely exists.

WMD-E does not just involve finding the weapons. Many of the inputs to the WMD production process (especially chemical precursors) are dangerous themselves; these inputs and the production equipment for WMD need to be secured and then eliminated. The experts (especially scientists) who have worked on WMD need to be identified,

---

[39] "Seoul Suspects About 100 Sites in N.K. Linked to Nuclear Program," *Korea Herald*, October 5, 2009

[40] Louis Charbonneau, "U.N. Told North Korea Has More Secret Atomic Sites: Envoys," Reuters, January 31, 2011.

[41] Demick, 2003.

[42] "'The North's Strategic Rocket Forces' Status Reinforced Directly Under the National Defense Commission," *DailyNK*, April 19, 2012.

debriefed, and placed in alternative, meaningful jobs to prevent their becoming a resource to third parties trying to build WMD. WMD-related documentation also needs to be collected and examined. Fortunately, many of these items will be collocated at the major complexes used to produce and weaponize WMD, along with some actual weapons or bulk stores. WMD production complexes should therefore be a major focus for WMD-E. The airfields, ports, and border transit areas where WMD may be sent to third parties also need to be controlled

In the process of looking for WMD, ROK and U.S. forces will also find many other weapons. Given the reported size of the North Korean active duty and reserve forces, North Korea must be saturated with such military weapons. In addition to major weapon systems, such as tanks, ships, and aircraft, if the North Korean government provides a small arm for each of its personnel, some 9 million military small arms may need to be found. These will also need to be secured to keep them away from insurgents or criminals and eventually eliminate them.

WMD-E is the process required to resolve the WMD threats. Because hundreds and perhaps thousands of facilities will need to be searched to find and eliminate the WMD, the ROK and the United States need to decide how rapidly WMD must be controlled and whether WMD needs to be captured and exploited or whether they can destroy the WMD with standoff attacks. For example, the ROK and U.S. presidents will likely want to have North Korean nuclear weapons controlled within a week or so of a collapse, a requirement that will be very difficult (likely impossible) to accomplish. Because it will take at least weeks and likely months to reach even a limited set of priority WMD sites with ground forces, there may be some pressure to use standoff attacks against likely storage sites. But there are several problems with such an approach:

- It is necessary to know the locations of the WMD to be effective with standoff attacks. When the ROK and the United States do not know the locations, they could increase collection in an effort to find the facilities. But unless such efforts succeed, the alternative is to put "boots on the ground" to search for WMD.

- It will be difficult to account for the WMD that has been destroyed in any given standoff attack, making it difficult to determine at some future point that "all WMD have been resolved." If such a determination cannot be made, efforts to find WMD may need to continue for a very long time (likely years).
- Attacks on WMD facilities will almost certainly kill some of the WMD experts. This could set a bad precedent and perhaps convince other WMD experts that the ROK and the United States want to eliminate them, too, making it difficult to obtain their surrender.
- Attacks on WMD sites may also kill or injure other North Koreans, especially guards around the WMD facilities. The survivors and their families will likely not feel that unification has been a good thing for them. They are far more likely to be involved in or to support insurgency or criminal activities.
- Attacks on UGFs may only seal the facilities, not destroy the WMD. Therefore, at some future time, these facilities would need to be checked for leakage. In addition, well-prepared and -trained personnel would likely need to enter the facilities to resolve any remaining WMD.
- There is also a serious risk that attacks against WMD weapons, bulk storage, and even production facilities will create and spread WMD contamination. With most forms of WMD, this would cause a potential local hazard around the former WMD site. But the spread of contagious biological weapons would create a much wider societal problem.

These problems notwithstanding, the ROK and/or U.S. president could order such strikes, and ROK and U.S. forces need to be prepared to deal with the consequences. Alternatively, the presidents may order the implementation of a "no-move" zone (where no vehicle traffic is allowed) within some distance of known WMD facilities. Attacks on vehicles moving in such a zone would run some of the same risks as attacks on the WMD facilities themselves.

Strategies for Eliminating the North Korean WMD

The focus of this subsection is on WMD-E that ROK and U.S. ground forces perform, although with air support. This aspect of WMD-E would focus on the advance of the ground forces, as constrained by poor roads and terrain, opposing forces, and logistical support, all of which would be issues in North Korea. The negotiating teams mentioned above should work with the North Korean military commanders in each area to identify where WMD is located, especially if the WMD and related assets have been dispersed (a highly likely outcome for some of the WMD and related assets because of how long it will take ROK and U.S. ground forces to reach all of the facilities). If the North Korean military commanders claim to not know about WMD locations or refuse to divulge such locations, other intelligence sources will need to be employed and other headquarters contacted to determine this information.[43]

Tasks to Be Performed

Once ground forces reach WMD facilities, they would be expected to seize control of them (or perhaps just take control in a permissive environment), secure the facilities, assess the contents of the facilities, expediently disable any WMD production processes, resolve the experts and records at the facility, and prepare for destruction of the WMD and related research and development and production equipment. The following are some specifics of the process:

- Reach the WMD facilities. North Korean ground forces, especially if mobilized, could prove a significant risk to the WMD-E operations. If the ROK and the United States have been able to achieve a cease-fire and to start demilitarizing North Korean forces, the WMD-E effort will be easier but could still run into

---

[43] For example, if many WMD warheads are intended for use with the North Korean ballistic missile forces, ROK and U.S. forces could visit the newly designated North Korean Strategic Rocket Force headquarters and obtain information from individuals and/or records located there. While there is no guarantee, at least one media article suggests that the commander of the strategic rocket forces would be involved in authorizing tactical ballistic missile launches. See "Who Has His Finger on the Nuclear Button in N.Korea?" *Chosun Ilbo*, February 23, 2012.

some fairly large North Korean forces that are not being demilitarized. Therefore, the WMD-E task force assigned to handle each WMD facility needs to be at least battalion sized for both security and command and control purposes, augmented by specialty forces to assess the WMD, debrief scientists, and perform other tasks at the facility. A task force of perhaps 1,000 personnel could easily be required, task organized to deal with the specific facility to be addressed.

- Seize the WMD facility. In a nonpermissive environment, the ROK-U.S. WMD-E task force would first isolate the WMD facility from outside contact and then seize it. In a permissive environment, the task force might simply need to arrive at the facility and take control, although this is more likely to be successful if the task force is prepared to offer some incentives to the facility guards and others, such as food, medicine, and money.
- Secure the WMD facility. The maneuver elements of the task force would next establish defensive positions around the facility, in particular hedging against any external North Korean unit that decides to intervene. They would also establish control of the facility so that people or weapons or other items are not allowed to leave without permission. In truly permissive circumstances, the former North Korean facility security guards could perform some of these functions, under supervision of a ROK-U.S. monitoring force to prevent leakage of WMD assets from the facility or a compromise of the facility defenses.[44]
- Reconnaissance of the WMD facility. After a facility is secured, the task force will want to send reconnaissance elements to survey the WMD facility. They will especially want to identify areas of WMD contamination and areas where WMD weapons and other materials might be stored. They would also want to identify documents and other records that should be examined (securing

---

[44] North Korean WMD facility security guards could well defect to insurgent or criminal activities if they lose their security guard jobs. They are also the people who would best know the security failings of the facility. Thus, retaining them in a security role may limit the damage they could do, especially if they are fed and paid well.

such) and identify WMD experts and others at the facility who should undergo debriefing.

- Debriefings at the WMD facility. One of the elements of the task force would be a multifunctional team that would, in part, include a group of debriefers who would interview facility leaders, WMD experts, and even some guards. The immediate concern would be identifying WMD experts who could help advise the assessment of WMD at the facility and others who could help locate the WMD, people, or other assets at the facility (e.g., finding unmarked UGFs) or that had been dispersed. The debriefers would want to verify the credentials of the North Koreans they would be interviewing (some North Korean personnel could feel they would be treated better if they put on a lab coat and appeared to be a scientist) and to identify key personnel who might be disguising themselves (some senior personnel could fear imprisonment or worse and thus not want to draw attention). After the immediate concerns are dealt with at the facility, key North Korean personnel would likely be transferred to other ROK and U.S. intelligence units for more thorough debriefing.[45] ROK and U.S. forces should then turn over the remaining personnel to ROK government organizations that would identify jobs for these individuals and keep them fed. While WMD experts pose a particular proliferation threat, even WMD technicians could know enough in their specialty areas to pose a proliferation threat.
- Document exploitation at the WMD facility. Another part of the multifunctional team would be document exploitation experts. They would examine the files and other documents at each facility, initially looking for information to help assess the WMD at the facility or locate WMD, people, or other assets at the facility or that had been dispersed. They would then seek to prioritize documents that should be evacuated for further analysis. But they

---

[45] This concept raises an important issue: According to the ROK constitution, the North Koreans at the WMD facilities are all Korean citizens. ROK and U.S. forces may not have the authority to detain these personnel if they refuse to cooperate. This area is thus one where the ROK legal framework may need adjusting to impose necessary debriefings.

may also find information about personnel, contamination, and other issues that would help the task force perform its tasks.

- WMD sampling and analysis at the WMD facility. Once WMD or related materials had been located at a facility, chemical, biological, radiological, and nuclear (CBRN) experts would examine the WMD and, in many cases, take samples for analysis. Because much of North Korea's stored WMD has been in place for years and probably reflects less-than-ideal weaponization or packaging, a fair number of WMD leaks can be expected, likely forcing the CBRN experts to operate in protective clothing. The North Koreans managing WMD facilities could also spread contamination before the ROK and U.S. forces arrive,[46] trying to complicate the WMD-E effort and slow it down, thereby giving them time to move dispersed WMD beyond the initial dispersal sites that ROK and U.S. forces may discover fairly quickly. While the CBRN experts will have some capabilities for analyzing any WMD that is found, they will also want to send samples to WMD laboratories that have better capabilities for detailed characterization of the WMD.
- Dealing with contamination at a WMD facility. ROK and U.S. forces will want to decontaminate any WMD contamination as best as possible at WMD facilities. They will do so in part to avoid inadvertent spread of WMD but also to prepare these facilities for return to civilian activities, if possible. At some level of contamination, ROK and U.S. forces will need to abandon WMD facilities, not having enough forces to adequately resolve heavily contaminated sites when other sites must still be visited. Before they do abandon the facilities, they will want to eliminate health risks to people who subsequently venture into the facilities. When adequate decontamination is not possible, ROK and U.S. forces

---

[46] North Korean WMD facility managers may decide to blow up some of their WMD to complicate the facility resolution process. Alternatively, ROK and U.S. military strikes against the WMD facility may also have caused WMD spills. While resolving WMD facilities will be challenging even if the facilities are left in their precrisis ("pristine") condition, many of them may well become heavily contaminated, also causing problems in the areas around the facilities.

will want to close and seal the contaminated areas and mark them as hazards to keep people out. In addition, a stay-behind security force may be required.

- Consolidating WMD. As noted above, ROK and U.S. forces will likely not be sufficient to provide security for all the WMD facilities (including dispersal locations) that are discovered. Therefore, ROK and U.S. forces will want to consolidate the WMD into a limited number of facilities. That consolidation will require decontamination and explosive ordinance disposal personnel to prepare the WMD for movement and ordinance and transportation personnel to actually move the WMD. Actual WMD destruction could later be organized at the consolidation sites, or the WMD could be moved again to a destruction location. But all this would entail some risk, both of contamination and attacks from insurgent or criminal groups. In some cases, commanders may decide that they have insufficient forces to secure the WMD they have acquired and could consider expedient "explosive" disposal of WMD. This may not be the preferred approach (explosive disposal may spread the WMD, rather than destroy it), but it may nevertheless be the choice of some commanders.

Getting to the WMD Facilities

Most North Korean WMD sites are located around Pyongyang and further north.[47] It will thus take some time for ROK and U.S. ground forces to reach these facilities. The time required is well illustrated with the Yongbyon nuclear complex, where several high priority WMD facilities are located. Yongbyon is located north of Pyongyang and is some 320 km by road from the DMZ. Deploying a significant ROK-U.S. military force to Yongbyon could take weeks, especially if it encounters opposition. Thus, the negotiating teams described above have a role not only in the Yongbyon area but also all along the route of advance to Yongbyon and elsewhere.

---

[47] See, for example, "North Korean Nuclear Facilities," *WMD Around the World*, Washington, D.C.: Federation of American Scientists, October 10, 1997, or "North Korea Chemical, Biological, Nuclear, and Missile Facilities," map, Washington, D.C.: Nuclear Threat Initiative, 2013.

The Yongbyon complex in North Korea is large. Securing it and performing thorough reconnaissance would likely take a force of two or more brigade combat teams (BCTs), each with thousands of personnel. Because the nuclear Nonproliferation Treaty requires many nuclear materials (which one would expect to find at Yongbyon) to be handled by a nuclear power, such as the United States, the force sent to Yongbyon would have to consist primarily of U.S., as opposed to ROK, personnel. Against this requirement, the U.S. 2nd Infantry Division, the U.S. major ground command in Korea, has only one BCT. The division would probably need to wait until a second BCT arrived in Korea as part of U.S. force flow, likely a couple of weeks after deployments to Korea start, although there is a prepositioned BCT equipment set in Korea that could be used. Still, even if the 2nd Infantry Division were focused on Yongbyon, it could take at least six weeks or so to get there (about two weeks waiting for a second BCT and a month or more trying to reach Yongbyon), giving the North Korean authorities considerable time to disperse weapons, people, and other WMD resources. In fact, both the currently deployed and prepositioned BCTs are armored BCTs that could have difficulty with many of the bridges between the DMZ and Yongbyon, likely slowing their advance.

Several means of accelerating the arrival of the 2nd Infantry Division at Yongbyon exist. One would be to deploy a second U.S. BCT as part of 2nd Infantry Division in Korea. Until 2004, there had been two U.S. combat brigades in Korea, but one was then removed and sent to Iraq; when finished in Iraq, it did not return to Korea. Its removal from Korea contributed to the force downsizing from 37,000 U.S. military personnel to 28,500, eventually completed in 2008. But this addition is unlikely in the current U.S. military budget climate.[48] An alternative would be to store an air assault or Stryker BCT equipment set in Korea (in addition to current prepositioned Army equipment). With conflict in Iraq over and conflict in Afghanistan ending, this might be the most

---

[48] The U.S. Army is pursuing a change in BCT structure in which all heavy BCTs like the one in Korea would increase from two battalions to three. When that happens, the number of U.S. personnel in Korea could increase by just less than 1,000 total. But that is well short of adding another BCT.

attractive alternative to enhancing the WMD-E capabilities because it would provide a lighter force more able to exploit the roads in North Korea. Another alternative would be to create a combined 2nd Infantry Division, an option that is apparently being discussed.[49] This alternative would remove the requirement to deploy a further U.S. force to Korea before the 2nd Infantry Division can advance toward Yongbyon, although it would require using the ROK maneuver forces mainly for security at Yongbyon (and presumably not for finding or investigating nuclear materials at Yongbyon). A fourth alternative might seek to deploy forces to Yongbyon by helicopter or airlift aircraft, well ahead of the ground advance. Such an option would require a relatively permissive environment around Yongbyon (an insertion of a force of this size would be vulnerable if landing in a less-than-permissive environment) and silencing of the air defenses en route before projecting significant forces. Moreover, once the force deployed to Yongbyon, it would be difficult to resupply it or to provide the provisions needed as incentives to secure North Korean support, at least until a ground line of communication is firmly opened. Would such an operation be viable?

If the delays suggested here are too long for national decisionmakers in the United States and the ROK (as might be expected), airpower could help bridge the gap. While the United States might not want to destroy a facility like Yongbyon with a standoff attack, it may be prepared to close the entrances to selected UGFs at Yongbyon, fill the Yongbyon area with scatterable munitions that would explode if people or vehicles come in contact with them,[50] and/or create a no-move zone 3 or 5 km from Yongbyon in which any vehicle traffic would be destroyed. North Korean roads would likely be filled with vehicles carrying internally displaced persons searching for food and other things, making general interdiction of vehicle traffic inappropriate because of the innocent people who would be hurt or killed. Extensive strategic communications would be required to inform North Koreans of these no-move areas to minimize collateral damage. But a no-move zone as

---

[49] Choi He-suk, "U.S. Forces Korea Bolsters Ground Units Ahead of Wartime Control Transfer," *Korea Herald*, June 18, 2012.

[50] Scatterable munitions have a sufficient dud rate that they become scatterable mines.

suggested here can only be declared around known or presumed WMD facilities, and to the extent that facility locations are not known, such a no-move zone policy would not be effective.

Chinese Cooperation

China may well intervene in North Korea following a government collapse there. If it does, it will likely secure many North Korean WMD sites first. For example, Yongbyon is only about 130 km by road from the China but is some 320 km by road from the DMZ. There also appears to be a train line from the Chinese border to Yongbyon. Because there are far fewer North Korean forces along the Chinese border, Chinese forces should reach Yongbyon well before ROK and U.S. forces can. Chinese leaders have apparently considered this possibility; as noted in Chapter Three, China has considered intervening, "to secure nuclear weapons and fissile materials."[51]

Chinese interest in securing nuclear weapons and fissile materials will almost certainly drive Chinese forces to occupy Yongbyon, a place where these materials would almost certainly be found. Within the purview of the nuclear Nonproliferation Treaty, the Chinese would be allowed to secure North Korean nuclear weapons and fissile materials because China is a recognized nuclear power. But the Chinese could also turn these materials over to a faction they support for control of North Korea, hoping to make that faction appear empowered. Doing so would be a clear violation of the nuclear Nonproliferation Treaty; the ROK and the United States should be prepared to make an international case for China not doing so, hoping to deter such actions. Given the likely Chinese sensitivity to U.S. forces going as far north as Yongbyon, the United States could agree to not send forces to Yongbyon if China promised to secure that facility rapidly and eliminate the nuclear weapons and related assets there. Of course, the Chinese will be concerned about ROK acquisition of North Korean nuclear weapons or fissile material. The United States must prevent such an outcome with the same rigor that it would expect China to

---

[51] Glaser, Snyder, and Park, 2008, p. 19.

secure WMD in the areas where it establishes control. See Chapter Nine for more discussion of Chinese intervention.

Collecting Dispersed WMD and Related Assets

Depending on the aggressiveness of North Korean WMD dispersal efforts after a collapse, a significant amount of WMD and related personnel, records, materials, and equipment may be dispersed before ROK and U.S. forces can secure the peacetime WMD facilities. While the ROK and U.S. task forces need to visit WMD facilities and collect what is left there, a different kind of unit is needed to pursue dispersed assets.

WMD collection units would focus on dispersed WMD using three methods. The first method would seek the voluntary surrender of the WMD or related assets, including WMD experts turning themselves in to ROK and U.S. authorities. The leverages for voluntary surrender would be patriotism (ridding Korea of this serious threat) and such incentives as food, medicine, jobs, and money. For example, senior North Korean WMD scientists might be offered $50,000 and a ROK science and technology job if they turn themselves in. These messages could be augmented by television and radio commercials in which former North Korean WMD scientists talk about how well the ROK has treated them and their families, how interesting their new jobs are, and their new quality of life. Alternatively, people who have received rewards for turning in WMD could testify about what the reward has allowed them to buy, while people who postponed WMD surrender could talk about the negative health effects they suffered from having WMD around (especially radioactive materials).

The second method would use the incentives offered in the first method to inspire third parties to act, seeking to have them turn in WMD, experts, or other WMD assets. Thus, anyone in North Korea might be offered $20,000 to identify a senior North Korean WMD scientist, the sum to be paid when the scientist's expertise is confirmed. Experts in information operations and civil affairs would be needed to formulate appropriate messages and seek the voluntary or third-party actions, while ROK scientists would be needed to confirm the expertise of the individuals identified as senior WMD scientists.

The third method for collecting WMD would involve typical police skills for finding WMD and related assets, augmented by military surveillance. Investigators would need to develop and pursue leads about where WMD is located, then search locations and investigate other possibilities. ROK and U.S. military police might conduct some of these activities, and ROK national police or other civilian investigators might do some searching.

ROK personnel could conduct most of the WMD collection. But when dealing with nuclear technologies, the Nonproliferation Treaty would require to U.S. personnel to take the lead. The ROK will not want to appear to be violating this treaty. These personnel need to be trained and prepared for these activities and given the resources and authorities to use to elicit cooperative behavior where possible. Note that these efforts will likely need to continue for years, in part because the ROK and the United States are unlikely ever to know how much WMD and related assets existed before a collapse and therefore how much has yet to be collected.

Stopping Proliferation

Some North Koreans will view WMD as a way to make money in the aftermath of a North Korean government collapse. Worried about having the money to buy food and other necessities, they may be prepared to offer WMD and related assets to the highest bidder, and many bidders would likely be terrorist organizations.

The ROK and the United States must act against proliferation in several ways. When WMD assets are offered on the market, the ROK and the United States must have people in a position to offer winning bids to purchase these assets. They must also seek to disrupt the North Korean criminal organizations that would often be involved in proliferation, reducing their activities and gaining control of some WMD assets in their possession. The ROK and the United States must also seek to interdict WMD movement out of Korea by sea, air, and land. Interdiction of movement by sea can be supported by inspections at all ports and by naval forces acting in support of the PSI. The ROK and the United States can interdict air movement by performing inspections at airfields and stopping aircraft flights where the aircraft have not been inspected. Movement by land can be addressed by setting up inspection points throughout North Korea and especially at border areas.

Given the established strength of North Korean criminal organizations and their likely connections with Chinese and Russian gangs, the ROK and the United States will also need to work with Chinese and Russian authorities to carefully secure their border areas. The Chinese border in particular is very long and rough and has regularly been crossed by North Korean merchants who are often associated with the black market. The ROK and the United States must do their best to elicit Chinese action against such proliferation. They need to explain to Chinese authorities that, if WMD does flow across the Chinese border and is eventually used against the United States or even against China itself, China will not appear to be the great power that it desires to be, having allowed such a disaster to occur. Being a great power is not just a reflection of military and economic strength; it also reflects the assumption of responsibility for supporting global peace and security.

Other Preparations Required

To be ready to perform both the basic WMD-E discussed above and the WMD collection activities, the ROK and the United States will need to make a number of other preparations.

Setting North Korean Beliefs and Expectations

North Koreans involved in WMD programs should find attractive all the concepts described above that would improve their quality of life after unification. In addition, it will be far easier to secure North Korean cooperation in WMD-E if the WMD scientists and others feel that the ROK will treat them well, as opposed to treating them as criminals. Knowing this, North Korea has likely told these personnel that the ROK will imprison them as war criminals if they defect or otherwise fall into ROK control. Thus, an important preparation would be an effort to send leaflets and other communications into North Korean WMD facilities that show ROK scientific facilities and offers rewards for defectors from the WMD programs, thereby expressing the value the ROK would associate with these scientists.

International Coordination

The key international coordination in this area will be with countries having sufficient expertise in countering WMD to provide counter-WMD specialty forces to augment ROK and U.S. WMD-E efforts. The key WMD-E teams are often small (a dozen personnel or so), but they use highly specialized equipment and have many years of appropriate training. While only a few countries would have such capabilities, even small numbers of forces could provide significant support to the ROK and the United States. A particular specialty area of interest would be the ability to breach UGF entrances that have been secured, a situation that ROK and U.S. forces will discover in likely hundreds of locations.

The ROK and the United States will also want to work with the countries in Northeast Asia to prevent as much WMD proliferation as possible. Cooperation on PSI will help this effort, but as noted above, cooperation with China in particular will be critical. This will be particularly true if China intervenes in North Korea and secures some of the WMD facilities, as discussed above. Well before a North Korean government collapse, the United States and the ROK will need to share an understanding of the treaty agreements relating to WMD internationally, seeking to establish international expectations. These efforts should then be repeated in the aftermath of a North Korean government collapse to continue the pressure on all regional countries to abide by the international agreements.

Supply, Equipment, and Financial Preparation

The ROK and the United States will need to have food, medicines, money, and other incentives to offer North Korean military leaders and others to gain access to the North Korean WMD more rapidly. Because of the potential rapidity with which events could develop and the likely delay in bringing these items in from the outside, the ROK and the United States will need to have the supplies to cover the first two months or so on hand in the ROK. These will mainly be for gaining cooperation with North Korean military units and the scientists and other experts associated with the WMD program and their families. ROK and U.S. forces will also need the authority to use such incentives and will need reasonable expectations about what they should offer. They will also need the authority to grant amnesty or otherwise reassure the key North Korean personnel and their families that they will be taken care of and have a good quality of life. And the ROK government will need to have identified jobs for North Korean scientists and others to transition them out of the North Korean WMD program.

Building ROK Political Consensus

As noted above, many in the ROK community will likely be opposed to providing incentives to the North Korean military and the North Korean civilians responsible for WMD development. The ROK will thus need to explain the costs of fighting to gain control of WMD (including likely North Korean use of WMD) relative to the costs for negotiating WMD surrender for various incentives. While providing the incentives will appear inappropriate to some, the net costs will likely be far less. These trade-offs need to be discussed over time, well before unification, so that the ROK population generally supports such efforts.

Legal Challenges

Under the ROK constitution, all North Koreans are citizens of Korea. That implies that U.S. forces, in particular, and likely also ROK forces will not be able to detain North Korean military personnel or WMD experts without their approval or a specific legal reason. The ROK legal system therefore needs to be prepared before unification to allow detention of these personnel for some time to prevent them from fleeing to third parties and to secure critical information from them. The alternative would be to accuse the WMD developers of "crimes against humanity," but such accusations would taint their future even if they were thoroughly cooperative. Thus, the detention privilege should exist without designating an individual as a criminal and should allow enough time, given everyone else to be debriefed, for thorough debriefing of all personnel. This could amount to several months, although in some cases, personnel could be released much sooner.

Military Preparation and Training

The ROK and the United States are preparing specialty forces (such as nuclear experts) for performing the WMD-E process. But the numbers of specialty personnel required and the range of skills needed will likely exceed current preparations. These requirements need to be continuously updated, and training plans will need to be revised. Particular emphasis should be placed on language skills for debriefing North Korean WMD-related personnel, WMD records, and the markings on WMD and WMD facilities. In many of these specialty areas, the vocabulary in use in North Korea will be different from comparable vocabulary in the ROK; thus, special translation dictionaries will likely be required to help normal language experts. In addition, all military personnel should be trained in North Korean danger signs, for example, those designating places that are contaminated or artillery shells containing chemical weapons. Finally, ROK and U.S. forces will require a range of specialty equipment and supplies to characterize North Korean WMD, to monitor potential spills or other threats, and to treat personnel who are affected by the WMD.

CHAPTER SEVEN

Challenges of and Responses to Security Services and Human Rights Disasters

North Korea maintains large security services in addition to the military forces discussed in Chapter Six. If anything, these security services would be expected to be more loyal to the regime and more hostile toward any outside intervention. And while the security services are mainly lightly armed, they also possess some heavy military equipment. Therefore, any ROK and U.S. intervention in North Korea would need to plan for the "demilitarization" of these forces as well. This report addresses them separately from the military forces because there are some important differences in how these forces should be handled. One major difference with the security forces is that they also have responsibility for North Korea's political prisons, places where the intense suffering of the prisoners could be exacerbated by extermination orders in the context of government collapse and anticipated ROK and U.S. intervention.

The Challenges of North Korean Security Services and Potential Human Rights Disasters

The North Korean security services include some 50,000 to 90,000 members of the State Security Department,[1] some 210,000 members of the Ministry of Public Security (which also includes the normal

---

[1] The lower estimate is from Gause, 2012, p. 17. The higher estimate adds the 30,000 to 40,000 personnel of the border guards who were recently attached to the Ministry of State

police forces),[2] and some 10,000 members of the Military Security Command.[3] In addition, there are some 50,000 to 120,000 personnel in the Guard Command,[4] which provides security for the regime elite in addition to performing other functions. These numbers are highly uncertain, in part because of North Korea's efforts to deny information on these forces.

The North Korean security services pose challenges in the post-collapse context, as illustrated in Figure 7.1, that correlate strongly with some of those the North Korean military poses. To contrast the two, the North Korean security services are less likely to pose major combat challenges (because they are not organized as combat forces) but are more likely to pose threats of insurgency and criminal activity, especially given their loyalty to the North Korean regime and their greater tendency to work in smaller groups or even individually. In addition, these personnel have been responsible for imposing the regime's discipline on the public, creating many incentives for the public to practice retaliation and revenge against security service personnel in the aftermath of a collapse. Their disappearing into insurgency and/or criminal behavior may partially shield them against such actions.

North Korea is well established as a human rights disaster. Six major North Korean prison camps contain perhaps 200,000 or so political prisoners in extremely abusive conditions, and another 180 or so detention and reeducation facilities house thousands more.[5] These camps support the regime by brutally suppressing any perceived dissidents and their relatives. The regime takes care of the camps by denying that there are human rights abuses and by protecting the guards from the human rights accusations that they would otherwise have to deal

---

Security. See Joseph S. Bermudez, Jr., *The Armed Forces of North Korea*, London, England: I.B. Tauris & Co. Ltd., 2001, p. 174.

[2]   Gause, 2012, p. 27.

[3]   Gause, 2012, pp. 36–37.

[4]   The lower estimate is from Bermudez, 2012, p. 196. The higher estimate is from "Guard Command," North Korea Leadership Watch website, April 29, 2012.

[5]   Shin Hyon-hee, "Up to 200,000 Incarcerated in N.K. Prison Camps," *Korea Herald*, June 20, 2012.

Figure 7.1
Security Service and Human Rights Challenges in North Korea

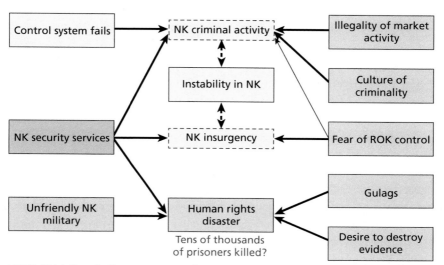

NOTE: Thick lines indicate a strong influence; thin line indicates a moderate influence.
RAND *RR331-7.1*

with. As discussed in Chapter Three, once the North Korean government fails, an even more severe human rights disaster could develop: the execution of the prisoners to prevent them from testifying of the abuses they have suffered. The Ministry of State Security personnel, in particular, are responsible for running the North Korean political prisons. The guards and others at the political prisons and detention facilities could attempt to exterminate the prisoners, in addition to the abuses they have already committed.

Dealing with the Security Services

As noted in Chapter Four, many of the security service personnel are guilty of serious crimes, particularly torture and other human rights abuses in arrests, interrogations, and imprisonment. Many security service personnel have also been actively involved in taking bribes. And some significant number appear to be involved in black market and related activities. But as noted previously, the ROK will lack the prison capacity or the judicial system capacity to deal with all these crimes and must therefore decide which ones to subject to criminal charges and which to excuse through amnesty or similar provisions.[6] The more security service personnel subjected to criminal charges, the more likely this population will be to try to transition to criminal and insurgent activities. Seeking to imprison too many security service personnel will make stabilization of North Korea far more difficult and costly.

Determining Which Security Service Personnel to Characterize as Criminals

The ROK government should pursue a more thorough analysis of North Korean security service personnel. It should identify their activities in terms of the likely level of abusive behavior in each job and the numbers of personnel involved in each job at any given time. It should also seek to determine the degree to which prison guards and others practicing highly abusive behavior tend to stay in such positions, as opposed to being promoted or transferred to other positions, to permit a more complete assessment of those who have committed highly abusive behavior over time. Simultaneously, an assessment should be made of each job to determine the likely variation in criminal behavior for those holding the job. This could be accomplished, for example, by talking with former prison camp guards or prisoners who have defected. In jobs for which the criminal behavior varies significantly, more investigation and analysis of each person would be required to achieve a reliable legal outcome. For jobs in which the criminal behavior is highly similar across individuals, it may be far easier to assemble the evidence needed to convict the truly guilty.

Identifying and Detaining the Security Service Personnel

A key effort in dealing with the security service personnel will be in identifying them. Some security service personnel operate in large

---

[6]   This author believes that criminals should be held to account for their crimes but that, in the difficult circumstances of a North Korean government collapse, some compromises may be required, focusing criminal action against the most serious North Korean criminal behavior, especially against prison camp guards and others who have practiced torture and other serious human rights violations.

units, not unlike North Korean military personnel. These units would include border guards who are now part of the Ministry of State Security,[7] as well as many of the elements of the Guard Command. The ROK military should be able to identify these personnel, much as it does the North Korean military, going to the security service units to disarm them as units and putting the unit largely into some form of public service. In practice, these units should also be treated as part of the unified Korean military for the first couple of years after unification, imposing military discipline and allowing debriefings and the application of biometric screenings to these individuals.

The same concept would apply to the North Korean prison camps and other detention facilities: The security service personnel should normally be with their units. But many of these security service personnel would expect to be arrested and treated as criminals; they may well attempt to flee their units before U.S. and ROK forces arrive, complicating the efforts to identify these personnel. ROK and U.S. forces could identify and detain these personnel still with these units but would then have to pursue the personnel who have escaped. Once these personnel are identified, they will more than likely require detention because they will be investigated for criminal behavior and would likely try to escape to avoid prosecution. Thus, to keep from losing individuals, ROK and U.S. forces may need to hold these personnel in the very prisons and detention facilities they once ran.

The local police forces would also need to be identified and assembled. The ROK will need to decide how to handle the police, who have tended to be corrupted by bribery and related crimes. In some cases, the retention of the local police could be a bad idea because they are too corrupt and too opposed by the local population. In other cases, retaining the local police may be the better option, providing officers familiar with local conditions and able to restrain local criminal organizations. In some cases, this may also be an individual decision, retaining some police but removing those perceived as being more corrupt or abusive. Where police are not to be retained, they should likely be replaced by a combination of North Korean military personnel and ROK personnel

---

[7]   Kim and Choi, 2012.

who are prepared to work with and monitor the North Koreans. The ROK personnel assigned to local leadership positions (such as mayors) should be involved in such decisions. If the police are replaced, decisions would need to be made on whether they would be criminally prosecuted and, if not, how they would be employed in some form of public service. To limit the movement of local police into criminal organizations, the police not retained and not prosecuted should likely be moved to a new geographic area.

Many other security service personnel operate individually or in smaller units. These would include agents who have monitored individuals, seeking to identify those who were "disloyal." These personnel would likely want to disappear to avoid both criminal prosecution and revenge attacks by those they have acted against. Some of these individuals may be found by examining identification cards, but others will have created fake identification cards to help them hide. Thus, it will be important to find local and/or national records of security service personnel, which might also provide information helpful for criminal prosecutions. Local and national headquarters of the security services should thus become early targets for visiting and securing records.

Once records of the security service personnel are available, they need to be made available in a distributed manner, to check against personnel everywhere. Thus, the ROK should plan checkpoints in major transportation hubs and potentially use face-recognition software to identify potential matches. In addition, North Koreans who are well dressed, who appear well fed, or whose hands suggest that they have not performed manual labor should receive particular attention.[8] Investigating teams should also be created to track down security personnel, with a particular focus on individuals who are likely to be subject to criminal prosecution. Many security personnel may seek to hide in criminal organizations or insurgent groups, so identifying these groups and examining these individuals should receive special effort.

---

[8]   North Korean security personnel use similar procedures for identifying North Koreans who have lived in China for some time. See Barbara Demick, *Nothing to Envy*, New York: Spiegel & Grau, 2009, pp. 229–230.

The security service personnel who initially escape detection will need to be detained once caught. Otherwise, they are likely to try to escape again, despite being put in "military" units and subjected to military justice. To easily justify detention, the ROK should declare all security service organizations to be part of the combined military when unification occurs, thereby making individual disappearance a violation of military discipline: desertion. The ROK should widely broadcast this plan so that North Korean personnel could not claim that they were unaware of having violated military rules. The major challenge that the ROK may face is in finding sufficient housing for detaining the security service personnel until they can be sorted out and a decision made on whether to hold them over for criminal prosecution or to assign them to public service activities. The ROK also needs to decide whether to employ some of the security personnel not designated as criminals to help track down their counterparts; North Koreans may be more capable of doing so than others, given their knowledge of locations and personnel in North Korea.

Dealing with Criminal Behavior

The ROK will have to deal with two groups of criminals. The first are security service personnel it determines to be subject to prosecution. The second are North Koreans imprisoned for criminal as opposed to political reasons. Both groups will need to be detained and analyzed, with the former requiring judicial action and the latter requiring at least judicial review (as some of them may not have really committed serious crimes). The ROK will not want to send North Koreans who were truly guilty of murder and burglary and other crimes into society, fearing repetition of their criminal behavior.

The challenge will be finding places to detain these individuals and providing adequate ROK judges and lawyers to handle the criminal proceedings in a reasonable time frame. ROK prisons are already essentially full, as noted above, and the ROK would probably not want to move criminals from North Korea into the South. The ROK will not want to use the North Korean political prisons to detain criminals other than former the guards of those prisons, given the international stigma that would be associated with these locations. But the North has capacity for tens of thousands of detainees in detention and reeducation centers and criminal prisons that could be used. In preparation for unification, the ROK needs to identify these locations and their capacities, then decide whether the total capacity will likely be sufficient, based on ROK decisions for providing selective amnesty. The ROK is unlikely to have sufficient judges and attorneys to try several hundred thousand security service personnel for their misdeeds and needs to study these capabilities and use them to define a reasonable set of selective amnesty decisions. The ROK personnel will also have to prevent desertions of both soldiers and security service personnel to avoid overwhelming detention and judicial facilities. Indeed, some criminal or insurgent groups may become strong enough to be able to attack detention facilities, seeking to free the prisoners. Thus, the ROK may need to retain significant military presence around these facilities to deter and/or defeat such attacks.

While senior North Korean military personnel should eventually be retired after a period of public service, retirement will less likely be applicable to security service personnel. Most senior security service personnel will have been aware of especially the most serious crimes their subordinates have committed. The ROK must decide how to handle the senior personnel who may or may not have committed crimes during their early years in the security services but then ordered criminal behavior, such as human rights violations, when they assumed more senior security service responsibilities. For example, the ROK needs to determine whether to allow these personnel to retire with reasonable pensions to avoid confrontation and their likely efforts to join insurgent or criminal groups, or to hold them to account for the crimes that they committed or at least sanctioned.

In the end, the ROK will need to decide how large a prison population it is willing to hold. It will also have to decide whether to end the moratorium on capital punishment, as many of the crimes that have been committed especially in the political prisons would surely warrant such sentences. If a significant percentage of the security service personnel are imprisoned, there may not be adequate facilities in North Korea, and the price of keeping these individuals imprisoned may be very high. But if the ROK fails to deal with especially the crimes against humanity that many North Korean security service personnel have committed, the stigma of these crimes may taint Korea for many years.

Taking Care of Security Service Personnel Not Determined to Be Criminals

As noted above, most security service personnel who are determined not to be criminals should be placed in "public service" activities similar to those for the military personnel, as discussed in Chapter Six. But these personnel should also be monitored closely because they may have a tendency to want to escape, potentially to join insurgent or criminal groups. In addition, the ROK needs to decide how many North Korean police will be retained in that function. The police need to be monitored to confirm that they are not being bribed or participating in other illegal activities. It will be important to keep all these noncriminal former security service personnel available for follow-up debriefings and for testimony against the security service personnel undergoing criminal prosecution. The noncriminal personnel may provide major sources of information on previous misbehavior; desertions of such personnel may undermine the ability of the courts to take action against security service personnel who had been involved in serious crimes. But if the judicial cases take years to resolve, it will be problematic to keep these personnel in public service—another reason to limit the number of criminal prosecutions through selective amnesty.

However long the prosecutions take in any given area, the noncriminal security personnel should eventually be released from public service when appropriate jobs are available. At least some of these personnel will probably be held longer than the North Korean military personnel in public service to participate in additional debriefings and criminal trials, as required.

Preparing the Legal System for Handling Security Service Personnel

The ROK must plan to administer true justice against North Korean security service personnel. North Korea is well established as a country that imprisons many people without judicial proceedings and exposes them to torture and other forms of severe punishment.[9] The ROK will want to apply due process and the rule of law in taking legal action against the North Korean security service criminals in a way that meets the scrutiny of the world. In practice, this means employing the same judicial procedures that would normally be used in the ROK to convict citizens of serious crimes.

This requirement will help set the number of criminal cases that the ROK could pursue. In addition to security service personnel, there will be other employees of the North Korean government and members of North Korean criminal organizations who should be subjected to criminal proceedings. The limitations of prison space were examined above, but the limitations of judges and lawyers must also be considered. While the author could find no definitive statistics on the degree to which the ROK judicial system is currently employed, a number of references suggested that the ROK judges and lawyers are already being used to the existing capacity and perhaps beyond. In recognition of this fact, the ROK enacted a new law in 2007 that significantly modifies its system for training lawyers, seeking to increase the number and quality of lawyers over time.[10]

The ROK must therefore prepare in various ways to meet the standards of due process and the rule of law, which would include handling North Korean criminals relatively promptly. The number of individuals who may be subject to criminal proceedings is thus a key factor in the ROK preparations. The material above indicates that there

---

[9] Marzuki Darusman, "Report of the Special Rapporteur on the Situation of Human Rights in the Democratic People's Republic of Korea," New York: Human Rights Council, UN General Assembly, February 1, 2013.

[10] The old system required prospective lawyers to earn an undergraduate LL.B. degree, followed by several years of preparation for the bar examination, which few (5 percent) passed. This kept the number of lawyers in Korea small. The new law that went into effect in 2009 requires prospective lawyers to first obtain a bachelors degree and then enter a three-year JD program, after which they take a bar exam that is not as restrictive. The new system admits 2,000 students to law schools throughout Korea each year and anticipates that 75 percent of those admitted will pass the bar examination. This approach is intended to significantly increase the number of ROK lawyers. See Harvard Law School, Program on the Legal Profession, "The Legal Profession of the Republic of South Korea," 2011, and "Too Many Lawyers?" editorial, *Korea Herald*, December 9, 2010.

are some 320,000 to 430,000 security service personnel (counting the Guard Command). Of these, perhaps 70 percent or so would likely be guilty of some form of criminal behavior, assuming that the acceptance of bribes is included. Presumably at least 100,000 would have committed more serious crimes,[11] such as crimes against humanity, for which amnesty is unlikely to be offered. These numbers are huge and would require significant preparation of the ROK legal and prison systems.

The author had difficulty finding authoritative data on the number of judges and lawyers in South Korea—different sites presented fairly different numbers. The best estimate suggests that the ROK had about 2,000 judges of all kinds in 2008, which likely extrapolates to about 2,400 today, including judges with little or no experience in criminal matters.[12] The ROK also has some 9,600 lawyers.[13] In addition,

> a three-judge panel is mandatory in such serious cases as civil cases in which the value in question exceeds 50 million Won (equivalent to about U.S.$37,000), and criminal cases in which the defendant can be sentenced to death, penal servitude or imprisonment of more than one year.[14]

Presumably, all the North Korean personnel not provided amnesty would be subject to imprisonment for more than one year, requiring

---

[11] See the later discussion on taking control of the camps that suggests that the Ministry of State Security might have some 24,000 to 47,000 political prison staff, many of whom would likely be considered for criminal prosecution based on anecdotal evidence, such as found in Harden, 2012, pp. 25, 44–53.

[12] See data from 2003 to 2008 for the ROK at UN Office of Drugs and Crime, "Total Professional Judges or Magistrates as at 31 December," Criminal Justice Resources Excel Workbook, 2011. A more recent reference on authorized judges says: "The number of judges to be assigned to various levels of courts under the main sentence of Article 5 (3) of the Court Organization Act shall be 2,844 persons." See "Act on the Fixed Number of Judges of Various Levels of Courts," *Statutes of the Republic of Korea*, April 12, 2011.

[13] The *Korea Herald*, citing a report from the Korean Bar Association, said that "there is one lawyer per 5,178 Korean residents" ("Too Many Lawyers?" 2010). The Korean population is about 49.8 million people, which if divided by 5,178 people per lawyer, yields a lawyer population of about 9,600.

[14] "The Judiciary System in Korea," Asian Info website, 2010.

the use of three judges under current law. If roughly half of the judges (some 1,200) could try criminal cases in North Korea, that would allow no more than 400 simultaneous cases. If, in turn, the average North Korean case took three days to conclude, only some 30,000 could be done per year. In practice, because of the seriousness of the cases to be tried, they will likely take much more than three days on average, especially given the heinousness of the crimes against humanity. Thus, one-half of the ROK judges or more could be tied up for several years just to try the more serious cases. Such a development would make judicial proceedings in the ROK unacceptably slow.

As noted above, the limits of the ROK judicial and prison systems should encourage the ROK to identify a variety of criminal offenses, such as bribery, for which selective amnesty would be applied.[15] The ROK must also consider how it will staff the prisons where North Koreans will be detained. The ROK needs to make systematic estimates of the number of North Korean personnel, both in the security services and elsewhere, who would be guilty of crimes and not subject to amnesty and who would thus require judicial proceedings and potential incarceration. These numbers need to be measured against the capacity of the judicial and prison systems, and a purposeful estimate needs to be made of the amnesty to be offered to keep the judicial and prison requirements within acceptable limits.

The ROK could seek to expedite judicial action on accused North Korean criminals by adjusting its legal arrangements. It could allow a declaration of a legal emergency in which judges, normally retired at ages 63 to 65,[16] could be recalled and/or kept in service, hopefully adding a few hundred in the short term. Provision could be made for having only one or two judges preside over serious cases during a legal emergency. And some lawyers with more than, say, 10 or 15 years criminal law experience could be converted to judges during a legal

---

[15] According to a UN report, South Korea had 14,928 staff for its adult prisons that had a capacity of 45,250 individuals without overcrowding in 2009. See UN Office on Drugs and Crime, "Criminal Justice System Resources," data for 2009. The ROK will not likely be able to use many North Korea prison staff to manage prisoners because many of them will be among those being held for criminal charges.

[16] "The Judiciary System in Korea," 2010.

emergency. And some prospective lawyers who had almost passed the Korean bar exam could be accepted as lawyers during a legal emergency, with their legal actions to be reviewed during and after the emergency to make sure the North Koreans are being treated fairly and to determine whether these individuals would continue as lawyers after the emergency.

If as many as 100,000 North Koreans would need to be detained awaiting legal action, with many of them eventually imprisoned for their crimes, the ROK would need to add 25,000 or so prison staff. Initially, these personnel may need to come largely from a combination of ROK and North Korean military personnel and/or the ROK national police, all of whom would require special training. The ROK military and national police should provide that training now to several thousand personnel, a hedge that would make the ROK partially prepared should the North Korean government collapse.

The ROK should also survey North Korean detention centers other than the political prisons to identify the capacity for housing both those being detained for trial and those who have been given prison sentences. In making these arrangements, the ROK needs to decide whether criminal cases will be tried in North Korea, in South Korea, or in some combination. Moving judges and other court officials to North Korea may be difficult, but finding jail space to hold North Koreans undergoing trial in the South could also be challenging.

Preventing Human Rights Disasters

Massive murders at the political prisons would be morally repugnant in both the ROK and the United States. Only prompt ROK and U.S. intervention to take control of these camps will prevent such a human rights disaster. But the six major camps are all well north of Pyongyang, making it difficult for ground forces to promptly reach and free these camps.[17] This mission will compete with others to be performed

---

[17] Three of the camps are located about 80 km north of Pyongyang, while the other three are in the far northeast of North Korea. See One Free Korea, "North Korea's Largest Concentration Camps on Google Earth," March 2012.

by ROK and U.S. forces but needs to be done with ground forces that can secure the camps and protect the prisoners. This could be one of the most time-urgent tasks.

Taking Control of the Camps

It will be difficult for the ROK and United States to send adequate military personnel promptly into all these camps to seize them and take control: The size and potential hostility of the security service personnel and the surrounding North Korean military forces will require major force commitments. Even ignoring the surrounding North Korean military forces, the number of political prison staff who could be armed to oppose ROK and U.S. intervention would apparently be too large for securing these political prisons with a few special forces teams. The author could not find estimates on the number of political prison staff either across the political prisons or for individual prisons. Nevertheless, as noted above it is usually estimated that there are 150,000 to 200,000 prisoners incarcerated in the main six prisons.[18] The UN maintains data on the aggregate numbers of adult criminal prisoners and prison staff across many countries that help suggest the potential prisoner to staff ratio.[19] In 2009, some 59 countries reported both adult prisoners and staff, and 75 percent of these countries had a prisoner-to-staff ratio of 4.3 or less, while 90 percent of the countries had a ratio of 6.3 or less.[20] From these ratios and the uncertainty in the number of prisoners, North Korean political prisons could have between about 24,000 (150,000/6.3) and 46,500 (200,000/4.3) prison staff. Several of the political prisons (e.g., Camps 14 and 18, both near

---

[18] Shin Hyon-hee, 2012, reports that, "[a]ccording to Amnesty International, 150,000 to 200,000 are incarcerated in six sprawling gulag-style prisons—Camp No. 12 in Hoeryeong, No. 14 in Gaecheon, No. 15 in Yodeok, No. 16 in Hwaseong, No. 18 in Bukchang and No. 25 in Cheongjin."

[19] UN Office on Drugs and Crime, "Data: Statistics on Criminal Justice," 2013, spreadsheets on "Criminal Justice System Resources" and on "Persons Detained."

[20] North Korea would be expected to have a relatively high prisoner-to-staff ratio, given the extent to which brutality is used to control the prisoners and the limited total size of the Ministry of State Security personnel (50,000 to 90,000, noted earlier). The author performed these calculations using the UN data.

Kaechon) are believed to have 50,000 or so prisoners, which would mean about 6,000 to 12,000 prison staff each. Others (e.g., Camp 25 at Chongjin and Camp 16 at Hwasong) are believed to have perhaps 10,000 to 15,000 prisoners or about 1,200 to 3,600 prison staff.[21] In practice, these numbers could be far smaller. For example, in Camp 14, the garment factory reportedly included about 2,500 prisoners but only one prison staff member—the factory superintendent. The other managing roles were played by prisoners selected to be foremen. And many of these foremen also committed serious crimes,[22] highlighting the fact that not only prison staff but also some prisoners could eventually require criminal proceedings. Thus, ROK and U.S. intelligence need to make a more purposeful estimate of the number of prison staff at each prison; presumably, the numbers at the larger political prisons could be as few as 1,000 or so, given the nature of the political prison organization. More likely, the numbers of prison staff are around 2,000 for the larger prisons and 500 for the smaller ones. But the prisons might also be defended by nearby North Korean military personnel, which could add to the number of defenders.

If the prison staff expect to be taken into custody for criminal prosecution, they would likely be armed and prepared to confront any ROK and U.S. force arriving at each prison. This suggests that a force of at least a battalion of soldiers would be required to promptly secure the smaller camps (arriving with overwhelming force), and a force of about a ROK and U.S. ground force BCT may be required to secure each of the larger political prisons, assuming no major intervention by the North Korean military. It will take some time (perhaps at least weeks) for sufficient ROK and U.S. forces to reach as far north as the major political prisons, although the smaller prisons might be handled by air assault, if sufficient helicopters could be committed and the air defense environment mitigated. Specific ROK and U.S. forces should be allocated to each prison and a plan established to deliver them to the prisons as rapidly as possible.

---

[21] The numbers of prisoners come from One Free Korea, 2012. The six political prison camps are listed below the first map.

[22] Harden, 2012, p. 92.

This potential for delay in reaching the political prisons raises questions about alternative approaches. For example, the prisoners significantly outnumber the guards but yet generally do not act against the guards because of the known consequences. To give the prisoners a chance to survive, should ROK and U.S. airpower be used to attack guard weapon facilities, guard towers, and other places guards use in controlling the prisoners? Should airpower be used to open holes in the security fences keeping prisoners in the facilities and to kill the power at camps to disable electrical fences and lights used at night for monitoring the prisoners? Should ROK and U.S. special forces be sent to the camps either to assist the prisoners in escaping or to assist the prisoners in seizing control from the guards? Under such circumstances, are the prisoners more likely to survive by rebelling against the guards? Or will such a rebellion just give the guards the excuse they want to exterminate many of the prisoners? All these actions carry considerable risk but potentially no more so than waiting for weeks before dealing with each camp, thereby allowing the camp officials time to exterminate many prisoners. Should the camps be closely monitored and these interventions begun only when extermination efforts start? Or would delaying that long give the guards too much of an advantage in killing the prisoners? All these factors need to be considered and trade-offs analyzed to determine preferred courses of action. Some of the prisons that may be easier for ROK and U.S. ground forces to access may be treated more aggressively than are the prisons where it will take longer for ROK and U.S. ground forces to reach.

Once ROK and U.S. forces reach the prisons, they should try to promptly secure them. To do so, these forces will need considerable intelligence on the activities of the prison staff, their potential preparations to defend or destroy the camps, the defenses in and around the camps (e.g., any minefields or electrified fences), and information about the camp command staff. A ROK-U.S. negotiating team should be first sent to the camps, several days before the full force can arrive,[23]

---

[23] The ROK and U.S. forces might insert an airborne or air assault battalion to support such a negotiating force and provide it air cover to minimize the chances that the negotiators could be taken hostage.

seeking the surrender of the prison staffs and to prevent the need for combat to secure the camps. This effort might actually work with some camps because the prison command staffs are likely to abandon the camps, hoping to evade identification and capture. It could be supported by air drops of food and other supplies to each prison to suggest that the ROK and the United States are concerned about the condition of those in the prisons. And selected air cover might be provided to try to stop wholesale executions. The ROK and U.S. forces need to decide whether to interdict major movements of prison staff away from the prisons, although allowing the escapes will undoubtedly facilitate rapid seizure of the prisons and thus be an expedient short-term measure.[24]

Still, the process of seizing the camps should not be delayed by negotiations, especially if the prison staffs use that time to kill more prisoners. Thus, a continual feed of information from throughout each camp will be required, which may be challenging, given the sizes of the camps. ROK-U.S. forces can anticipate having to engage in combat with the prison staff in at least some cases, and the prison staff may use prisoners as human shields to complicate ROK and U.S. attacks. ROK-U.S. forces involved in securing the camps must thus be prepared for such combat situations, having developed the tactics, techniques, and procedures required to minimize the collateral damage to prisoners. Care should be taken to identify any fatalities at the camps so that as complete a record as possible can be created on the prison staff and prisoners. In addition, some prisoners should be recruited to help identify prison staff who may seek to hide among the prisoners.

An alternative overall approach would be to encourage Chinese military intervention to secure some of the political prisons. The most obvious candidate prison is near Hoeryong and only some 10 to 15 km

---

[24] ROK and U.S. forces would prefer not to have to fight their way into each camp, delaying the relief of the prisoners and likely causing substantial collateral damage. The ROK and the United States might even want to encourage the prison staffs to escape to make securing the camps easier, likely saving the lives of many prisoners. But letting the prison staff escape would complicate subsequent efforts to arrest and try these individuals for their crimes. If ROK and U.S. air forces attack early to prevent prison staff escape efforts, other prison staff members may abandon hope of escape and focus on defending the prison. Thus, the ROK and the United States need to decide how to handle such escape efforts instead of leaving the decision to be made ad hoc, with little thorough thought.

from the Chinese border. The Chongjin political prison is perhaps 100 km or so from the Chinese border, although it is also only about 10 km from the coast, if a port or amphibious landing could be staged in that area. Chapter Nine will discuss the potential Chinese role in dealing with these camps.

Actions to Be Taken at the Political Prisons

As ROK-U.S. forces secure each North Korean political prison, they will want to determine which individuals present are prison staff and prisoners serving as abusive foremen, and which are purely prisoners. The forces will then want to move the prison staff and abusive foremen to locations where they can be detained but also protected from former prisoners who may wish to seek revenge against at least some prison staff. This may mean swapping housing for the prison staff with some of the prisoners and leaving a large enough military force at the camp to secure the prisoners and maintain order. Moving the prison staff would be complicated because at least some of them will have their families living with them; the ROK and the United States should plan to move the families to some other part of the prison to avoid implying that the families are also being incarcerated (as the current North Korea would do). ROK-U.S. forces should then focus on collecting personal information and biometrics from the former prison staff to assist in the investigation process and to provide means of tracking these personnel should any of them escape. In particular, camp personnel files should be a major target of the intervening forces because these files should provide substantial information to assist in criminal proceedings.

Some of the prisoners will also be guilty of criminal activities. Many will have served as foremen in different parts of the prison and committed brutal acts against their fellow prisoners. The ROK needs to decide how to handle these individuals (in particular, in which cases, if any, to extend amnesty). The military forces securing the prison then need to identify prisoners who have committed crimes not covered by amnesty and detain them along with the prison staff. The military forces will need to get substantial assistance from the other prisoners to identify these individuals.

On the prisoner side, the major changes that ROK-U.S. forces should enact immediately on reaching the prison would be providing the prisoners more food, medical care, and information about what is happening. This would imply that ROK-U.S. forces would need to bring with them substantial quantities of food and medical supplies and make provision for regular resupply.[25] In addition, clothing, coats, shoes, blankets, and other basic life items should also be supplied.

Meanwhile, ROK-U.S. forces should be identifying the prisoners, taking pictures, and collecting biometrics. The forces should seek to determine who among the prisoners' family members have also been incarcerated, so that families can be reunited. The forces should also collect several kinds of information on each prisoner. First, the forces should seek to determine the jobs and activities that the prisoners had before incarceration. Some of the former prisoners may be very valuable in filling governmental positions and other jobs (such as doctors) for the unified Korea, having been taken from such positions for political reasons. Second, testimony should be taken on the crimes of the former prison staff, information that could be used in subsequent criminal trials.

While it would be ideal to move the prisoners out of the prisons, doing so would take them away from housing (however poor), sanitation facilities, and jobs. For most political prisoners, the housing and jobs they had before imprisonment have likely been given to others, particularly because entire families have often been incarcerated together. Finding housing and jobs outside the prison camps will take time.

---

[25] For subsistence-level consumption, about 30 tons of food would be required per day for 50,000 prisoners, suggesting that more adequate consumption would run about 50 tons of food per day. This estimate is based on the national subsistence requirement of about 5 million tons per year for 24 million people. See Chapter Four.

Building housing inside the prisons would require creating construction work teams and the ROK providing building supplies. Prison conditions could be substantially improved with the addition of new buildings supported by a more reliable flow of energy to provide heat in the winter. In some places, the military public service units in the vicinity could provide this construction, but it would likely be better to form such construction teams from the former prisoners.

ROK-U.S. forces will need to establish rules for handling the former prisoners at each camp. Some former prisoners will insist on leaving the prisons, which they should presumably be allowed to do once they have been identified and their testimony about the criminal activities of the former prison staff has been taken. Careful records should be maintained to recall any departing former prisoners who have critical testimony. In various places around North Korea, ROK-U.S. forces should seek to build housing, identify jobs for the departing former prisoners, and give them priority in transfer to these homes and jobs.

Some former prisoners may have escaped from the prisons during the collapse period, likely after ROK and U.S. military air attacks against the camps. Once ROK and U.S. forces arrive at the camps, some of these personnel may want to "break back in" to take advantage of improved conditions and lacking other places to go. Given the likely shortages of food and other critical supplies in the surrounding area, even individuals who had not been prisoners might want to enter the prisons for the food, medical care, and other resources being provided. The ROK and the United States need to develop rules for how non-prisoners should be handled, but presumably the preferred solution is to provide adequate food and other supplies also to the civilians in the vicinity of the prison camps to encourage them to stay in their homes and jobs and discourage them from flocking to the prisons after ROK and U.S. forces have secured the prisons.

Preparing for Freeing the Political Prisons

The process of freeing those in political prisons will have extremely high intelligence requirements during a time when there will also be other serious intelligence requirements (e.g., locating WMD). It is therefore critical to compile substantial intelligence information on these camps now to allow the real-time intelligence collection to focus on changes and new developments as the assaults are staged. Information that should be collected now would include the identities and personalities of the key leaders in each camp, the nature of camp facilities and potential defensive positions, the locations of prisoners and potential escape routes, the nature of camp jobs, where prison staff could be detained after the camps are seized, and the key infrastructure improvements the camps need to improve the lives of the former prisoners. This information could then be augmented in the real time with information on the actions prison staff members take to prepare defenses and/or kill prisoners, any efforts to remove the families of prison staff from the prisons, the potential departure of senior camp leadership, and movements of North Korean military units to potentially support the prison staff.

The intelligence organizations would also want to assemble information on the prisoners. This would include the extent to which some prisoners are also involved in criminal activities, generally as a function of the jobs they perform, and plans made to detain these individuals in addition to the prison staff. Some prisoners might also be former North Korean government officials who could be valuable in supporting the unified Korean government. Intelligence on these individuals should be compiled so that the forces going into a prison could look for these individuals and get them promptly transferred to the proper authorities.

As noted above, the forces assigned to free the political prisons will require special training. In particular, they will need to prepare to defeat opposition from the prison staff and neighboring North Korean military forces and to do so even if the North Koreans use prisoners as hostages or human shields. The forces going to the political prisons would also have to be trained in detaining the prison staff, in doing some basic interrogations (requiring basic language skills for any U.S. units assigned), and in applying biometrics to both prison staff and prisoners. This kind of training cannot wait until the collapse occurs, after which time the assigned ROK and U.S. forces will need to be deploying and making final preparation for the assaults. The forces therefore need to be assigned long before a collapse, and the training needs to be done now, in peacetime. In addition, some backup units should also be trained in case one of the primary units is diverted to a more significant mission or in case the force defending a prison camp is determined to be larger than expected.[26]

For the forces going to the political prisons to be successful, they will also need to take a variety of supplies or have the supplies promptly delivered by air. These supplies would include food, medicine, clothing, coats, blankets, shoes, construction materials (especially for housing), and prison-specific supplies for providing meaningful jobs for the prisoners. For example, Camp 14 is reported to have large numbers of jobs associated with making North Korean military uniforms.[27] After this prison is secure, these jobs might be converted to making clothing first for the prisoners and then for sale, but doing so would require providing the material, thread, and other needed items, as well as some instruction in sewing something other than a military uniform. Means for promptly providing these resources would need to be identified; in some cases, as with rice, a supply might simply have to be stored in peacetime for rapid deployment. A food supply would need to be rotated every couple of years to maintain its quality. Once the operation starts, follow-on supplies, such as food, would also have to be acquired, and transportation would need to be arranged for regular deliveries (and could well require military escort).

International humanitarian organizations or third countries could handle provision of these supplies in part. These organizations would be anxious to become involved in helping, especially with the North Korean political prisoners. And these organizations distributing supplies within the prisons should not have the difficulties of military or criminal expropriation that could be associated with supplies delivered to the civilian population. But to take advantage of this assistance, the

---

[26] For example, if it suddenly became known that a nuclear weapon storage site existed along the line of advance of a force assigned to secure a political prison, the National Command Authorities might decide to have that unit focus on securing the nuclear weapons, with priority, because even one nuclear weapon delivered against a ROK city could kill and injure far more people than there are prisoners in any given political prison.

[27] Harden, 2012, pp. 90–96.

ROK and the United States would need to make agreements on what assistance is to be provided and what the ROK and the United States would need to do to secure this assistance. For example, an international humanitarian organization or third country might be prepared to deliver food or other supplies to the port at Chongjin but might require the ROK and the United States to provide transportation (and security) from the port to the political prison nearby.

The former prisoners in the political prisons will also require education. At least some will not even be familiar with North Korean life and culture outside the prisons, having been raised there. And everyone will require education on life in a democratic, market economy. In addition, some job training should also go on to prepare the former prisoners for assuming jobs outside the prisons. Both the materials for this education and appropriate instructors need to be identified and prepared. While some of these materials may be similar to what is used with the former North Korean military personnel, some would need to be even more basic because of the isolation of many former prisoners.

CHAPTER EIGHT
Challenges of and Responses to Ownership Issues

In discussions with ROK experts on North Korea and unification, I discovered their serious concerns about North Korean ownership issues in the aftermath of a North Korean government collapse and Korean unification. The key question is: After the collapse of the North Korean government and subsequent unification, who will own the property of North Korea and the North Korean businesses? This question requires the ROK government to make several decisions, although partial and probably poor decisions already exist in ROK law. The decisions on this question will have significant implications for the North Korean people's satisfaction with unification and also whether they will stay in place or become refugees seeking to enter China or the ROK. It will also affect the ability of the North Korean economy to obtain the capital needed to replace dilapidated infrastructure and begin serious growth. Poor decisions on this question could have serious negative consequences for many parts of the unification process.

The Challenges of North Korean Ownership Issues

Figure 8.1 shows the challenges associated with ownership issues. Today, the North Korean government owns almost all businesses and property in North Korea. But how this property is treated in the aftermath of a North Korean government collapse will have major consequences for the people of North Korea and the viability of business in the former North Korea after unification.

Figure 8.1
Ownership Challenges in North Korea

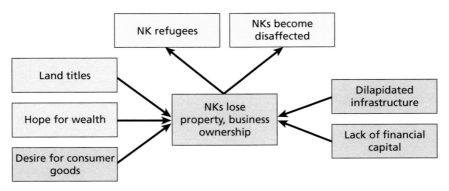

RAND *RR331-8.1*

Until the late 1940s, individual Koreans owned property through-out Korea. Kim Il-Sung nationalized most of that property in North Korea in 1946 and had the former landowners designated as a hostile class in the North Korean class system. Fearing for their future, many of these individuals and their families immigrated to the ROK before the borders were strictly controlled, some 60 or more years ago. Often, these people brought with them their land titles, hoping for the even-tual restoration of their properties after the fall of the North Korean government. While these former landowners have not lived in North Korea for many decades, and may not move back after unification, they at least hope for the financial windfall that they were denied by nationalization of their property.[1]

On the other hand, North Koreans occupy and use the prop-erty of North Korea today. They have residences that, while govern-ment owned, are theirs as far as they are concerned. Many work on farms that are collectively run, but where the farmers likely perceive that they have a right of ownership. Any initiative to take this property away from them will create significant problems and serious animosity toward the South Koreans who could be responsible for doing so.

[1]   See the description of this challenge in Andrei Lankov, "A Legal Minefield for Korean Unification," *Asia Times*, July 30, 2011a.

Of course, simply transferring the title of homes to the current residents in North Korea is not necessarily a solution. Many of them may decide to sell their homes to entrepreneurs ready to offer cash, the North Koreans anxious to secure a windfall to obtain consumer goods. But if many North Koreans acquire and then sell their residences shortly after unification, the limited supply of consumer goods and the sharply increased demand will drive prices up significantly, erasing much of the windfall for many people.

With regard to business ownership, the key challenge is the dilapidated capital stock of most North Korean businesses and of the surrounding infrastructure (the electrical system, roads, rail lines, and so forth). In practice, most North Korean firms will not be worth much; as in the German case, ROK companies may need to be paid to assume ownership. The exception will likely be North Korean firms associated with mineral resources, and these firms may be worth a very large amount of money, although Chinese firms have already acquired much of this value.[2] Most North Korean firms will need an infusion of capital to make them viable and eventually competitive. While sales of the firms may seek to raise this capital, the ROK government will likely need to look for additional means of raising the necessary capital. Meanwhile, the employees of the firms, especially the managers, may hope for a financial windfall that in reality is unlikely to occur when their firms are privatized. And few of the employees will be able to contribute any significant amount to the capital needed to make the firms viable.

If the North Koreans were to lose "their" homes and other property, many may decide to become refugees and head to South Korea or China for what may appear to be excellent job opportunities. As noted above, some ROK sources suggest that 3 million or so North Korean refugees may come to the ROK alone. Marcus Noland notes that, in analysis of German unification, home ownership was robustly

---

[2] The unified Korean government will need to decide the extent to which the transfers of property rights to China will be recognized, although the ROK planning to not recognize these transfers makes Chinese intervention (to secure Chinese property rights) more likely. See Chapter Nine.

correlated with staying in that home;[3] thus, the decision on owner-ship could significantly affect the number of refugees who try to enter the ROK and China. And as noted in Chapter Three, massive refugee flows could be destabilizing in both countries and could lead China, in particular, to intervene in North Korea to stop the refugee flow.

The combination of the population's hopes and expectations is thus unlikely to be realized. For example, the North Korean people will generally not suddenly find themselves rich like their South Korean brothers. They will probably blame the ROK-led unification govern-ment for their dissatisfaction.

Establishing an Ownership Framework

As noted above, the unified Korean government, likely a direct succes-sor of the ROK government, will need to set the conditions for own-ership in North Korea in the aftermath of Korean unification. Thus, ROK government policy in this area is critical.

Concepts and Policies for North Korean Ownership

The ROK government will need to establish concepts and policies for both business ownership and property ownership.

Business Ownership

The ROK can choose either of two extremes in dealing with busi-ness ownership: Sell the ownership or vest ownership in the existing employees of the firms. The ROK could also select some combination of these two extremes (e.g., sell 60 percent of the ownership of the firms and give 40 percent to the employees).

If the ROK selects the latter extreme, the North Koreans will own the businesses but have no financial capital with which to make them viable. To sustain the viability of the businesses and their jobs, the employees would have little choice but to sell a least part of their own-

---

[3] Noland notes that job security was also critical to the East Germans staying in place. See Marcus Noland, "Some Unpleasant Arithmetic Concerning Unification," Washington, D.C.: Peterson Institute for International Economics, 1996.

ership in exchange for the capital needed for improvements. In short, the extreme of vesting ownership in the employees may actually not be much different from selling the firms, except that the employees would be managing the sales and may not be qualified to do so.

If the ROK decides to sell ownership, it could follow the example of the German government in dealing with East German businesses. The West Germans set up a privatization trust fund called Treuhand: "The Treuhand approach required potential buyers to submit detailed business plans, including binding agreements on future employment and investment; the success of the bidder depended on a combination of the bid and the business plan."[4] While cases of incompetence or corruption led to some inappropriate purchases of businesses, this approach worked very well in most cases, providing a roadmap for firms to become economically viable while ensuring jobs for most employees. Investment was close to the business plan commitments, and employment fell only a small amount (more due to the negotiated wage increases than to the privatization approach).[5] These outcomes reflected a major success for privatization.

The ROK could select an interim approach, selling part of the ownership and giving part of it to the existing employees. The North Korean employees would likely find such an approach more acceptable, but it might make it more difficult to find buyers with the desired capital for many North Korean businesses. Moreover, this approach is unlikely to be viable if the employees hold the controlling share—few external firms will be willing to make major investments in North Korean businesses that they do not control. Most external firms will want all owners to bear an equal share of the investments, which the North Korean employees will normally not be able to do; alternatively, the external firms will want to gain increased ownership in proportion to their investment, which would be difficult to manage.[6] Instead of

---

[4] Holger Wolf, "Korean Unification: Lessons from Germany," in Marcus Noland, ed., *Economic Integration of the Korean Peninsula*, Washington, D.C.: Peterson Institute for International Economics, January 1998, p. 182.

[5] Wolf, 1998, p. 182.

[6] Wolf, 1998, p. 183.

offering the North Korean employees ownership, it would be less complicated to offer them a profit-sharing arrangement based on actually achieving some level of profitability, an arrangement that would also tend to induce more-effective labor.

Property Ownership

There are two basic options for property ownership in North Korea. The first is restitution of the North Korean property to anyone who can establish a historical deed or other proof of ownership. The second alternative is to cancel historical ownership (while providing some compensation for the loss) and in some way give the ownership to the North Koreans currently utilizing the land and the homes or other associated buildings.

The East German experience provides a useful example:

> Germany opted for restitution. In practice, however, the determination of property rights turned out to be highly complicated because of repeated transfers, partial or missing documentation, and disputes over the treatment of investments made after the expropriation. In consequence, claimants took their cases to the courts: soon, more than 1.2 million cases were logged, creating multiyear judicial backlogs. These delays curtailed both the ability of the Treuhand to dispose of assets and the ability, and certainly the incentive, of individuals to embark on major investments until the ownership issue was resolved. The gridlock eventually forced a shift in policy emphasis from restoration to compensation.[7]

A German colleague of mine argues that, even after more than 20 years, many of these cases are still ongoing.

If restitution is applied in North Korea, the Korean case could be just as serious or even worse:

> It would be a minor exaggeration to say that any piece of well located flat land in North Korea has a potential claimant lying in wait, somewhere in Seoul. The number of such claimants is esti-

---

[7]   Wolf, 1998.

mated at some 1.2 million—even though the actual number of claims must be significantly smaller, since there is a large number of multiple claims when few descendants of the same person claims [sic] the rights to the same parcel of land.[8]

The author goes on to note the Kangnam development experience in southern Seoul, in which the value of land increased 1,000-fold in 20 years as farmland was transformed into the posh part of the city of Seoul. Many of the holders of North Korean land deeds yearn for exactly such a development in North Korea to make them rich: "[U]nder current South Korean laws, the claims of the descendants of North Korean landowners are technically valid."[9] One can imagine the animosity that would be created with the North Koreans as these landowners who have lived in the ROK for over 60 years went north after unification and tried to take control of "their" property; North-South conflict, at least at the individual level, might be difficult to avoid.

To take the compensation approach, the ROK would need to amend its laws. It would need to nullify the deeds of the former landowners, while potentially providing them some compensation for the nullification. Because the Japanese government issued many of the deeds, the source of the deeds could be the focus of nullification so as to gain broader support in the ROK. The ROK would then need to decide the principles on which property would be given to the occupants or held by the ROK government for disposition (which should likely be the case for North Korean businesses, as discussed above). In turn, the key challenge will be to avoid giving property to the North Korean occupants, then seeing many of them sell all or part of their property to achieve a prompt financial windfall for purchasing consumer goods. Since a key objective is to keep North Koreans in place so that they do not become burdensome refugees, a vesting period to obtain land ownership should be a part of any transfer of ownership. But establishing the rules for ownership and the vesting period will

---

[8] Lankov, 2011a.

[9] Lankov, 2011a.

need to be done wisely to avoid a vast number of lawsuits, as happened in the restitution case in East Germany.

Strategies for North Korean Ownership

The ROK needs to adopt laws to specifically deal with the owner-ship issue when unification occurs. Unfortunately, because the exist-ing ROK laws provide one solution, likely the least attractive one, any changes need to be made before unification. But getting changes will be difficult. The former North Korean landowners and their descen-dants are a politically powerful and wealthy group that would oppose any such changes. This political sensitivity explains why this issue has not been addressed and why it may not be until it is too late.

But if the issue is addressed, the ROK should consider a com-pensation approach to previous ownership, seeking to avoid the North Koreans feeling that they will lose their homes and livelihoods at uni-fication. The North Koreans would likely blame such losses on "greedy South Koreans," creating a level of animosity that Korea needs to avoid. The ROK needs to get most North Koreans to stay at home and in their jobs to keep humanitarian aid requirements and the overall cost of unification within manageable levels and to avoid a massive influx of refugees into the ROK and China that would disrupt the economy of both countries.

Ownership of businesses should be assumed by a privatization trust fund, as was the case in Germany. The fund should control the future ownership of all North Korean businesses and should seek acqui-sition of those businesses by ROK and other companies able to provide the financial capital needed to keep the businesses operating (and the people employed) while modernizing the businesses. Purchase should be based on both the amount to be paid and the business plan for making the business viable over time. Full ownership should vest over three to five years so that outside companies do not purchase North Korean businesses, strip out the assets of value, and then abandon the remains. Indeed, the ROK may want to retain approval authority for any business sales within ten years of unification to reduce purchases by speculators not interested in the long-term development of the econ-omy in North Korea.

Particular attention needs to be paid to the ownership of mining and other businesses that would have access to North Korea's mineral wealth: "The South Korean government believes that North Korea may have as much as $6 trillion USD [U.S. dollars] in rare earth elements."[10] If North Korea does have such wealth, the ROK government will want to take advantage of it to help cover the various costs of unification. It should therefore retain interest in any businesses sold with mineral wealth potential.

In terms of property ownership, the ROK government should favor an arrangement where ownership is given to the North Koreans utilizing the land and buildings at the time of unification. This type of ownership would apply to homes and apartments and modest tracts of associated land. Collective farms and similar properties should normally be divided among the farmers, allowing them to decide whether to work independently in the future or to work together. For all properties, a vesting approach will help keep people in their homes during the critical period after unification. The ROK will probably want to require North Koreans to remain on their properties for three to five years to gain the full ownership. Absences in excess of a couple of weeks would have to be cleared with a government authority, with the ownership opportunity forfeited if this does not happen or if the property is abandoned. The government would retain ownership of public properties (administrative buildings, parks, and the like) and would also retain ownership of land areas without immediate inhabitants (mountainous areas, reservoirs and lakes, and so forth).

Of course, in every case there will be exceptions that would need to be handled. The privatization trust fund would be allowed to deal with changes in business plans and needs to sell properties that are not yet vested. One or more other government agencies could handle private lands, residences, farms, and other properties, including the need to deal with absences exceeding a few weeks.

The structure for these arrangements should likely be formalized into a "special administrative zone" that would exist in North Korea

---

[10] Scott Thomas Bruce, "North Korea's Six Trillion Dollar Question," *The Diplomat*, August 30, 2012.

for ten or more years. It would create a Korea that was one country but with two systems for business and property issues. Because some of these provisions are less likely to be controversial, the ROK president and National Assembly could seek to enact these provisions first, such as the creation of a privatization trust fund. Any actions taken before unification will better prepare the ROK for dealing with a North Korean government collapse and help reassure North Koreans of reasonable treatment in a Korean unification.

Other Preparations Required

North Korean ownership issues will require a number of other preparations.

Setting North Korean Beliefs and Expectations

As noted above, decisions on ownership will significantly influence the attitudes of North Koreans toward Korean unification. This can be no more clearly demonstrated than to realize that North Korean propaganda has focused on this issue:

> For decades North Korean propaganda has made it clear to North Koreans that the collapse of the Kim family regime will herald the return of greedy, brutal landlords who are always ready to make North Korean farmers into their powerless tenants. It is remarkable that even in the stories of the post-communist East Europe, presented by the North Korean propaganda, there is a recurrent topic of greedy landlords who are allegedly ready to grab their estates, depriving the Russian or East German farmers of their livelihood.[11]

ROK efforts to address ownership would belie the North Korean propaganda.

At the very least, the ROK wants to avoid North Korean refugee flows that are significantly stimulated by North Koreans thinking that they will lose their homes and jobs. The ROK can at least begin to address this issue by discussing plans for business ownership, even if

---

[11] Lankov, 2011a.

presenting only examples rather than stating a general principle. North Koreans need to learn that a major ROK objective is sustaining and strengthening North Korean jobs both in the short and medium terms.

Supply, Equipment, and Financial Preparation

Property issues in North Korea will require very large bureaucracies to manage the assignment of ownership. The personnel in these bureaucracies will require considerable training followed by the development of systematic plans for how to handle property ownership. This will be particularly true of the privatization trust fund, if established: It will need to begin operating rapidly to sustain operations of business that will likely be short of operational capital and could fail before being sold. The privatization trust fund would need a substantial amount of money to keep North Korean businesses operating until they can be sold.

Building ROK Political Consensus

Former North Korean landowners make up a politically and economically powerful group in the ROK. They will likely resist even discussion of changes in ROK laws that could hurt their perceived financial interests. The ROK government therefore needs to begin a discussion on the implications of business and property ownership after unification, describing the example of East Germany, the options that were available for dealing with ownership, and the implications of each option. In the end, the former North Korean landowners will dominate politics on this issue until a broader constituency in the ROK feels that a change in ROK laws is needed for this case to be equitable to the North Korean people and to reduce the costs and likely conflict of unification.

CHAPTER NINE

Challenges of and Responses to Potential Chinese Intervention

As noted above, China can choose whether or not to intervene in a North Korean government collapse. The ROK and the United States have no force available to secure the Chinese–North Korean border either to prevent refugee flows that would, in part, stimulate Chinese intervention or to stop a Chinese intervention itself. There are reasons for believing that the Chinese might intervene and also reasons for believing that they would not. The ROK and the United States might even decide to invite Chinese intervention, especially in future years, when the ROK Army will likely become too small to handle Korean unification after a North Korean government collapse. Thus, the ROK and the United States should be prepared to coordinate with China on a Chinese intervention.

This chapter addresses a Chinese intervention. It begins by examining the challenges that could push China to intervene. It also looks at the challenges that could cause China to oppose unification and the challenges that could lead to conflict between China and the ROK-U.S. alliance. It then turns to options for moderating these challenges and the preparations needed now to facilitate mitigation.

The Challenges of Chinese Intervention

Figure 9.1 identifies some of the challenges that could induce Chinese intervention. Those on the left are primarily repeated from Figure 5.1. China has been explicit about its concerns relative to North Korean

Figure 9.1
The Challenges Leading to Chinese Intervention

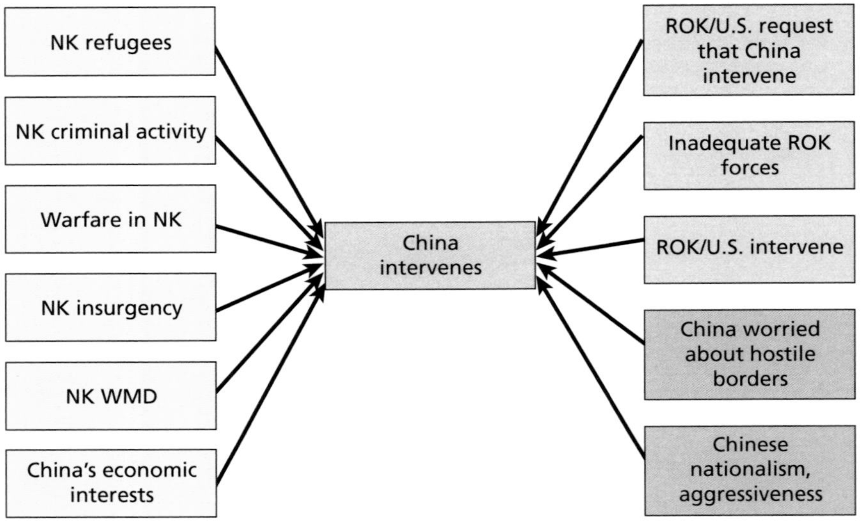

RAND *RR331-9.1*

refugees; it fears, in part, growth in the already large ethnic Korean population in Manchuria that could destabilize Manchuria and/or induce ROK intervention in Manchuria.[1] China would also be concerned about North Korean criminal activity, conflict, and insurgency and, in particular, with the possibility that these could spill over into China. China also recognizes that North Korean WMD could be fired at China, especially by groups that perceive that they will not survive. As noted in Chapter Three, such behavior would be consistent with Kim Jong-Il's claim that in such circumstances, "'I will be sure to destroy the Earth! What good is this Earth without North Korea?'"[2] Some aspects of North Korean WMD might also be traceable back to some Chinese entities, a situation that may lead to international censure of China if the ROK and the United States document it. Finally, China has extensive economic interests in North Korea that it may

---

[1]   See the discussion of China's Northeast Project in Chapter Three.

[2]   Kim, Hyun Sik, 2008.

wish to safeguard, including rights it has purchased to North Korean mineral resources and North Korean ports.

In addition, China could decide to intervene for the reasons shown on the right side of Figure 9.1. As noted in Chapter Three, the ROK and the United States could request a Chinese intervention, likely when the ROK military becomes too small to allow the ROK and the United States to secure and stabilize North Korea adequately. This is still a challenge for the ROK and the United States as they seek to avoid conflict with China. China may also decide to intervene on its own if it perceives that the ROK and U.S. force commitment will be too small and lead to chaos in North Korea potentially worse than seen in Iraq from 2004 through 2007. China could also decide to intervene simply because the ROK and the United States have, giving China a convenient excuse but also helping China address its worries about hostile forces deploying near its borders (especially U.S. forces but perhaps also ROK forces). Finally, Chinese nationalism and aggressiveness may also play a role in a Chinese intervention,[3] much as it has affected Chinese actions in the South China Sea or in its conflict with Japan over the Senkaku/Diaoyu Islands.

Chinese intervention in North Korea after a North Korean government collapse could become a serious consequence because of ROK and U.S. conflict with China or because China decides to disrupt Korean unification (see Figure 9.2). Conflict with China would most likely occur as an accident that escalates out of control, but the accident and subsequent escalation would be more likely if China decides to press its forces deep into North Korea to prevent ROK and U.S. forces from approaching its borders or because of Chinese nationalism and a desire to demonstrate its military prowess. Conflict could also result in part because the ROK and the United States do not know either Chinese strategic or tactical objectives, and the two sides make overlapping choices. The conflict could escalate because China (and the ROK and the United States) had not adequately assessed the costs and benefits of its actions at each step in the escalation process. These fac-

---

[3]   The Northeast Project discussed in Chapter Three could also be used to justify historical Chinese claims to some of the North Korean territory.

Figure 9.2
The Challenges That Might Lead to Conflict or Cause China to Oppose
Unification

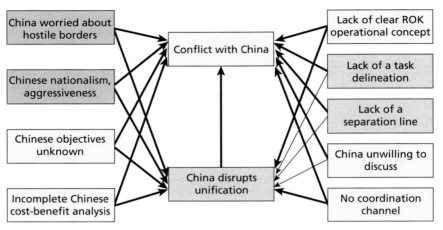

NOTE: Thick lines indicate a strong influence; thin lines indicate a moderate influence.
RAND *RR331-9.2*

tors might also lead China to conclude that it should disrupt Korean unification.

The lack of a clear ROK and U.S. concept for operating in this environment could also lead to conflict with China. As both sides rushed toward similar ground objectives, such as the Yongbyon nuclear plant, the lack of delineation of which side would deal with each area in North Korea could contribute to conflict. In practice, the risks associated with each side advancing into the same areas could be mitigated by creating a separation line that the two sides would agree not to cross, but such a separation line may not get set up. This could happen in part if China refuses to discuss these military operations or if there is no means of coordination between China and the ROK and the United States.

The Feasibility of Chinese Intervention

During the Korean War, the Chinese committed over 3 million personnel to operations in Korea, including more than 600,000 civilian laborers.[4] The PLA is no longer of a size to support such a massive commitment of troops to Korea. Moreover, the full PLA is spread throughout China and could not be committed to operations in North Korea without significant, visible movements of its forces.

Table 9.1 describes the ground maneuver forces that China would have available for operations in North Korea under plausible scenarios. It makes the point that China actually keeps relatively limited PLA ground forces in the Shenyang Military Region (MR), which adjoins Korea: only just over eight division equivalents of maneuver forces.

Table 9.1
Chinese PLA Versus ROK Forces for Intervention in North Korea

Force	Active Duty Forces[a]			
	Heavy Divisions	Infantry Divisions[b]	Cumulated Divisions	Cumulated Personnel
China				
Shenyang MR	3-2/3	4-2/3	8-1/3	250,000
+ Beijing MR	6	2-1/3	16-2/3	550,000
+ Jinan MR	4-2/3	1-1/3	22-2/3	740,000
+ Nanjing MR	17	3-2/3	29	990,000
ROK				
Army + Marines, 2013	6-1/3	20-1/3	26-2/3	528,000
Army + Marines, 2022	6	10-2/3	16-2/3	415,000

SOURCES: For Chinese forces, IISS, 2012, pp. 238–240; for ROK forces, ROK MND, 2010, p. 340, and the author's interviews.

[a] Counts maneuver divisions as one and maneuver brigades as one-third; does not include special forces.

[b] Does not include the Chinese 15th Airborne Corps, which consists of three airborne divisions.

---

[4] See Xiaobing Li, *A History of the Modern Chinese Army*, Lexington, Ken.: University Press of Kentucky, 2007, pp. 110–111. See also Ron Brackett, "Korea: The Forgotten War 1950–1953: Questions and Answers," *St. Petersburg Times*, July 20, 2003.

This force is organized into three group armies,[5] of which the Chinese government might consider using two or so in North Korea, perhaps leaving the third behind as a hedge against Russian action.[6] This force of two to three group armies (five to eight division equivalents) might be sufficient to create a limited buffer zone in North Korea of, say, 50 to 100 km deep,[7] depending on the degree of North Korean military cooperation or opposition, on the number of displaced persons China had to handle, and on the number of refugees likely to penetrate the buffer zone and cross into China.[8] If the North Korean forces (especially reserve divisions) vigorously opposed the Chinese entrance, this could be too small a force to place at risk in North Korea.[9] But with North Korean military cooperation, perhaps associated with Chinese support of the faction in North Korea controlling these forces, a limited buffer zone should be quite feasible with the Shenyang MR forces.

---

[5]   Office of the Secretary of Defense, *Annual Report to Congress: Military and Security Developments Involving the People's Republic of China 2012*, Washington, D.C.: Department of Defense, May 2012, p. 30.

[6]   Note that if Russia decides to intervene in North Korea in these circumstances, it would do so along a route that would cut the Chinese line of communication to the Rajin-Sonbong ports and the Chongjin port, ports that are extremely important to China's view of the future of its northeast territory. China may well want to rapidly project some military force along the routes to the Rajin-Sonbong ports to prevent Russia from cutting the route; in the end, a group army would almost certainly hold this flank to deter Russian advances. The potential for Chinese-Russian conflict is also very real.

[7]   At a recent conference, Cheng Xiaohe of Renmin University talked about North Korea creating a 100-km buffer zone in North Korea if intervention became required (Cheng Xiaohe, "Refugees and Neighbors," panel session, ASAN Plenum 2013, Seoul, May 1, 2013; see the video for the day 2 session), and his talking points (Cheng Xiaohe, "Refugees and Neighbors," talking points, ASAN Plenum 2013, Seoul, May 1, 2013) identified three conditions associated with North Korean collapse that could differentiate a Chinese response.

[8]   While the Chinese People's Armed Police should be able to handle such refugees, the Chinese border with North Korea is *very* long, stretching even these forces.

[9]   This is not to say that the Chinese forces would be defeated, but rather that the losses they could sustain would likely not be acceptable in China. Moreover, with the force heavily focused on combat, it would not have the resources to simultaneously handle the displaced persons. Chinese People's Armed Police could perform the latter task, assuming that the number of displaced persons was not too large (e.g., hundreds of thousands would be a problem).

Still, since North Korean factional allegiances could change, China would likely be very careful with such an intervention and should limit the distance of its penetration to one that would allow prompt extraction of its forces should North Korean attitudes change.

If China wishes to commit more forces, perhaps to take control of North Korea above Pyongyang or even more, it would have to move forces forward from the other MRs, as shown in Table 9.1. China is not well prepared to move these forces and would have to divert substantial rail traffic and many trucks to make such a move—and this would be further delayed by the likely lack of plans for doing so. Any such mobilization and movement would take at least weeks for even a single division and many months for a force of multiple divisions. The movement of these forces would be very visible. Moreover, China will likely be reluctant to move all the PLA forces from any of these MRs; the cumulative numbers in Table 9.1 are thus higher than the forces China would likely employ. For example, the combined PLA force in the Shenyang and Beijing MRs would provide almost 17 division equivalents of ground maneuver forces, although China would likely prefer to deploy no more than about 14 of these to North Korea. With North Korean cooperation, this force could be sufficient to occupy much of the area north of Pyongyang. By drawing on the forces of four of China's seven MRs,[10] China could provide up to 29 PLA maneuver division equivalents to operations in North Korea, although a force of something less than 25 PLA divisions would be more likely. That force could probably occupy and secure all of North Korea with North Korean military assistance and would be fairly likely to occupy and generally control the North with some modest North Korean opposition. As Table 9.1 suggests, ROK Army and Marine forces of roughly 26 maneuver division equivalents would similarly be available today and, with U.S. assistance, should be able to occupy and generally control the North.

Table 9.1 does not take into consideration China's three airborne divisions. If China decided to occupy North Korea as far south

---

[10] China's other three MRs (Guagzhou, Chengdu, and Lanzhou) are far from Korea and are responsible for sustaining security in other border regions.

as Pyongyang or beyond, China might try to insert these divisions well into North Korea ahead of its ground advance, perhaps at the Pyongyang airport.[11] With assistance from the North Korean military in that area, China could take this action relatively securely and rapidly. However, such a projection would be risky unless China had already deployed forces along the North Korean border from at least the Beijing MR and preferably also the Jinan MR. This kind of Chinese airborne insertion would be dependent on continued support from the North Korean faction providing access to the Pyongyang airport. If China lost the support of this North Korean faction before Chinese ground forces could connect a ground line of communication from China to the Pyongyang airport, a situation could develop like the one the British 1st Airborne Division experienced in Operation Market Garden during World War II, which operation was chronicled in the movie, *A Bridge Too Far*.[12] This risk might lead China to wait until its ground forces had advanced significantly into North Korea before trying a forward insertion into the Pyongyang airport.

Table 9.1 also notes the planned ROK Army reduction by 2022 or so. Once the ROK ground forces have been reduced to 16 or so division equivalents, the ROK may also have to limit the parts of North Korea that it occupies and secures unless considerable North Korean military cooperation can be achieved.

How Quickly Might China Intervene?

Chapter Three discusses the serious security challenges that China would perceive from a North Korean collapse. The severity of these challenges would push China to intervene rapidly in North Korea. Its ability to intervene more quickly than the ROK and the United States would be a function of the following:

---

[11] The Pyongyang airport is referred to as such here, although its formal name is the Sunan International Airport.

[12] In that event, a highly trained and very capable British airborne division was surrounded by German forces with considerable armor and artillery advantages; the British force suffered almost 80 percent casualties.

- The Chinese government would likely have better intelligence on the situation in North Korea and, with that intelligence, should have better warning of a potential government collapse in two ways: (1) It should have more information on the level of dissatisfaction of the North Korean elites with Kim Jong-Un and thus the potential for action (such as an assassination) against him, and (2) it should be able to follow developments after an assassination of Kim Jong-Un more closely and thus have a better sense of the stages of government failure through which the North proceeds.
- This intelligence should cue the Chinese government, giving it time to decide that it will likely need to intervene. Given the serious threats that a North Korean collapse would pose to China, the Chinese leadership would likely face an easier decision to intervene than would the ROK. Thus, this would be a decision that China should be able to make more quickly and sooner than the ROK and United States can.
- China would also likely mobilize its military forces in at least the Shenyang MR soon after obtaining the intelligence cues and prepare them for prompt intervention.
- China would likely feel extreme urgency to seize control of North Korean WMD-related sites. It would worry about its own vulnerability to WMD. But the driving factor would more likely be its desire to secure these sites before U.S. forces are committed against the facilities, thereby (China would hope) averting the commitment of U.S. forces near the Chinese border.
- China would feel pressure to protect Chinese citizens and economic interests in North Korea against the actions of North Korean factions or (especially with regard to Chinese economic interests) those of the ROK and United States. China has made major investments in the North and would be distressed to lose them; prompt action would likely allow China to secure many investments before ROK and U.S. forces could reach the facilities.

There is no guarantee that China would act so promptly and before the ROK and United States, but the likelihood seems high.

Dealing with a Chinese Intervention

The ROK and the United States have failed to develop military capabilities to deny Chinese intervention in a North Korean collapse. The ROK might have constituted such capabilities by building five or six airborne divisions and the means for inserting them rapidly into North Korea, just below the Chinese border. These forces would then have been positioned to largely block the North Korean refugee and related threats to China, removing major Chinese incentives (but not all of them) for intervening. The ROK forces could also have served as a tripwire against Chinese intervention.[13]

Having failed to create such a force, the ROK has given China the initiative in deciding whether or not to intervene in North Korea. The ROK and the United States must therefore prepare to deal with a Chinese intervention. The ROK and the United States might even need to invite Chinese intervention, especially if they perceive that they have inadequate forces to fully handle unification on their own (which the ongoing ROK force reductions may cause within a few years, as suggested in Table 9.1). The Chinese might decide not to intervene, but they will have many incentives to intervene, making that course of action most likely. The ROK and the United States must set goals for preventing the negative consequences discussed in Chapter Three, then take actions to achieve these goals. Preparation now will be essential to minimizing the potential negative consequences.

Possible Chinese Strategic Objectives

If China does intervene in North Korea, it will select its own strategic objectives. The following are the most likely options it would consider:

---

[13] In practice, this force would be more than a tripwire but still very vulnerable. China reportedly has six divisions (three of them heavy) plus seven combat brigades (two heavy) in the three group armies and other forces in the Shenyang MR, adjoining North Korea. China also has three airborne divisions that could be swung to this area. If this entire force were committed to attack North Korea (an unlikely development, since this would leave the MR without major defenses against Russia), five or six ROK airborne divisions could be inadequate to withstand them. See IISS, 2012, pp. 238–241.

1. China might recognize a North Korean faction as the true North Korean government, supporting that faction as the new North Korean government and as the sole legal authority in all North Korea. If this faction were weak, China would effectively be establishing a puppet government, likely supported by Chinese forces.

2. China might secure parts of North Korea for defensive purposes and then turn them over to the ROK as soon as the ROK can adequately secure these areas, allowing Korean reunification to occur.

3. China could seize and hold ground as a bargaining chip in eventual Chinese negotiations over the contours and conditions of postunification Korea.

4. China could secure major parts of North Korea and annex them into China, potentially as a new province.

In either the first or fourth options, China would essentially be attempting to thwart Korean unification. While this might provide China with some advantages in terms of territory controlled (especially the ports on the East Sea/Sea of Japan) and access to minerals and cheap labor in that territory, it would also impose burdens on China to stabilize and rebuild the territory controlled while likely fighting both criminal activity and a North Korean insurgency. These Chinese strategic objectives would also likely infuriate the ROK population, increasing the potential for conflict in both economic and military terms. The ROK might also control some North Korean territory if it has also intervened while China is pursuing the first and last options, although China might insist on ROK withdrawal from North Korean sovereign territory. In contrast, Chinese intervention in the third option would be temporary, with these longer-term issues turned over to the ROK as soon as China determines that the ROK is able to maintain stability (which would be the likely ROK preference).

In practice, the ROK is unlikely to know the real Chinese intent when China intervenes. Even if China declares one option or another, it may actually pursue a different strategic objective, or it may change its strategic objective based on the developing situation. For example, if China initially selects the third option but the ROK proves unable to stabilize even the areas that it occupies, China may conclude that it cannot afford to turn the rest of North Korea over to the ROK and may feel forced to select the first or fourth strategic objectives, since regional stability will still likely be the principal Chinese goal. Alternatively, some in China might want to annex major parts of North Korean territory but urge the Chinese government to declare that it is simply trying to help the ROK establish stability in the short term, making China appear to be a true regional great power concerned about the interests of its neighbors. They might do so expecting the ROK to have difficulty stabilizing the parts of North Korea that it secures, giving China the opportunity to change objectives and appear justified in annexing North Korean territory or supporting a North Korean faction.

ROK and U.S. Objectives

Thus, the ROK cannot and may not want to prevent Chinese intervention in a North Korean government collapse. At the same time, the ROK will not have a close alliance with China the way it does with the United States. Therefore, the ROK must work with its U.S. ally to shape and moderate Chinese intervention and the effects it causes. In doing so, the ROK would presumably focus on four key objectives:

- Avoid conflict with Chinese forces, given the potential for such conflict developing into war with China.
- Secure as much of North Korea as possible to provide the ROK leverage toward unification.
- Demonstrate the ROK and U.S. ability to stabilize that territory promptly. This would imply taking the actions discussed in Chapters Five through Eight.
- Seize and secure North Korean WMD that could otherwise threaten the security of both China and the ROK and the United States.

At the same time, the ROK would want to avoid Chinese selection of a North Korean faction to become the new North Korean government, exercising sovereignty over a significant portion of North Korea. And the ROK would want to encourage China to plan to relinquish North

Korean territory to ROK control as soon as the ROK is able to maintain stability in that territory; at that time, China should withdraw its forces from that territory.

Formulating ROK and U.S. Strategy Relative to China

Korean unification will depend on ROK control of much of North Korea. If the ROK allows China to establish control over most of North Korea after a government collapse, China would be in a position to thwart unification. Unfortunately, the ROK and the United States will not know the Chinese intervention objective. Therefore, they will likely want to "race" China to secure relatively large amounts of North Korean territory,[14] seeking the most leverage possible for achieving unification. In particular, the ROK will likely want to secure Pyongyang as a symbol of Korean unification even if China is able to control most of the area north of Pyongyang. If China controls only North Korean territories north of Pyongyang, they will not constitute a viable independent country, especially from a food perspective (much of North Korean food production occurs south of Pyongyang). Such an outcome would bound China's options in terms of a long-term solution and would make full Korean unification much more likely.

In racing China for Pyongyang, the ROK and the United States have the advantage of starting with many of their forces very close to the border with North Korea. ROK forward defense, in particular, also facilitates a rapid offensive. Even the Chinese forces in the Shenyang MR do not have this advantage, let alone the forces coming from the other MRs. But this is a fleeting advantage—unless the ROK decides to intervene promptly after a North Korean government collapse, China will have time to deploy its forces to its border with North Korea. At that time, China's relations with North Korean personnel may well turn the situation to China's advantage, probably allowing China to intervene with cooperation of one or more factions in North Korea. In contrast, at least at the current time (and before the ROK fully implements actions to win North Korean cooperation, as discussed in

---

[14] In similar circumstances at the end of World War II, the United States and its allies raced Russia for control of Berlin.

Chapter Four), the ROK will likely have to fight its way into North Korea, a much slower process than China would experience with local cooperation.

The ROK must therefore prepare to intervene in North Korea promptly, soon after a North Korean government collapse. There will likely be considerable reluctance in the ROK to do so, fearing that intervention may not be successful and that the costs will be very high. For early intervention to be feasible, ROK society must discuss North Korean government collapse more extensively and decide that it should act if collapse occurs; otherwise, the ROK positional advantage and as a result much of North Korea could be lost.

This ROK positional advantage could also be lost if China is able to send its airborne forces into the Pyongyang airport or some similar location well inside North Korea. Still, as noted above, such an airborne insertion will depend on North Korean cooperation. Should the North Korean forces around the Pyongyang airport oppose the insertion of the Chinese forces, that insertion could fail, and China could suffer serious force losses. It is therefore unclear whether China would take that risk. But if China does, the ROK needs to be prepared to intervene promptly, if it has not already, and to accelerate its advance to avoid being seriously disadvantaged in the race for Pyongyang.

To offset China's insertion capabilities, the ROK should create its own significant capability to project a substantial infantry force to a forward North Korean airport to offset some of the advantages that China would gain from projecting forces into the Pyongyang airport. If ROK efforts to develop cooperation in North Korea advance significantly, the ROK may actually secure cooperation from North Korean forces in the vicinity of the Pyongyang airport and forward deploy into it. In addition, ROK and U.S. Marines could execute an amphibious landing along North Korea's west coast, perhaps just north of the Pyongyang airport. But a marine landing would take a fair amount of preparation time to move the amphibious ships to the needed locations, suggesting that the ROK and the United States should plan to move amphibious shipping to Korea whenever North Korea shows significant signs of instability (rather than waiting for a North Korean government collapse).

Shaping and Moderating the Effects of Chinese Intervention

Intervention in North Korea will involve serious risks for both China and the ROK and the United States. But since the most serious potential consequence of intervention would be conflict between China and the ROK and the United States, the most effective way to shape and moderate the consequences is to cooperate with China in a mutual intervention. This proposal will surprise many readers and perhaps even be offensive to some in the ROK. After all, according to the ROK Constitution, North Korea is also part of Korea, and Chinese intervention could therefore be interpreted as a hostile act against Korea. But as argued above, Chinese intervention cannot be prevented and may be needed. If China does intervene, a cooperative intervention effort with the ROK and the United States would have the lowest risks by far compared to any other alternative.

Unfortunately, China has largely refused to discuss the possibility of a North Korean collapse with the ROK and the United States. After all, North Korea is China's ally, and China has therefore been reluctant to speak of the demise of its ally, even in "what if" terms. But in the aftermath of North Korea's provocations in recent years, some Chinese have begun talking positively about the potential for change in North Korea.[15] This is thus a good time to pursue a dialogue with China. Indeed, such a dialogue may already be occurring, as a confidential dialogue on this sensitive topic would be far preferable to a public dia-

---

[15] According to one report, "Deng Yuwen, deputy editor of *Study Times*, the journal of the Central Party School of the Communist Party of China, writing Thursday in *Financial Times*, said, 'China should consider abandoning North Korea. The best way of giving up on Pyongyang is to take the initiative to facilitate North Korea's unification with South Korea'" (Choi Hyung-kyu and Kim Hee-jin, "'Give up on Pyongyang,' Says China Insider," *Joongang Ilbo*, March 2, 2013). According to another,

> Retired major-general Luo Yuan, a prominent foreign policy hawk, wrote in the column [in China's quasi-official Global Times], "It does not matter if you were a comrade and brother-in-arms in the past, if you harm our national interest then we'll get even with you." If (a nuclear-armed) North Korea faces an attack or spirals into a regime collapse, there will be a massive influx of refugees into China, Luo wrote. "This would create a huge political and economic burden on China's remote regions."

"Chinese State Media Hints at Implosion of N.Korean Regime," *Chosun Ilbo*, March 11, 2013.

logue, at least initially. But before going too far, the ROK and the United States need to coordinate their thinking on involving China and need to develop a combined concept and strategy for working with China. Only a closely agreed approach between the ROK and United States will provide maximum leverage in negotiating with China.

The key to a cooperative Chinese and ROK-U.S. intervention in North Korea is preventing forces from the two sides from blundering into each other. Accidents could happen with major force advances in the race to Pyongyang, with special forces operating around key North Korean facilities (such as the Yongbyon nuclear facility), with interactions between air forces and air defenses, and in trying to suppress North Korean missile launches and related activity in areas being secured by the other side. The best way to minimize such accidents is to define a separation line for Chinese forces versus ROK and U.S. forces, insisting that the Chinese forces stay north of the line and ROK and U.S. forces stay south of it. The separation would apply to all military forces—ground, air, navy, and special forces. Such an approach would not be popular in the ROK, with the precedent of the separation lines after World War II having led to the partitioning of Germany throughout the Cold War. Thus, the ROK would at least want Chinese agreement to eventual withdrawal from North Korea and likely a UN Security Council resolution to ratify the conditions of such an agreement. But achieving a Security Council resolution would take time, eroding the ROK advantage of being forward deployed, especially if China seeks to delay an agreement. Thus, it would be far preferable to make an agreement on a separation line and provisions for operations before a North Korean collapse.[16]

---

[16] According to Michael Finnegan,

> early discussions—long before instability is evident—to reassure China that the resolution of the situation will not be to China's detriment, that the allies will not "take advantage" of the situation in a way that threatens Chinese interests, will go a long way toward ensuring that China takes a cooperative, rather than a competitive, approach to reestablishing stability in North Korea.

Michael J. Finnegan, "Preparing for the Inevitable in North Korea," PacNet 28B, Pacific Forum CSIS, April 28, 2009.

Figure 9.3 offers three possible separation lines, although others could also be selected. The first is roughly 50 km into North Korea, reflecting what the Shenyang MR forces could do with some North Korean cooperation. The second is a line north of Pyongyang that would likely be the minimum territory the ROK would like to secure. The third is a line that goes through the centers of Pyongyang and Wonsan and reflects a split of these major cities.

Figure 9.3
Possible Separation Lines with China

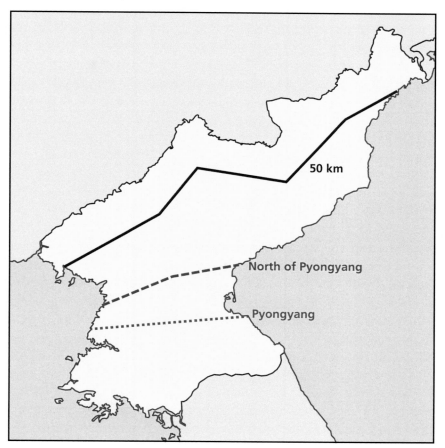

Assuming that the ROK intervenes promptly after a North Korean collapse, the "North of Pyongyang" line provides a reasonable separation, although the "50 km" line may be more appropriate if China decides that it only wants a limited buffer zone and if the ROK has sufficient force to handle the full area south of it. But if China secures North Korean cooperation to enter the Pyongyang airport early, the ROK may be forced to accept the "Pyongyang" line for separation. Alternatively, if the ROK develops cooperation with the North Korean forces around the Pyongyang airport and has the force projection capability to secure that area or if the ROK and the United States can promptly execute an amphibious landing on North Korea's west coast, the ROK and the United States should be able to achieve a separation line north of the "North of Pyongyang" line, at least near the west coast.

In addition to negotiating a separation line with China, the ROK and the United States will also want to negotiate some rules of engagement. For example, in territory that China secures, the ROK and the United States will want China to secure WMD promptly and not turn that WMD over to a faction that it may be trying to legitimize (which would be a violation of the nuclear Nonproliferation Treaty or other WMD control measures). If a North Korean faction were to launch a ballistic missile against the ROK, the ROK and the United States would want China to promptly secure the related ballistic missiles and launchers so that such a launch would not be repeated. But note that the ROK and the United States would need to make a similar commitment on their side of the separation line against any missile launch, especially launches toward China. Early in an intervention, neither China nor the ROK and United States may have advanced as far as a missile base executing such launches, forcing the responsible side to use airborne insertion or air strikes to deal with the threat. Getting the other side to take action in such cases may be challenging.

To avert problems in such a cooperative effort, a "Resolution Board" should be created, which would likely operate via a hotline between the two sides. This board would be constituted from senior officers on each side and would address problems implementing the intervention agreement. The political leadership of each side would need to pressure its Resolution Board members to be prompt and responsive or risk a breakdown of the cooperative intervention. For example, if a North Korean faction launched a missile at a ROK city and then, a day later, launched another missile before Chinese intervention to prevent such behavior, the cooperation could fail, something that would not be in either side's interest. Because many lives could depend on faithful implementation of the cooperation, there will be little willingness to accept a failure to follow the agreement. In addition, the Resolution Board would need to promptly address any accidental conflict between Chinese units on the one side and ROK and U.S. units on the other, including the potential crossing of the separation line.

The other issue to be addressed in such an agreement would be handling a Russian intervention. As noted previously, while Russia may well not be involved, even a modest Russian intervention could cut the line of communication between China and the North Korean ports (Rajin and Sonbong) it has bargained for. China may be able to negotiate with Russia to maintain access to the ports across territory that Russia occupies, but otherwise, there is the potential for conflict between China and Russia. While the ROK and the United States would not be directly involved in this issue, its potential for causing conflict implies that the ROK and the United States would be better off if they could help resolve the conflicting interests.

Short-Term Implications of a Separation Line

If China will control some part of North Korea, at least for a time, it will bear the responsibility for humanitarian aid, military demobilization, and the other issues discussed above within the area of Chinese control. The ROK should address these issues as part of any agreement with China, seeking to establish standards for treating the North Koreans to avoid alienating them.

The humanitarian aid issue will be particularly important. China would fundamentally have two options in this area: Filling the humanitarian needs of the population north of the separation line or allowing the ROK and the United States to deliver humanitarian aid into these areas. Of course, some combination of these two would also be possible. If China wants ROK and U.S. humanitarian aid in the area it initially controls, which it may, especially if the ROK and the United States encourage Chinese intervention, China will need to provide access to aircraft and/or ships that would deliver that aid north of the separation line. China may even want ROK and U.S. trucks and drivers provided that would then deliver the aid. These are all issues that would require discussion before intervention to properly prepare.

China may intervene in North Korea and insist that ROK and U.S. aircraft and ships stay some distance south of the separation line. If so, the ROK and the United States need to let China know that it will be fully responsible for the delivery of humanitarian aid in these areas. Given the population numbers in the 2008 North Korean census, it is possible to estimate for China the quantity of daily aid that it would need to provide, depending on the location of the separation line. China should do so before a collapse by identifying the daily aid transportation requirement north of the separation line and the food supplies that would need to be stockpiled for, say, meeting three months of requirements. The ROK and the United States should welcome China's preparation to meet these needs and publicly treat China's preparations as an indicator of whether China really is a great power prepared to take major international responsibilities. The ROK and the United States should then set a precedent for China by stockpiling in the ROK a similar three-month supply of aid so that the ROK and the United States do not delay aid donations until the required aid can be transported to the ROK.

Longer-Term Chinese Withdrawal

Any plans for a separation line in North Korea should be accompanied with conditions for Chinese withdrawal from North Korean territory. The Chinese will want these conditions to identify levels of stabilization that the ROK must achieve south of the separation line before China will turn territory over to the ROK. But the ROK will also want conditions set on WMD-E and providing humanitarian aid, such that, if China cannot meet them, it will withdraw to allow the ROK to assume these roles. China may want to implement a phased withdrawal back to something like its 50-km line to ensure the control of North Korean refugees on North Korean territory. To make decisions on such a withdrawal more obvious, the ROK will want very clear requirements established for North Korean demobilization, WMD-E, and provision of humanitarian aid. These clear requirements will be needed to then identify turning points in performing these roles, turning points that would trigger Chinese withdrawal. The ROK should be drafting such an agreement now (and may be doing so, just not publicly). It should then coordinate the approach with the United States before negotiating with China.

CHAPTER TEN

Addressing the Prerequisites of Collapse Preparation

In conclusion, if the North Korean government were to suddenly collapse today, the consequences of that collapse could jeopardize Korean unification and perhaps even the viability of South Korea. In particular, the North Korean elites and others are generally not prepared to accept ROK-led unification and may actively oppose it. The ROK and the United States need to make preparations now for a North Korean government collapse and should continue these preparations for potentially many years to facilitate unification.

The key preparations that are needed have been described in the preceding chapters: overcoming North Korean fears of unification and being ready to resolve the anticipated North Korean humanitarian disaster, to demobilize the North Korean military and security forces, to handle property and human rights issues, and to work with China to cooperatively address the consequences of the North Korean government collapse.

There are two key prerequisites that the ROK government needs to undertake to make progress in preparing for a North Korean collapse and the subsequent potential for Korean unification. First, the ROK population must be convinced of the importance of dealing with these topics, or the ROK government will face substantial political opposition in trying to prepare for a North Korean collapse, and potentially send the wrong messages, especially to the North Korean elites. Second, the ROK government needs to develop a plan for providing sufficient military and related capabilities to secure and stabilize North

Korea. While the ROK may have sufficient military forces today, it may not have them by 2020 or so because of the ROK demographic challenges that have reduced the size of the ROK age cohorts entering military service.

Convincing the ROK Population to Address North Korean Collapse

Many ROK citizens are not convinced that a North Korean government collapse and a subsequent Korean unification would be good things. The potential cost of such a unification is generally perceived as very high—just the financial costs would likely amount to several trillion dollars, much of it in the first five years after a collapse and unification but with some costs continuing for decades. Moreover, the negative consequences discussed in Chapter Three also appear daunting, and most people recognize only a modest subset of the potential consequences. Would preparation for unification really be worthwhile for ROK citizens? This question must be asked across a range of potential scenarios.

North Korean Government Collapse Appears to Be More a Matter of Time

In practice, this appears to be more a rhetorical question. The North Korean regime appears to be truly failing, as argued in Chapter Two. The question may thus not be whether a North Korean collapse will occur but when. This is not to argue that collapse will happen soon but rather that it could happen in the coming months or years. While the ROK government would need to decide whether or not to pursue unification after a North Korean government collapse, it is hard to imagine that the Korean people would ignore the plight of a divided North Korea or that they could afford the consequences that would develop with a potential civil war in North Korea; large refugee flows into the ROK, including many criminals; and a likely Chinese intervention.

It seems impossible to predict when a North Korean government collapse will occur. In the case of the failure of the East German government, very few experts predicted that it would happen as soon, as rapidly, or as painlessly as it did. In the case of North Korean government, it is even more difficult to determine when a collapse could occur, given the relative lack of information on conditions in North Korea. As noted in Chapter Two, the collapse could happen as quickly as Kim Jong-Un being assassinated and the residual leadership dividing into factions. It has been reported that Kim Jong-Un has already survived one assassination attempt.[1] Whether or not that report is true, assassination appears to be a possibility about which Kim Jong-Un and his supporters are concerned.[2]

One thing is clear: The cost of unification will be far less if proper preparation is made for North Korean collapse than if the current status quo prevails. In particular, the actions suggested in Chapter Four, but also in Chapters Five through Nine, should significantly reduce the potential costs of unification, as well as the serious risks. But there appears to have been little effort in the ROK to explain this comparison to the ROK leadership or population.

In the process of a collapse, the North Korean regime could well try to execute a diversionary invasion of the ROK, as described in Chapter Three. Such an invasion might fairly closely parallel a North Korean government collapse, at least in terms of outcome. The ROK and the United States believe that they would fairly quickly stop such a North Korean invasion and would then execute a counteroffensive to remove the residual North Korean threat and unify Korea. While the level of antagonism between the North Korean military and the ROK and U.S. military would likely be greater than in the North Korean government collapse scenario, the ultimate outcome would depend on many of the recommendations made in Chapters Four through Nine. Thus, preparations in these areas would also significantly reduce the risks and costs of defeating a North Korean invasion.

---

[1]   It is reported that "North Korean leader Kim Jong Un faced an assassination attempt in Pyongyang last year [in 2012] during a power struggle in a military bureau" (Chang Se-jeong and Ser Myo-ja, 2013).

[2]   Heavily armed, uniformed guards have been seen around Kim Jong-Un in a manner different from his father. See, for example, Lee Young-jong, "Kim Jong-un's Guards Bringing out the Big Guns," *Joongang Ilbo*, November 21, 2012.

Some of the ROK population appears to support preparing for unification, while others oppose such action. Most of the opponents fear alienating the North Korean regime and thereby possibly causing it to commit more provocations. They also fear the potential of contributing to a North Korean collapse. Nevertheless, if a collapse really is likely at some point in the future (as argued in Chapter Two), actions to prepare for it are really more likely to accelerate a collapse rather than cause it. On the positive side, accelerating a North Korean collapse would more quickly end the depravations and abuses of the North Korean regime, having a very positive humanitarian outcome overall. But some Koreans apparently oppose accelerating a North Korean collapse, hoping to postpone the prospect of paying the costs of unification beyond their lifetimes.

Preparing for a Peaceful Unification

Another possible future is a peaceful unification of Korea— possibly preempting North Korean collapse. In the current environment (summer 2013), this outcome seems far less likely, with North Korea refusing to negotiate on its nuclear weapons and other critical issues.[3] Still, over many years, Korea might unify peacefully. How would preparation for a North Korean collapse affect peaceful unification?

Most of the same preparations needed for unification after a North Korean government collapse would be needed for peaceful unification. Even in a peaceful unification, North Koreans would worry about their future, humanitarian crisis, military and security force demobilization, WMD-E, and property rights resolution. Because economic power tends to be dominant in peaceful unifications, the ROK industrial, economic, and other leaderships are likely to rise above their

---

[3] Because the ROK is a member of the nuclear Nonproliferation Treaty, North Korea would need to eliminate its nuclear weapons before a truly peaceful unification. In contrast, the Korean Central News Agency, North Korea's media spokesman, has stated that "North Korea's nuclear weapons are a 'treasure' not to be traded for 'billions of dollars,' . . . . They 'are neither a political bargaining chip nor a thing for economic dealings to be presented to the place of dialogue or be put on the table of negotiations aimed at forcing (Pyongyang) to disarm itself'" (Foster Klug, "North Korea: Nuclear Weapons Are a 'Treasure,'" *USA Today*, March 31, 2013).

North Korean counterparts, with the situation bearing some resemblance, over time, to a ROK absorption of North Korea that would come in the aftermath of a North Korean government collapse. As with a North Korean collapse case, peaceful unification would be far less risky and costly if preparations like those discussed in Chapters Four through Nine are made first.

Other Possible Futures

The Koreas could also experience other possible futures that do not involve the unification of Korea. For example, the current independence of North and South Korea could continue. Alternatively, the North Korean government could collapse, but South Korea could decide not to intervene and could leave some degree of anarchy dominant in the North, at least for a time. Or a collapse could occur, and China could intervene in a manner that allows it to secure much of North Korea. It could then annex the areas it occupies as a new Chinese province or set up a Chinese puppet government in the North to manage these areas.

These scenarios appear to be far less likely as ultimate outcomes for the Korean peninsula. Nevertheless, any work done as part of the preparations recommended in Chapter Four would likely be beneficial in these cases, reducing the level of antagonism between the ROK and its northern neighbor. The ROK might also need to provide humanitarian assistance to the North in ways consistent with the preparation proposals in Chapter Five. If the ROK and the United States might need to deal with China, they would find the preparations suggested in Chapter Nine to be of value. The preparations recommended in Chapters Six through Eight would appear to be less relevant, although they may aid in some conventional force reductions in North Korea.

Summation

In short, across the scenarios discussed here, the preparations for collapse recommended in Chapters Four through Nine would be valuable. If a North Korean government collapse leads to Korean unification, as appears to be the most likely outcome at some point in the future, the reduction in risks and costs would be particularly substantial. But even in the other scenarios, these preparations should have a positive or, at worst, neutral effect.

This conclusion suggests that the ROK government and general population need to have the future prospects better explained. They need to understand that a failure to prepare will make the ROK worse off in the range of potential futures. It is hard to get people to consider such future situations, but for the ROK, it is important to do so.

An Approach to Preparing for the Korean Future

The fact that a similar preparatory approach works across a range of future ROK scenarios allows some flexibility in that approach. In particular, if a similar set of preparations will help the ROK prepare for peaceful unification, peaceful unification should be the centerpiece for planning. Preparations for a North Korean collapse will almost certainly be rebuffed by North Korea, but preparations for peaceful unification would likely be far more agreeable to the leaders and population in both North and South Korea.

For example, even in preparation for peaceful unification, the North Korean populace, and the elites in particular, would need assurances about their futures. They need to feel that they will have a good future, that selective amnesty will be applied, that they will be able to obtain jobs, and so forth. The ROK would need to provide humanitarian aid, for at least some time, and to resolve property and related issues. The North Koreans also need to see a path to demilitarization of parts of the North Korean military and security services, which are disproportionally large compared to similar services in other countries. ROK plans in all of these areas can be explained for peaceful unification, while similarly applying (from an overarching, strategic perspective) to the collapse of the North Korean government.

In practice, the ROK Ministry of Unification is apparently assigned to make plans across these areas. But the lack of broader population exposure to these plans limits their usefulness and fails to provide the ROK and North Korean populace what they need to know about a potential unification. While the ROK and North Korean people do not need to know great details, they do need to become comfortable about how their lives would evolve in such circumstances. This is particularly true in seeking to derail the many negative consequences discussed in Chapter Three; the ROK and North Korean people need to know that many of these social, financial, and political consequences can be mainly avoided.

Providing Sufficient Military Capability

The large North Korean military and security services will make many unification tasks difficult or impossible without the support of adequate ROK and U.S. military forces. For example, humanitarian relief projected into North Korea is unlikely to get to those most in need without a military escort. The escort need not combat North Korean forces but must be prepared to prevent the misappropriation of the aid being carried. It should prevail by deterring North Korean military action and, hopefully, co-opting the North Korean military, not by fighting through the North Koreans. But the lack of psychological preparation of the North Koreans may make fighting inevitable. North Korea is a state in which the culture supports the strong over the weak, compelling the ROK and the United States to apply their power.

Chapter Six described the demographic problems the ROK is having and their likely effect on the size of the ROK military. As that chapter indicated, the ROK Army is planned to drop from 22 active duty combat divisions today to roughly 12 divisions in 2022. While 22 active duty ROK Army divisions may be adequate to handle much of a North Korean government collapse today, assuming U.S. and perhaps Chinese assistance, 12 active duty ROK Army divisions are undoubtedly not enough. Moreover, the ROK Army will almost certainly decline below that level in subsequent years.

This section discusses actions the ROK can take to sustain more of its military capabilities in support of handling a North Korean government collapse. Some of the actions involve maximizing the size of the active duty force that would be available and preparing to utilize it most effectively. Other actions involve creating more useful reserve forces. Chapter Nine has already discussed approaches to gaining the support of Chinese forces, but other countries could also provide important assistance.

Maximizing the Size of the Active Duty ROK Military

Chapter Six described some actions for the ROK to offset these military force reductions. Two key issues are associated with determining the feasible size of the ROK military, given the age cohort sizes that are projected. The first is the willingness of ROK youth to volunteer for military service, becoming officers or NCOs, and the willingness of the services to adjust to have more officers and NCOs.[4] Most of the changes in the number of officers and NCOs would be in the ROK Army. The ROK Defense Reform Act of 2006 required the ROK Army to increase its proportion of officers and NCOs to 40 percent by 2022, a difficult task in that the fraction was only about 25 percent in 2012. Such a change would also be costly because volunteers cost considerably more than draftees, significantly affecting the ROK Army budget.

The second key issue is the length of the conscription period. This period has gradually declined over time and is currently set at just over 21 months. Any reduction in the conscription period will, over time, cause an equal reduction in the number of conscripts serving in the military. This is an issue because the current ROK President, Park Geun-Hye, promised during her election campaign to reduce the conscription period from 21.5 to 18 months. This would reduce the number of conscripts by more than one-seventh—about 16 percent.[5]

---

[4] In the ROK military, all officers are volunteers, and all other volunteers immediately become NCOs. Thus, in the ROK, the designation "NCO" relates to a soldier's decision to volunteer and thereby commit to a longer service period than the basic conscription period, whereas in the United States an NCO is a soldier who has served several years and earned promotions that reflect the soldier's growing military capabilities.

[5] "Park's Team Reconsiders Cutting Military Service Period," *Korea Herald*, January 27, 2013. In DRP 1230, the ROK military of 2022 is projected to have about 522,000 active duty personnel. By ROK law, this force is to be 40 percent volunteers or more (which will be difficult to achieve) and thus only about 60 percent conscripts. The conscripts would thus amount to about 310,000 or so personnel. If the conscription period is cut from 21.5 months to 18 months, that would reduce the number of conscripts by about 16 percent (3.5 divided by 21.5), or about 50,000 personnel.

Table 10.1 suggests the trade-offs that exist for the ROK military across these two issues, including some historical data.[6] In 2000, the ROK had a total military force of roughly 690,000, of which 560,000 personnel made up the ROK Army. At that time, the conscription period was 26 months for the ROK Army. Across the MND, volunteers (officers and NCOs) made up about 23 percent of the force, although only 19 percent of the ROK Army personnel were officers or NCOs. By 2012, the force size had declined fairly significantly, but the proportion of officers and NCOs in the force had increased—a good thing, to gain the experience of these people. Despite its reduction in force size, the ROK Army had chosen not to reduce the number of active duty divisions. But it faces the need to do so in the coming years.

The projected information in Table 10.1 is based on a RAND Corporation model, not the plans of the ROK MND. By 2022, that model suggests that the ROK military could have varying sizes, depending on the two issues mentioned earlier. The military can reach its targeted size (522,000) by either expanding the percentage of officers and

Table 10.1
ROK Army Active Duty Size: Past, Present, and Projected

	Actual		Projected Alternatives			
	2000	**2012**	**2022**	**2022**	**2022**	**2022**
MND volunteers (percent)	~23	29	40	30	40	30
Army volunteers (percent)	~19	25	38	26	38	26
Army conscription period (months)	26	21	21	21	18	18
MND manpower	690,000	636,000	585,000	523,000	530,000	466,000
Army manpower	560,000	500,000	449,000	387,000	394,000	330,000
Divisions	22	22	14–15	12	12	10

NOTE: Numbers are author estimates.

---

[6] The manpower projections for 2022 are based on a spreadsheet model I developed. It calculates potential manpower in terms of volunteers and conscripts from the age cohort over time, and estimates from it the total military force size.

NCOs in the force or by sustaining the 21-month conscription period. Indeed, if both of these choices are selected, the ROK Army may actually be able to sustain more of its force size than has been planned (at least through 2022) and retain a few more (14 to 15 total) active duty divisions. But if neither of these choices is selected, the ROK Army could actually become even smaller than planned, perhaps losing two more active duty divisions than currently planned, dropping down to about 10 active duty divisions in 2022 and to lower levels thereafter.[7]

If the ROK were serious about maintaining as much as possible of the current active duty force structure through 2022, it could chose to increase its conscription period rather than decrease it. As Table 10.1 suggests, a conscription period of 21 months provides roughly 55,000 personnel more than going to an 18-month conscription period. Thus, increasing the conscription period from 21 months to 24 months would add roughly another 55,000 military personnel, which in combination with a higher level of officer and NCO volunteers would roughly sustain current ROK Army manpower levels through 2022. More would need to be done after 2022 because of the continuing age group population decline shown in Figure 6.4. But increasing the conscription period to between 27 and 30 months after 2022, assuming that the size of the age cohort stabilizes, as shown in Figure 6.4, could sustain the current ROK active duty military force size. Of course, such increases in the conscription period would be hugely unpopular in the ROK and politically infeasible to obtain unless the North adopts a consistent, more threatening approach.

Preparing to Use ROK Active Duty Forces Most Effectively

How can the ROK deal with the reduction in the size of its active duty military? The ROK MND should chose to use its active duty forces, across the services, more effectively. There are two basic options for doing so.

---

[7] A simple calculation will illustrate this point. If we assume that the ROK military of 2022 is roughly 500,000 active duty personnel, of whom 70 percent are conscripts, there would be 350,000 conscripts. If the conscription period is changed to 18 months from 21 months, one-seventh of the conscripts would be lost, or about 50,000 personnel.

The first is to modify ROK Army active duty divisions to include a significant reserve component.[8] For example, each ROK Army division could have two active duty infantry regiments and one reserve infantry regiment, or each infantry regiment could have two active duty infantry battalions and one reserve infantry battalion. Such a change could provide sufficient ROK infantry to sustain 18 divisions instead of reducing to 12 divisions. The ROK Army would also have to introduce reserves into other elements of a division to make such an expansion, such as the artillery regiments and support units.

This use of reserves in ROK active duty units could help sustain ROK Army force size but only if three significant issues can be resolved. First, the reserve battalions or regiments would still need active duty cadres (officers and NCOs). Assuming that the ROK Army increases to about 40 percent officers and NCOs, appropriate active duty personnel should be available to provide this needed leadership (but not if the ROK Army is only 30 percent officers and NCOs). Second, the reserve personnel in these units would need more than three days of training per year; sustaining reasonable proficiency for these personnel would require something more like the one weekend per month, two weeks each summer that U.S. Army reserve forces train. Third, the ROK Army would require the funding to pay for such a reserve system.

The greater funding would largely be for personnel costs. Increasing reserve training would be politically unacceptable in the ROK unless it were done for a limited number of reserves and unless they were paid a reasonable salary to perform this training. Twelve fully active duty ROK Army divisions in 2022 would amount to about 130,000 personnel. Expanding to 18 divisions, one-third or so of their manpower being reserve, would therefore require assigning about 65,000 more reservists to these divisions than is currently the case and providing them extra training. If these personnel accepted two-year reserve commitments to these positions, about 33,000 personnel would be needed per year, or about 15 percent of those leaving the military each year in 2022. Assuming that the required training would be about 40 days per year, the cost would be about 1,600,000 Korean won per soldier at the

---

[8]   Today, the ROK Army divisions include perhaps 20 percent reservists at the squad level.

ROK minimum wage (not much more than conscripts are paid each year),[9] or about 100 billion Korean won (about $100 million) for the full reserve force. Even if the pay were set at 50 percent more than the minimum wage, the total salary cost of reserves for augmenting active duty units would be only about 160 billion Korean won per year, or less than 0.5 percent of the ROK military budget. As the size of the ROK Army falls from roughly 500,000 today to about 390,000, with the loss of mostly conscripts, salary for the conscripts could be transferred to pay for salary for these reservists at almost no increase in the military budget. The ROK Army would also require the funding for equipment and operations and maintenance for 18 divisions. As the ROK Army reduces from 22 active duty divisions, the equipment and operations and maintenance funding to sustain 18 divisions should not cause any significant increase in the short-term budget required for the ROK Army.

Another option for more effective use of ROK military forces is to employ elements of the ROK Air Force and ROK Navy in support of operations in North Korea after a collapse. Of course, the ROK Marines, part of the ROK Navy, would be actively involved in handling a North Korean collapse, working in conjunction with the ROK Army. But some of the rest of the ROK Navy could be assigned to secure North Korean ports and naval ships and to demobilize North Korean Navy personnel. Similarly, some of the ROK Air Force could be assigned responsibility for securing North Korean Air Force bases and aircraft and for demobilizing North Korean Air Force personnel. In practice, such assignments would likely be better than having the ROK Army deal with the other North Korean services and personnel. But the ROK Navy and Air Force are unlikely to have prepared the required manpower for these tasks and would need to train sufficient personnel for handling the collapse circumstances.

---

[9]   The ROK minimum wage in 2013 is just short of 5,000 won per hour. That would be about 40,000 won for an 8-hour workday and 1,600,000 won (about $1,500) for 40 days of training per year.

Creating More Useful ROK Reserve Forces

For nearly 60 years, ROK defense planning has focused on a North Korean invasion of the ROK. The ROK Army reserves include some 20 reserve divisions that have one of two functions in such a case: roughly eight mobilization reserve divisions that would support the active duty divisions and some 12 homeland reserve divisions that would support homeland defense. But these divisions constitute only about 10 percent or so of the ROK Army reserves. The vast majority of the ROK Army reserves consist of individual riflemen who could be introduced as replacements for casualties as the defense proceeds.

As the number of both the active duty and reserve personnel has been declining, the ROK MND has recognized that it needs to better utilize its reserve personnel and is examining whether it should organize more of them into units to fill the gaps created by reductions in active duty force units. For example, the ROK Army could create in its reserves many of the specialty forces it would need to support WMD-E, drawing in particular on training ROK personnel who have served in chemical defense units on active duty. The ROK Army could create reserve intelligence units from personnel who worked in intelligence on active duty to assist in debriefing North Korean personnel, finding critical documents, and other functions.

These specialty reserve units would be similar to the reserve regiments or battalions that could be added to ROK Army divisions: They would require a leadership cadre and more training. The ROK Army probably will not have many of the officers and NCOs for these specialty units. Instead, it will need to train many of the officers and NCOs within the reserve force, taking some time to develop full capabilities. The ROK Army could begin doing so while conscripts or short-term officers and NCOs are on active duty, putting them through key training for eventually leading reserve units, and potentially having them serve their final months on active duty as cadre of appropriate reserve units. They would then become part of the manning of the reserve units. The members of these units would require more like 40 days of training per year and should be paid more appropriate salaries, as noted above. While it is difficult to estimate how large these specialty reserve forces should become, they should likely amount to at least 50,000 or so personnel, costing over 100 billion won if salaries averaged 50 percent more than the minimum wage. Alternatively, the Korean government could offer to provide scholarships or fellowships for students returning to college after concluding their active duty military service, thereby supporting development of reserve forces with stronger educational backgrounds. While this cost would not be trivial, it would provide key force capabilities at much lower costs than using active duty forces and would fill the gaps created as the active duty manpower declines in the coming years.

Utilizing the Forces of Other Nations

Since the Korean War, a number of countries other than the ROK and the United States have remained interested in ROK security. Some of these countries, such as the United Kingdom and Australia, remain ready to provide manpower in defense of the ROK and would likely be prepared to also support operations in North Korea after a North Korean collapse. These partner countries could be asked to prepare to perform specific military functions in the aftermath of a collapse, thus reducing requirements for ROK or U.S. forces. For example, some of these partner forces might be deployed to North Korean ports to secure the delivery of humanitarian aid in the ports and its transfer to ROK forces for distribution in North Korea. At the same time, they could also inspect ships in port before they sail, trying to prevent the export of WMD on ships leaving the ports. To support partner forces in such roles, some ROK personnel would be required to provide Korean language translation and interpretation, although it may be possible to provide this assistance through ROK contract civilians rather than military personnel. Operating in a port area would make it easier to provide logistical support for these partner forces. They could also potentially provide security and inspection at airfields in North Korea or perform various other functions. Indeed, some partner countries may be prepared to offer specialty forces, such as personnel trained in handling WMD.

Conclusions

The projected ROK force reductions could significantly impair the ROK ability to unify Korea in the aftermath of a North Korean government collapse. But the structure of the ROK active duty force could provide more military capability than currently expected, and appropriate use of ROK reserve forces and partner country forces would also make up for some of the expected force reductions. Providing forces to replace the expected active duty reductions will be a critical part of sustaining a ROK ability to take the lead in Korean unification.

References

"Act on the Fixed Number of Judges of Various Levels of Courts," *Statutes of the Republic of Korea*, April 12, 2011. As of July 11, 2013:
http://elaw.klri.re.kr/eng_service/lawTotalSearch.do?key=Act%20on%20the%20
Fixed%20Number%20of%20Judges%20of%20Various%20%20Levels%20
of%20Courts

Ahmed, Azam, "Afghan Amnesty Program Falls Short, Leaving Ex-Insurgents Regretful and Angry," *New York Times*, January 9, 2013. As of July 11, 2013:
http://www.nytimes.com/2013/01/10/world/asia/many-afghan-ex-insurgents-regret-laying-down-arms.html?_r=0

Albright, David, and Christina Walrond, "North Korea's Estimated Stocks of Plutonium and Weapon-Grade Uranium," Washington, D.C.: Institute for Science and International Security (ISIS), August 16, 2012.

Bank of Korea, "Economic Statistics System," database, 2010, item 17.2.1. As of July 11, 2013:
http://ecos.bok.or.kr/flex/EasySearch_e.jsp

Barry, Mark P., "A Window of Opportunity with North Korea," World Policy Blog, January 31, 2012. As of July 11, 2013:
http://www.worldpolicy.org/blog/2012/01/31/window-opportunity-north-korea

Bennett, Bruce W., "North Korea's WMD Capability and the Regional Military Balance: A US Perspective," *The Korean Journal of Security Affairs*, Korea National Defense University, December 2009.

———, *Uncertainties in the North Korean Nuclear Threat,* Santa Monica, Calif.: RAND Corporation, DB-589-NDU, 2010. As of July 11, 2013:
http://www.rand.org/pubs/documented_briefings/DB589.html

Bennett, Bruce W., and Jennifer Lind, "The Collapse of North Korea: Military Missions and Requirements," *International Security*, Vol. 36, No. 2, Fall 2011.

Bermudez, Joseph S., Jr., *The Armed Forces of North Korea*, London, England: I.B. Tauris & Co. Ltd., 2001.

————, "Behind the Lines—North Korea's Ballistic Missile Units," *Jane's Intelligence Review*, June 14, 2011.

Brackett, Ron, "Korea: The Forgotten War 1950–1953: Questions and Answers," *St. Petersburg Times*, July 20, 2003. As of August 13, 2013:
http://www.sptimes.com/2003/webspecials03/koreanwar/qanda.shtml

Brown University, "Costs of War," August 2012. As of July 11, 2013:
http://costsofwar.org/

Bruce, Scott Thomas, "North Korea's Six Trillion Dollar Question," *The Diplomat*, August 30, 2012. As of July 11, 2013:
http://thediplomat.com/2012/08/30/north-koreas-six-trillion-dollar-question/

Cathcart, Adam, "How Weibo 'Killed' Kim Jong-un," *The Diplomat*, February 11, 2012. As of July 11, 2013:
http://thediplomat.com/2012/02/11/
how-weibo-%E2%80%9Ckilled%E2%80%9D-kim-jong-un/

Central Bureau of Statistics, *2008 Population Census: National Report*, Pyongyang, DPR Korea, 2009. As of July 11, 2013:
http://unstats.un.org/unsd/demographic/sources/census/2010_PHC/North_
Korea/Final%20national%20census%20report.pdf

Central Intelligence Agency, "Korea, North: Economy—Overview," World *Factbook*, 2012. As of July 11, 2013:
https://www.cia.gov/library/publications/the-world-factbook/geos/kn.html

Chang Se-jeong and Ser Myo-ja, "Attempt to Kill Jong-un Took Place in 2012: Source," *JoongAng Ilbo*, March 14, 2013. As of July 11, 2013:
http://koreajoongangdaily.joinsmsn.com/news/article/Article.aspx?aid=2968561

Chang, Jennifer, "Korean Propaganda Soars with Balloons," Al Jazeera, September 29, 2012. As of July 11, 2013:
http://www.aljazeera.com/indepth/features/2012/09/2012924788960487.html

Charbonneau, Louis, "U.N. Told North Korea Has More Secret Atomic Sites: Envoys," Reuters, January 31, 2011. As of August 13, 2013:
http://www.reuters.com/article/2011/01/31/
uk-korea-north-un-idUKTRE70U6QW20110131

Cheng Xiaohe, "Refugees and Neighbors," panel session (video), ASAN Plenum 2013, Seoul, May 1, 2013. As of August 12, 2013:
http://www.asanplenum.org/multimedia/videoArchive.asp

————, "Refugees and Neighbors," talking points, ASAN Plenum 2013, Seoul, May 1, 2013. As of August 12, 2013:
http://www.asanplenum.org/programme_detail/talkingPointsDetail.asp?seq=590

"Chinese State Media Hints at Implosion of N.Korean Regime," *Chosun Ilbo*, March 11, 2013. As of August 13, 2013:
http://english.chosun.com/site/data/html_dir/2013/03/11/2013031101079.html

Cho Jong Ik, "Government Agrees to Maintain Analogue TV," *DailyNK*, December 25, 2012.

Choi He-suk, "U.S. Forces Korea Bolsters Ground Units Ahead of Wartime Control Transfer," *Korea Herald*, June 18, 2012. As of July 11, 2013: http://view.koreaherald.com/kh/view.php?ud=20120618001100

Choi Hyung-kyu and Kim Hee-jin, "'Give up on Pyongyang,' Says China Insider," *Joongang Ilbo*, March 2, 2013. As of July 11, 2013: http://koreajoongangdaily.joinsmsn.com/news/article/Article.aspx?aid=2967922

Choi Song Min and Kim Kwang Jin, "Starvation Deaths Reported in Southern Areas," *DailyNK*, May 20, 2012.

CIA—*See* Central Intelligence Agency.

Collins, Robert, *Marked for Life: Songbun; North Korea's Social Classification System*, The Committee for Human Rights in North Korea, 2012.

Darusman, Marzuki, "Report of the Special Rapporteur on the Situation of Human Rights in the Democratic People's Republic of Korea," New York: Human Rights Council, UN General Assembly, February 1, 2013.

"Defense Officials of S. Korea, U.S., Japan Say N. Korea 'Stable,'" *Korea Herald*, January 31, 2012. As of July 11, 2013: http://www.koreaherald.com/national/Detail.jsp?newsMLId=20120131000689

Demick, Barbara, "Vision on Tunnels Drives N. Korean Defense," *Boston Globe*, November 28, 2003.

———, *Nothing to Envy*, New York: Spiegel & Grau, 2009.

Eberstadt, Nicholas, "A Skeptical View," *Wall Street Journal*, September 21, 2005, p. 26.

"Economic Gap Between 2 Korea Remains Huge," *Chosun Ilbo*, January 6, 2011. As of July 11, 2013: http://english.chosun.com/site/data/html_dir/2011/01/06/2011010600980.html

Ertel, Manfred, "South Korea's Unification Plan: 'No One Wants to Just Swallow up the North,'" interview with Yu Woo-ik, *Spiegel Online International*, March 10, 2012. As of July 11, 2013: http://www.spiegel.de/international/world/south-korea-s-unification-plan-no-one-wants-to-just-swallow-up-the-north-a-820577.html

"Evidence Points to N.Korea in Hacker Attack on Bank," *Chosun Ilbo*, May 4, 2011. As of July 11, 2013: http://english.chosun.com/site/data/html_dir/2011/05/04/2011050400576.html

Finnegan, Michael J., "Preparing for the Inevitable in North Korea," PacNet 28B, Pacific Forum CSIS, April 28, 2009.

"Food Shortage Worsens in N. Korea: Official," *Korea Herald*, February 10, 2010.

Fund for Peace, "Failed States Index," 2011. As of August 8, 2013:
http://ffp.statesindex.org/rankings-2011-sortable

Gates, Robert M., "Remarks by Secretary Gates at the Shangri-La Dialogue, International Institute for Strategic Studies, Singapore," Washington, D.C.: U.S. Department of Defense, June 3, 2011. As of July 11, 2013:
http://www.defense.gov/transcripts/transcript.aspx?transcriptid=4831

Gause, Ken E., "Coercion, Control, Surveillance, and Punishment: An Examination of the North Korean Police State," Washington, D.C.: Committee for Human Rights in North Korea, 2012.

Gertz, Bill, "N. Korea Elite Linked to Crime," *Washington Times*, May 25, 2010, p. 1.

———, "Inside the Ring: North Korea's ICBM," *Washington Times*, March 7, 2012.

Glaser, Bonnie, Scott Snyder, and John S. Park, "Keeping an Eye on an Unruly Neighbor: Chinese Views of Economic Reform and Stability in North Korea," Washington, D.C.: Center for Strategic and International Studies and the U.S. Institute of Peace, January 3, 2008.

Go Myong-Hyun, "Economic Improvement in North Korea," Seoul: Asan Institute for Policy Studies, Issue Brief 58, June 10, 2013.

Good Friends USA, website, undated. As of July 11, 2013:
http://goodfriendsusa.blogspot.com/

———, "News of 'Imminent Death from Starvation' Floods the Central Party," North Korea Today blog, No. 331, February 2010.

"Govt to Establish Research Center on Goguryeo Studies," *Chosun Ilbo*, January 15, 2004. As of July 11, 2013:
http://english.chosun.com/site/data/html_dir/2004/01/15/2004011561003.html

Greitens, Sheena Chestnut, "A North Korean Corleone," *New York Times*, March 3, 2012. As of July 11, 2013:
http://www.nytimes.com/2012/03/04/opinion/sunday/a-north-korean-corleone.html

"Guard Command," North Korea Leadership Watch website, April 29, 2012. As of July 11, 2013:
http://nkleadershipwatch.wordpress.com/dprk-security-apparatus/guard-command/

Gunjalm, Kisan, Swithun Goodbody, Joyce Kanyangwa Luma, and Rita Bhatia, "FAO/WFP Crop and Food Security Assessment Mission to the Democratic People's Republic of Korea," Rome: Food and Agriculture Organization of the United Nations, Economic and Social Development Department, and World Food Programme, November 16, 2010. As of July 11, 2013:
http://www.fao.org/docrep/013/al968e/al968e00.htm

Haggard, Stephan, "Guns vs. Rice: More on the UNICEF Nutritional Survey," Washington, D.C.: Peterson Institute of International Economics, May 29, 2013. As of July 11, 2013:
http://www.piie.com/blogs/nk/?p=9819

Haggard, Stephan, and Alex Melton, "Crisis, Food Prices and Rations," Washington, D.C.: Peterson Institute of International Economics, May 10, 2013. As of August 23, 2013:
http://www.piie.com/blogs/nk/?p=10286

Han Yong-Sup, "Politico-Military Repercussions of North Korean Crisis," Seoul: Ilmin International Relations Institute, Working Paper Series No. 4, September 2010.

Harden, Blaine, "In N. Korea, Resistance Is the New Currency," *Washington Post*, December 27, 2009. As of August 23, 2013:
http://articles.washingtonpost.com/2009-12-27/world/36820446_1_kim-jong-eun-new-currency-private-markets

———, "Dear Leader Appears to Be Losing N. Koreans' Hearts and Minds," *Washington Post*, March 24, 2010, p. 11.

———, *Escape from Camp 14*, New York: The Penguin Group, 2012.

Harlan, Chico, "N. Korea Reverses Stance on Markets," *Washington Post*, June 19, 2010, p. 8.

———, "In North Korea, Role of Foreign Currency Grows," *Washington Post*, February 15, 2012. As of July 11, 2013:
http://www.washingtonpost.com/world/asia_pacific/in-north-korea-role-of-foreign-currency-grows/2012/02/05/gIQAcRLdFR_story.html

Harvard Law School, Program on the Legal Profession, "The Legal Profession of the Republic of South Korea," 2011. As of July 11, 2013:
http://www.law.harvard.edu/programs/plp/pdf/Korean_Legal_Profession.pdf

Hassig, Ralph, and Kongdan Oh, *The Hidden People of North Korea*, Lanham, Md.: Rowman & Littlefield Publishers, 2009.

Havel, Vaclav, Kjell Magne Bondevik, and Elie Wiesel, *Failure to Protect: A Call for the UN Security Council to Act in North Korea*, Washington, D.C.: U.S. Committee for Human Rights in North Korea, October 30, 2006. As of July 11, 2013:
http://www.dlapiper.com/files/upload/North%20Korea%20Report.pdf

Hayes, Peter, and David Von Hippel, "DPRK 'Collapse' Pathways: Implications for the Energy Sector and for Strategies of Redevelopment/Support," Los Angeles: Korean Studies Institute, University of Southern California, and Washington, D.C.: Center for Strategic and International Studies, August 2010. As of July 11, 2013:
http://csis.org/publication/dprk-collapse-pathways

Hildreth, Steven A., *North Korean Ballistic Missile Threat to the United States*, Washington, D.C.: Congressional Research Service, February 24, 2009.

von Hippel, David, Scott Bruce, and Peter Hayes, "Transforming the DPRK Through Energy Sector Development," *38 North*, Special Report 11-3, March 4, 2011. As of July 11, 2013:
http://38north.org/wp-content/uploads/2011/03/38NorthSR_11-3_EnergySectorDev2.pdf

"How N.Korea's Ruling Family Swells Its Private Coffers," *Chosun Ilbo*, April 28, 2010. As of July 11, 2013:
http://english.chosun.com/site/data/html_dir/2010/04/28/2010042801309.html

"HQ-9/-15 and HHQ-9 (RF-9/-15, FD-2000 and FT-2000)," *Jane's Strategic Weapon Systems*, December 22, 2011.

Hwang Chang Hyun, "Winds of Unification Still Blowing...," *Daily NK*, June 28, 2012.

IISS—*See* International Institute for Strategic Studies.

Im Jeong Jin, "Yangkang Province Gets New 10th Corps," *Daily NK*, December 16, 2010.

"In North Korea, Learning to Hate U.S. Starts with Children," *USA Today*, June 23, 2012. As of July 11, 2013:
http://usatoday30.usatoday.com/news/world/story/2012-06-23/north-korea-teaching-hate-united-states/55784168/1

Institute for Far Eastern Studies, "Two Years after the DPRK's Currency Revaluation," Seoul, December 8, 2011. As of July 11, 2013:
http://ifes.kyungnam.ac.kr/eng/FRM/FRM_0101V.aspx?code=FRM111208_0001

International Centre for Prison Studies, "World Prison Brief," website, undated. As of July 11, 2013:
http://www.prisonstudies.org/info/worldbrief/wpb_country.php?country=109

International Institute for Strategic Studies, *The Military Balance 2002*, London, 2002.

———, *The Military Balance 2012*, London, 2012.

"Joint Declaration in Commemoration of the 60th Anniversary of the Alliance Between the Republic of Korea and the United States of America," Washington, D.C.: The White House, Office of the Press Secretary, May 7, 2013. As of July 11, 2013:
http://www.whitehouse.gov/the-press-office/2013/05/07/joint-declaration-commemoration-60th-anniversary-alliance-between-republ

"Joint Vision for the Alliance of the United States of America and the Republic of Korea," Washington, D.C.: The White House, Office of the Press Secretary, June 16, 2009. As of July 11, 2013:
http://www.whitehouse.gov/the_press_office/Joint-vision-for-the-alliance-of-the-United-States-of-America-and-the-Republic-of-Korea/

"The Judiciary System in Korea," Asian Info website, 2010. As of July 11, 2013: http://www.asianinfo.org/asianinfo/korea/politics.htm#Judiciary

Jung Sung-ki, "US to Chart Steps Against N. Korea's Insurgency Tactics," *Korea Times*, June 29, 2008. As of July 11, 2013:
http://www.koreatimes.co.kr/www/news/nation/2008/07/205_26699.html

Kang Chol-hwan, "Power Struggle Looms in N.Korea," *Chosun Ilbo*, May 8, 2009. As of July 11, 2013:
http://english.chosun.com/site/data/html_dir/2009/05/08/2009050800706.html

Kaplan, Robert D., "When North Korea Falls," *The Atlantic*, October 2006.

Keller, Bill, "The Day After," *New York Times*, April 29, 2012. As of July 11, 2013: http://www.nytimes.com/2012/04/30/opinion/keller-the-day-after.html?_r=1

Kim Bumsoo, "N. Korea: Kim Jong-il Was Shot at (and Knocked Unconscious at His Family Compound)," *Future Korea* (in Korean), February 27, 2005.

Kim Eun-jung, "S. Korea Pushes to Cut Troop Levels to 522,000 by 2022," Yonhap News Agency, August 23, 2012. As of August 23, 2013:
http://english.yonhapnews.co.kr/national/2012/08/23/0301000000
AEN20120823007000315.HTML

Kim, Hyun Sik, "The Secret History of Kim Jong Il," *Foreign Policy*, September/October 2008.

"Kim Il-sung," *New World Encyclopedia*, April 2, 2008. As of July 11, 2013: http://www.newworldencyclopedia.org/entry/Kim_Il-sung

"Kim Jong Il," *Biography*, undated. As of July 11, 2013:
http://www.biography.com/articles/Kim-Jong-Il-201050

"Kim Jong-nam Says N.Korean Regime Won't Last Long," *Chosun Ilbo*, January 17, 2012. As of July 11, 2013:
http://english.chosun.com/site/data/html_dir/2012/01/17/2012011701790.html

"Kim Jong-nam Survived Assassination Attempt," *Korea Times*, June 15, 2009. As of July 11, 2013:
http://www.koreatimes.co.kr/www/news/nation/2009/06/120_46904.html

Kim Kwang Jin and Choi Song Min, "Border Security Goes Back to NSA," *DailyNK*, April 22, 2012.

Kim Yong Hun, "Alternative Ways to Unification Funding," *DailyNK*, August 18, 2011.

Kim Young-jin, "NK Parliament Closes with No Word on Heir's Promotion," *Korea Times*, April 7, 2011. As of July 11, 2013:
http://www.koreatimes.co.kr/www/news/nation/2011/04/116_84752.html

Kirk, Donald, and Clifford Coonan, "Uncle Jang Emerges as Real Power in North Korea," *The Independent*, December 22, 2011. As of July 11, 2013:
http://www.independent.co.uk/news/world/asia/uncle-jang-emerges-as-real-power-in-north-korea-6280298.html

Klug, Foster, "North Korea: Nuclear Weapons Are a 'Treasure,'" *USA Today*, March 31, 2013. As of July 11, 2013:
http://www.usatoday.com/story/news/world/2013/03/31/north-korea-nukes/2039783/

Korean Statistical Information Service, website, undated. As of July 11, 2013:
http://kosis.kr/eng

———, "Projected Population by Age," January 2013. As of August 8, 2013:
http://kosis.kr/eng/database/database_001000.jsp?listid=A&subtitle=Population/Household

Kristof, Nicholas D., "South Korea Welcomes Family Fleeing North," *New York Times*, February 9, 1987. As of July 11, 2013:
http://www.nytimes.com/1987/02/09/world/south-korea-welcomes-family-fleeing-north.html

Kwon Dae-yul, "China's Alleged Plot to Annex North Korea," *Chosun Ilbo*, October 19, 2004. As of July 11, 2013:
http://english.chosun.com/site/data/html_dir/2004/10/19/2004101961017.html

Lankov, Andrei, "The World According to Pyongyang," *Asia Times*, July 13, 2007.

———, "Pyongyang Puts Politics Above Dollars," *Asia Times*, November 26, 2008. As of July 11, 2013:
http://www.atimes.com/atimes/Korea/JK26Dg01.html

———, "A Legal Minefield for Korean Reunification," *Asia Times*, July 30, 2011a. As of July 11, 2013:
http://www.atimes.com/atimes/Korea/MG30Dg01.html

———, "Conditions Unripe for North Korea Revolt," *Asia Times*, November 17, 2011b. As of July 11, 2013:
http://www.atimes.com/atimes/Korea/MK17Dg01.html

———, "Costs Stir Korean Unification Dreamers," *Asia Times*, August 9, 2012. As of July 11, 2013:
http://www.atimes.com/atimes/Korea/NH09Dg01.html

Lee, Jiyeon, "North Korea Plans Prisoner Release to Mark Dead Leaders' Birthdays," CNN, January 10, 2012. As of July 11, 2013:
http://www.cnn.com/2012/01/10/world/asia/north-korea-prisoners/index.html

Lee Joon-seung, "Upgrade of N. Korea's Power Grid Needed for Electricity Aid," Yonhap News Agency, July 13, 2005. As of July 11, 2013:
http://www.geni.org/globalenergy/library/technical-articles/transmission/
yonhapnews.co.kr/upgrade-of-north-koreas-power-grid-needed-for-electricity-aid/
index.shtml

Lee Tae-hoon, "'NK Regards OPLAN 5029 as Declaration of Warfare,'" *Korea Times*, November 8, 2009. As of July 11, 2013:
http://www.koreatimes.co.kr/www/news/nation/2009/11/116_55089.html

Lee Wha Rang, "Wagging the Dog—The Korean Style," Kimsoft website, December 25, 1998.

Lee Young-jong, "Kim Jong-un's Guards Bringing out the Big Guns," *Joongang Ilbo*, November 21, 2012. As of July 11, 2013:
http://koreajoongangdaily.joinsmsn.com/news/article/article.aspx?aid=2962679

Levy, Jack S., "The Diversionary Theory of War: A Critique," in Manus I. Midlarsky, ed., *The Handbook of War Studies*, Ann Arbor: The University of Michigan Press, 1989.

Li, Xiaobing, *A History of the Modern Chinese Army*, Lexington, Ken.: University Press of Kentucky, 2007.

Lim, Benjamin Kang, "N.Korea Military, Uncle to Share Power with Kim's Heir," Reuters, December 21, 2011. As of August 8, 2013:
http://in.reuters.com/article/2011/12/21/
korea-north-china-idINDEE7BK09Y20111221

Lim, Jason, "If North Korea Collapses," *Washington Times*, December 17, 2004. As of July 11, 2013:
http://www.washingtontimes.com/news/2004/dec/16/20041216-081425-8021r/

Maddison, Angus, "Historical Statistics of the World Economy: 1-2008 AD," Excel workbook, undated. As of July 11, 2013:
http://www.ggdc.net/MADDISON/Historical_Statistics/horizontal-file_02-2010.
xls

Manyin, Mark E., and Mary Beth Nikitin, "Foreign Assistance to North Korea," Washington, D.C.: Congressional Research Service, R-40095, June 1, 2011.

Marine Corps Intelligence Activity, *North Korea Country Handbook*, MCIA-2630-NK-016-97, May 1997, p. 51.

Maxwell, David S., *Catastrophic Collapse of North Korea: Implications for the United States Military*, Ft. Leavenworth, Kan.: School of Advanced Military Studies, United States Army Command and General Staff College, May 1996.

McCreary, John, "NightWatch," blog, January 11, 2010. As of July 11, 2013:
http://www.kforcegov.com/Services/IS/NightWatch/NightWatch_10000053.aspx

306 Preparing for the Possibility of a North Korean Collapse

―――, "NightWatch," blog, October 19, 2010. As of July 11, 2013:
http://www.kforcegov.com/Services/IS/NightWatch/NightWatch_10000270.aspx

―――, "NightWatch," blog, November 17, 2010. As of July 11, 2013:
http://www.kforcegov.com/Services/IS/NightWatch/NightWatch_10000288.aspx

―――, "NightWatch," blog, February 2, 2012. As of July 11, 2013:
http://www.kforcegov.com/Services/IS/NightWatch/NightWatch_12000024.aspx

"Millions of N.Koreans Listen to Foreign Radio Broadcasts," *Chosun Ilbo*, April 30, 2010. As of July 24, 2013:
http://english.chosun.com/site/data/html_dir/2010/04/30/2010043001070.html

Mok Yong Jae, "North Korea's Unlikely 'Big 3,'" *DailyNK*, January 28, 2012a.

―――, "Cheong: Jang Has Passed His Peak," *DailyNK*, February 7, 2012b.

Moo Bong Ryoo, *The ROK Army's Role When North Korea Collapses Without a War with the ROK*, Ft. Leavenworth, Kan.: School of Advanced Military Studies, U.S. Army Command and General Staff College, January 2001.

Na Jeong-ju, "3 million NK Refugees Expected in Crisis: BOK," *Korea Times*, January 26, 2007.

National Intelligence Council, *Strategic Implications of Global Health*, ICA 2008-10D, December 2008. As of July 11, 2013:
http://www.state.gov/documents/organization/113592.pdf

Natsios, Andrew, "The Politics of Famine in North Korea," special report, Washington, D.C.: U.S. Institute of Peace, August 2, 1999.

"NK Defectors Fail to Assimilate Into S. Korean Society," *Donga Ilbo*, October 26, 2009. As of August 23, 2013:
http://english.donga.com/srv/service.php3?bicode=040000&biid=2009102687058

"N.K. Jamming Affects Flights: Seoul," *Korea Herald*, May 2, 2012. As of July 11, 2013:
http://www.koreaherald.com/national/Detail.jsp?newsMLId=20120502001100

"NK News Database of North Korean Propaganda," database, undated. As of August 8, 2013:
http://www.nk-news.net/index.php

"N. Korea Appoints New Security Chief," Yonhap News Agency, April 1, 2013. As of July 11, 2013:
http://english.yonhapnews.co.kr/northkorea/2013/04/01/0401000000
AEN20130401002900315.HTML

"N. Korea May Have Sea-Based Missile System: Report," *Korea Herald*, March 17, 2009. As of July 11, 2013:
http://view.koreaherald.com/kh/view.php?ud=20090317000035&cpv=0

"N. Korea Purged Senior Intelligence Official: Source," *Korea Times*, April 17, 2012. As of July 11, 2013:
http://www.koreatimes.co.kr/www/news/nation/2012/04/120_109120.html

"N.Korea's Nuclear Facilities 'a Disaster in the Making,'" *Chosun Ilbo*, April 19, 2011. As of July 11, 2013:
http://english.chosun.com/site/data/html_dir/2011/04/19/2011041901290.html

"N.Korean Military's Morale 'Weakening,'" *Chosun Ilbo*, July 5, 2011. As of July 11, 2013:
http://english.chosun.com/site/data/html_dir/2011/07/05/2011070500529.html

Noland, Marcus, "Some Unpleasant Arithmetic Concerning Unification," Washington, D.C.: Peterson Institute for International Economics, 1996. As of July 11, 2013:
http://www.iie.com/publications/wp/print.cfm?researchid=169&doc=pub

———, "Is the North Korean Economy Growing?" *North Korea: Witness to Transformation*, Washington, D.C.: Peterson Institute for International Economics, March 13, 2012. As of July 11, 2013:
http://www.piie.com/blogs/nk/?p=5290

———, "North Korea's Vulnerability to a China Shock," *North Korea: Witness to Transformation*, Washington, D.C.: Peterson Institute for International Economics, July 1, 2013. As of July 11, 2013:
http://www.piie.com/blogs/nk/?p=10778

"North Korea Chemical, Biological, Nuclear, and Missile Facilities," map, Washington, D.C.: Nuclear Threat Initiative, 2013. As of July 11, 2013:
http://www.nti.org/gmap/?country=north_korea&layers=biological,chemical,missile,nuclear

"North Korea Resumes Its Distribution of Food Rations," New Focus International, May 3, 2013. As of July 11, 2013:
http://newfocusintl.com/north-korea-resumes-distribution-of-food-rations/

"North Korean Nuclear Facilities," *WMD Around the World,* Washington, D.C.: Federation of American Scientists, October 10, 1997. As of July 11, 2013:
http://www.fas.org/nuke/guide/dprk/facility/other_nuke.htm

"'The North's Strategic Rocket Forces' Status Reinforced Directly Under the National Defense Commission," *Daily NK*, April 19, 2012.

"No 'Unification Tax' Right Now, Lee Promises," *Chosun Ilbo*, August 18, 2010. As of July 11, 2013:
http://english.chosun.com/site/data/html_dir/2010/08/18/2010081800232.html

Office of the Secretary of Defense, *Annual Report to Congress: Military and Security Developments Involving the People's Republic of China 2012*, Washington, D.C.: Department of Defense, May 2012. As of July 11, 2013:
http://www.defense.gov/pubs/pdfs/2012_CMPR_Final.pdf

One Free Korea, "North Korea's Largest Concentration Camps on Google Earth," March 2012. As of July 11, 2013:
http://freekorea.us/camps/

Park Sang-seek, "What's Behind N. Korea's Survival?" *Korea Herald*, May 1, 2012. As of July 11, 2013:
http://view.koreaherald.com/kh/view.php?ud=20120501000505

"Park's Team Reconsiders Cutting Military Service Period," *Korea Herald*, January 27, 2013. As of July 11, 2013:
http://nwww.koreaherald.com/view.php?ud=20130127000212

Petrov, Leonid A., "Neo-Cons Rule in Pyongyang," *Asia Times*, December 9, 2008. As of July 11, 2013:
http://www.atimes.com/atimes/Korea/JL09Dg01.html

Pollack, Jonathan D., and Chung Min Lee, *Preparing for Korean Unification: Scenarios and Implications*, Santa Monica, Calif.: RAND Corporation, MR-1040-A, 1999. As of July 11, 2013:
http://www.rand.org/pubs/monograph_reports/MR1040.html

Pritchard, Jack, "My New Year's Predictions for North Korea," The Peninsula blog, Korea Economic Institute, December 21, 2011. As of July 11, 2013:
http://blog.keia.org/2011/12/my-new-years-predictions-for-north-korea/

"Pyongyang Now More Than One-Third Smaller; Food Shortage Issues Suspected," *Asahi Shimbun*, July 17, 2010. As of July 11, 2013:
http://www.asahi.com/english/TKY201007160470.html

"Report: Assassins Targeted N Korean Leader's Son," *Irish News*, March 14, 2005.

Republic of Korea Ministry of National Defense, *Defense White Paper*, 2006.

———, *Defense White Paper*, 2008.

———, *Defense White Paper*, 2010.

"Rice Monthly Price—US Dollars per Metric Ton," Index Mundi website, August 9, 2012. As of July 11, 2013:
http://www.indexmundi.com/commodities/?commodity=rice&months=60

"Rice Reserve Exceeds 1.5 million Tons," *Korea Times*, March 1, 2011. As of July 11, 2013:
http://www.koreatimes.co.kr/www/news/biz/2011/03/123_82241.html

"Rodong Sinmun S. Korean Conservative Forces' Conspiracy with Their American Masters Under Fire," Korean Central News Agency, October 30, 2012. As of July 11, 2013:
http://www.kcna.co.jp/item/2012/201210/news30/20121030-06ee.html

ROK MND—*See* Republic of Korea Ministry of National Defense.

Roy, Denny, "China and Nuclear Standoff Over N. Korea," *Korea Herald*, August 25, 2009. As of July 11, 2013:
http://www.koreaherald.com/common_prog/newsprint.php?ud=20090825000036&dt=2

"S-300/Favorit (SA-10 'Grumble'/SA-20 'Gargoyle')," *Jane's Strategic Weapon Systems*, December 23, 2011.

Salmon, Andrew, "North Korean Reforms Are Smokescreen, Say Senior Defectors," *Washington Times*, August 28, 2012.

Savada, Andrea Matles, ed., "Industry," *North Korea: A Country Study*, Washington, D.C.: Library of Congress, 1993. As of July 11, 2013:
http://countrystudies.us/north-korea/48.htm

Savage, Timothy, "Big Brother Watching: China's Intentions in the DPRK," *China Security*, Autumn 2008.

"Scenarios—North Korea's Stability Paradox," *Jane's Intelligence Review*, October 1, 2007.

Scobell, Andrew, "Making Sense of North Korea: Pyongyang and Comparative Communism," *Asian Security,* Vol. 1, No. 3, 2005, pp. 245–266.

———, *Projecting Pyongyang: The Future of North Korea's Kim Jong Il Regime*, Carlisle Barracks, Pa.: Strategic Studies Institute, U.S. Army War College, March 2008.

———, "The View from China," in Gilbert Rozman, ed., *Asia at a Tipping Point: Korea, the Rise of China, and the Impact of Leadership Transitions*, Washington, D.C.: Korea Economic Institute, 2012, pp. 69–81. As of July 11, 2013:
http://www.scribd.com/doc/96297246/A-View-from-China-by-Andrew-Scobell

"Seoul Suspects About 100 Sites in N.K. Linked to Nuclear Program," *Korea Herald*, October 5, 2009. As of August 26, 2013:
http://view.koreaherald.com/kh/view.php?ud=20091005000097&cpv=0

Shin Hae-in, "Changes Brewing in 'Not so Isolated' North," *Korea Herald*, December 15, 2010. As of August 23, 2013:
http://view.koreaherald.com/kh/view.php?ud=20101215000870&cpv=0

Shin Hyon-hee, "Up to 200,000 Incarcerated in N.K. Prison Camps," *Korea Herald*, June 20, 2012. As of August 23, 2013:
http://view.koreaherald.com/kh/view.php?ud=20120620001036

Smith, Hazel, "Don't Expect a Pyongyang Spring Sometime Soon," Washington, D.C.: Center for Strategic and International Studies, PacNet #60, October 28, 2011. As of July 11, 2013:
http://csis.org/publication/
pacnet-60-dont-expect-pyongyang-spring-sometime-soon

Spitzer, Kirk, "Isles Key in S. Korea Defense," *Honolulu Advertiser*, March 3, 1994, p. 1.

Stafford, Jonathan, "Finding America's Role in a Collapsed North Korean State," *Military Review*, January–February 2008, p. 101.

Stares, Paul B., and Joel S. Wit, "Preparing for Sudden Change in North Korea," Washington, D.C.: Council on Foreign Relations, Council Special Report No. 42, January 2009.

"Sudden Unification Could Cause 3.65 Mln N. Koreans to Enter S. Korea: Report," Yonhap News Agency, January 24, 2012. As of July 11, 2013: http://english.yonhapnews.co.kr/national/2012/01/24/77/0302000000AEN20120124002900320F.HTML

Suh Jae Jean, "Social Consequences of North Korean Contingency," Seoul: Ilmin International Relations Institute, Working Paper Series No. 2, June 2010.

"Survival of the Wickedest," *Strategy Page*, June 26, 2008. As of July 11, 2013: http://www.strategypage.com/qnd/korea/articles/20080626.aspx

"System to Punish NK Leaders Needed After Reunification," *Dong-A Ilbo*, October 4, 2010.

Tandon, Shaun, "N. Korea Dissent on Rise: US Study," Agence France-Presse, February 1, 2011. As of July 11, 2013: http://newsinfo.inquirer.net/breakingnews/world/view/20110201-317768/Dissent-in-North-Korea-on-the-riseUS-study

"Too Many Lawyers?" editorial, *Korea Herald*, December 9, 2010. As of July 11, 2013: http://nwww.koreaherald.com/view.php?ud=20101209000705

Tran, Mark, "South Korea: A Model of Development?" *Guardian*, November 28, 2011. As of July 11, 2013: http://www.guardian.co.uk/global-development/poverty-matters/2011/nov/28/south-korea-development-model

UN FAO—*See* United Nations Food and Agriculture Organization.

Um Sang-hyun, "N. Korea: Kim Jong-il's Distant Relative Tried to Kill Him With Chinese Blessing," *Shin-Dong-A*, October 2004.

United Nations, "Integrated Disarmament, Demobilization and Reintegration Standards," New York, 2006.

United Nations Food and Agriculture Organization, FAO statistical database, undated. As of February 19, 2012: http://faostat.fao.org/site/567/DesktopDefault.aspx?PageID=567#ancor

United Nations Office of Drugs and Crime, "Total Professional Judges or Magistrates as at 31 December," Criminal Justice Resources Excel Workbook, 2011. As of July 11, 2013:
http://www.unodc.org/documents/data-and-analysis/statistics/crime/CTS12_Criminal_justice_resources.xls

————, "Criminal Justice System Resources," 2009 entries. As of July 11, 2013:
http://www.unodc.org/documents/data-and-analysis/statistics/crime/CTS12_Criminal_justice_resources.xls

————, "Data: Statistics on Criminal Justice," 2013, spreadsheets on "Criminal Justice System Resources" and on "Persons Detained." As of July 11, 2013:
http://www.unodc.org/unodc/en/data-and-analysis/statistics/data.html

U.S. Department of Defense, "Sustaining U.S. Global Leadership: Priorities for 21st Century Defense," Washington, D.C., January 2012. As of July 11, 2013:
http://www.defense.gov/news/Defense_Strategic_Guidance.pdf

"USFK Commander Warns of Possible N.K. Instability," *Korea Herald*, March 26, 2010.

"U.S. General Concerned by Threat to Seoul Posed by N. Korea's 800-Missile Arsenal," East-Asia-Intel.com, October 17, 2008.

"U.S. General Says Forces Ready to Counter N.Korean Attack," *Chosun Ilbo*, July 15, 2009.

"What China's Northeast Project Is All About," *Chosun Ilbo*, May 30, 2008. As of July 11, 2013:
http://english.chosun.com/site/data/html_dir/2008/05/30/2008053061001.html

"Who Has His Finger on the Nuclear Button in N.Korea?" *Chosun Ilbo*, February 23, 2012. As of July 11, 2013:
http://english.chosun.com/site/data/html_dir/2012/02/23/2012022301441.html

Wolf, Charles, Jr., and Kamil Akramov, *North Korean Paradoxes: Circumstances, Costs, and Consequences of Korean Unification*, Santa Monica, Calif.: RAND Corporation, MG-333-OSD, 2005. As of July 11, 2013:
http://www.rand.org/pubs/monographs/MG333.html

Wolf, Holger, "Korean Unification: Lessons from Germany," in Marcus Noland, ed., *Economic Integration of the Korean Peninsula*, Washington, D.C.: Peterson Institute for International Economics, January 1998, p. 182. As of August 8, 2013:
http://www.piie.com/publications/chapters_preview/26/9iie2555.pdf

World Bank, "World Development Indicators," December 15, 2011. As of August 8, 2013:
http://databank.worldbank.org/data/views/variableSelection/selectvariables.aspx?source=world-development-indicators

Yoo Ho-Yeol, "Current State of North Korea and Types of Its Contingencies," Seoul: Ilmin International Relations Institute, Background Paper Series No. 2, August 2010.

Yoon Hwy-tak, "China's Northeast Project: Defensive or Offensive Strategy?" *East Asian Review*, Vol. 16, No. 4, Winter 2004. As of July 11, 2013: http://www.ieas.or.kr/vol16_4/16_4_6.pdf